AF528011

Buddhist Studies Series: 3

General Editor: Prof. S R Bhatt

Ekayāna Philosophy of the Saddharmapuṇḍarīka Sūtra

Ven. NGUYEN XUAN KINH

(Thich Tam Duc)

Originals

Delhi-110052

© Ven. Nguyen Xuan Kinh (Thich Tam Duc) 2012

ISBN 13: 978-81-8454-114-4
ISBN 10: 81-8454-114-7

Published by
Originals
A-6, Nimri Commercial Centre,
Near Ashok Vihar Phase-IV,
Delhi-110052
Phone: 011-27302453, Fax: 011-47061936
e-mail: info@Lppindia.com
website: www.Lppindia.com

Printed at
D K Fine Art Press P Ltd.
Delhi-110052

No part of this book may be reproduced, stored in or introduced into a retrieval system, or transmitted in any form or by any means (electronic, mechanical, photocopying, recording or otherwise), without the prior written permission of the above mentioned publisher of this book.

PRINTED IN INDIA

Dedicated to
My Master,
Most Rev. Dr. Thich Minh Chau

Foreword

I have great pleasure and privilege to write Foreword to this erudite work on Saddharmapuṇḍarīkā Sūtra based on deep thinking, wide reading and subtle research by a learned scholar from Vietnam. It takes into account different versions of the text and analyses its contents with a remarkable philosophical acumen.

Out the nine well known Mahāyāna Buddhist sacred texts known as "*Vaipulya Sūtras*", the *Saddharmapuṇḍarīkā Sūtra* is the most important, the most representative and extraordinarily popular work. It is considered to be the last and the supreme teaching of the Buddha. It is at once the foundation and the culmination of the Buddhist thought and practices. It declares itself as the "*King of all Sūtras*." It is regarded as the quintessence and the most comprehensive of the teachings of the Buddha. It glorifies and divinizes the Buddha and extols the life of a bodhisattva. It promises that following the Buddhist way of life enables one to get enlightenment and to reach the final goal, the *summum bonum*, of life. It presents Buddhism as *emancipatory* or liberating religion and that is why it has provided solace and succor to millions of people throughout Asia. This also accounts for its prominence. Its language is highly symbolic, suggestive and evocative. Ideas are expressed, doctrines are propounded and messages are communicated through parables and analogies the implications of which need to be drawn out.

The *Saddharmapuṇḍarīkā Sūtra* advocates the theory of *Ekāyāna (Buddhayana)* which encompasses and reconciles the three *yanas* of *Śrāvakayāna, Pratyekabuddhayāna* and *Bodhisattvayāna.* It expounds the theory of ***Śūnyatā***. *Śūnyatā* is also expressed as *Tathatā*, *Samatā*, *Dharmakāya*, *Nirvāṇa*, *Paramārtha Satya*, *Pariniśpanna*, *Madyamāpratipad* etc. In a remarkable way it presents the Two-Truths theory of Nagarjuna as to how the Two Truths of *Samvṛtti* or *Samsāra* (Mundane Truth) and *Paramārtha* or *Nirvāṇa* (Higher Truth) are distinct, interrelated and yet ultimately one. The Mundane Truth is for living the worldly life and the Higher Truth is for gaining Nirvāṇa. The Reality (*Tattva*) is one but there are two ways of experiencing it. Ultimately there is not the slightest difference between the two. *Samvṛtti* is the ***upāya*** (means) and the *Paramartha* is the *upeya* (goal).

The title of this text is highly suggestive and significant. Different commentators and scholars have drawn out wide ramifications of this caption. The term "*Saddharma*" means true or real Dharma or the view and the way of life and reality. The term "*Puṇḍarikā*" stands for white lotus which is a symbol of purity and perfection and is an emblem of immaculacy. The Dharma preached and practiced by the Buddha is compared to a white lotus. One of the meanings is that just as a lotus grows in muddy water but is not sullied by its dirt and spreads its sweet fragrance all around, likewise the Buddha dharma has sprung out of the earthly turmoil but provides solace and succor to all beings. Further, a living being is exhorted to realize *Buddhatva* by leading the life of a bodhisattva who lives in the vicious world but is not affected by it just like a lotus flower which grows out of the mire and yet does not share its defilement. This analogy is available in the *Bhagavadgita* also which is another representative text of Indian culture.

Based on the *Saddharmapuṇḍarīkā Sūtra* the Tien-tai school of Chinese Buddhism came into existence. The school is named after the Mount Tien-tai where its founder lived. This school is regarded as the first distinctly Chinese school of Buddhism, though prior to this there were some earlier schools as well which were of Indian heritage. This school regards the *Saddharmapuṇḍarīkā Sūtra* as the most authoritative and comprehensive exposition of the Buddhist thought and culture. The distinctive feature of the Tien-tai school is advocacy of three-fold mode of comprehension, which is called as the "Perfected Comprehension", based on the Mādhyamika philosophy of Nagarjuna coupled with the Vijnanavada school of Vasubandhu and others. The three modes are as under:-

a. The Empty Mode of Comprehension which destroys the illusion of sensuous perception and constructs supreme knowledge (*prajña*).

b. The Hypothetical Mode of Comprehension which does away with the defilement of the world and brings about salvation from all sins.

c. The Medial Mode of Comprehension which destroys hallucination arising from *avidya* or ignorance and establishes the enlightened mind.

(Refer—2500 Years of Buddhism, p. 129, Edited by P.V.Bapat, Publication division, Government of India, New Delhi).

The basic philosophy of the Tien-tai school can be represented with the help of a concentric circle, i.e., circle within circle, all circles having a common center. It is one-in-three or three-in-one. One circle is that of *samsāra* or emptiness. The other is the circle of Nirvāṇa or real which comprehends the first circle. The third is the circle of identification of *samsāra* and Nirvāṇa. All blend in One

Supreme Circle. A circle has no beginning and no end and therefore it best represents the nature of reality. Chih-I is the founder of the school of Tien-tai. He was a yogic philosopher and a great thinker whose understanding and interpretation of Buddhist theory and practices were based on his vast study as well as his own realizations in the state of *Sāmadhi*, which led him to visualize and realize the Buddhist spirit in its purest and truest form as the *Madhyam Pratipad* (Middle way). He had a creative, original and penetrating mind. In order to expound his philosophy Chih-I chose to espouse the *Saddharmapuṇḍarīkā Sūtra* because according to him it incorporates the essence of all other *Sūtras*. It is permeated with the spirit of harmonization which was cherished by Chih-I and which was his guiding idea. In expounding and elaborating the contents of the *Saddharmapuṇḍarīkā Sūtra* he displays a rare hermeneutical skill, draws out several important, seminal and far-reaching implications of the analogy of the lotus and other analogies contained in the text. He brings to the fore deep and profound meaning of the Sutra, which is otherwise abstruse, and thereby reconstructs the Buddhist thought with authoritative knowledge of the extant Buddhist scriptures. He interprets them in such a way as to put them in tune with Confucian and Taoist ideologies.

Professor Ven. N.X. Kinh's work also is a scholarly, thoughtful and exhaustive presentation of *Saddharmapuṇḍarīkā's* philosophy which became the foundation for the formulation of the notable school of Tien-tai. Based on the analytical study of this text and other available expository literature in the field, it is a painstaking and enlightening research work which deserves all commendation. It exhibits the logical acumen, analytical skills and penetrating insight of the author. With detailed and well classified contents, minute and in depth analysis, exhaustive footnotes and extensive bibliography it presents a remarkable survey of the main contents of the text. It may therefore prove to be a landmark in and a significant contribution to the study of this text. He deserves to be congratulated for his scholarly contribution which will surely be a milestone in Buddhist studies. Though it takes for study and analysis only one of the several Mahāyāna sūtras, the choice of this sūtra is significant because it has the most powerful presentation of Buddhist thought. This single work, with its comprehensiveness and coherence, has fulfilled the gigantic task of presenting a holistic view of the whole Buddhist system. Most Buddhist theories and concepts that are scattered throughout various Buddhist scriptures have been incorporated into this text by reasserting and redefining them, so that they form a coherent whole of the Buddha's teaching, including all branches of Buddhist learning.

It is hoped that this work will receive serious attention it deserves from the world of scholars in the fields of Buddhism. It will surely help in proper understanding of the basic philosophy of Buddhism.

S.R.Bhatt

Former Professor and chair

Department of philosophy

University of Delhi

Delhi (India)

Srbhatt39@gmail.com

1-9-2011.

Preface

This book originates from the two main motivations: a) Professor S.R. Bhatt's suggestion and b) the writer's aspiration to study the *Saddharmapuṇḍarīka-sūtra,* or in short the *Lotus* in English, in a new way.

It was very happy for the writer when he met one day Prof. Bhatt in the office of the Department of Philosophy, University of Delhi, in September, 1997. The writer was longing and searching for the knowledge of Buddhist philosophy when he met the professor, a good advisor in this sphere. The professor said that an exposition of the philosophy of the *Lotus,* a very popular *sūtra* in the countries of East Asia, was a good thing. This suggestion corresponded to the writer's aspiration.

The *Lotus* has been popularly recited by the Buddhists in the countries of East Asia including Vietnam and most scholars have dwelt on the major points of each chapter of the *sūtra*. But very few have discussed and arranged the concepts and doctrines underlying the highly symbolic expressions of the *sūtra* in a philosophical system, which are *Ekayāna, Upāya-kauśalya, Bodhisattva, Buddhahood* and *Dhāraṇī*. So the method used in this book is an analysis of those concepts and doctrines. Here some accounts are repeated for the connection and understanding of the discussing questions.

An intensive study of the *sūtra* reveals that almost every word and phrase in it contains a number of important teachings related to the central issues of Ultimate Reality in the Mahāyāna Buddhist philosophy such as *Ekayāna, Gotra, Śūnyatā, Tathatā, Trikāya, Nirvāṇa, Madhyamā Pratipad,* etc. Particularly, the *sūtra* expounds the important treatises of the two Indian Buddhist philosophical schools, viz., *Mādhyamika* and *Yogācāra* (or *Vijñaptimātratā*). The *Lotus* also reveals and explains a way of life to reach the goal of *nirvāṇa*; accordingly, a complete symbiosis of theory and practice is necessary for bringing about such a saintly change.

Hochi Minh City
Vietnam

Ven. Nguyen Xuan Kinh

Abbreviations

Ava. Śa — *Avadāna-śataka,* edited by J. S. Speyer (St. Petersburg 1906, 1909). 2 vols. Bibliotheca Buddhica.

CWSL — *Ch'eng-wei-shih-lun*

Dh. S. — *Dharma-saṅgraha*, edited by F. Max Müller, H. Wenzel, and K. Kassawara (Oxford, 1885).

IBK — *Idogaku Bukkyōgaku Kenkyū* (Journal of Indian and Buddhist Studies).

Lal. V. — *Lalitavistara*, Ch. 7, ed. Lefmann, 1908.

M. K. — *Madhyamakakārikā.*

M. Vy. — *Mahā-vyutpatti*, edited by Sakaki, Kyoto, 1928.

P.P. - *Prasannapadā*

Pr. Pā. Śata — *Śata-sāhasrikā Prajñā-pāramitā* (chapters i-xii), edited by P. Ghosa, Calcutta 1902-13. Bibliotheca Indica.

T. T. — Tibetan Tripiṭaka

WSSSLS — *Wei-shih-san-shih-lun-sung*

Contents

Chapter I

Introduction

The Buddhist *Mahāyāna sūtra,* which was translated into many languages, was studied by number of scholars and was recited by many people, we can say, is the *Saddharmapuṇḍarīka-sūtra* or, in short, the *Lotus* in English. Its thoughtful contents, literary value and religious significance merit the highest position in the *Mahāyāna* Buddhist tradition. Consequently, the *Lotus* was raised to the high pedestal of the 'King of all *sūtras.*'

The *Lotus* which is of Indian origin was first translated from Sanskrit to Chinese and there have been many different translations thereafter. However, the version translated by *Kumārajiva* in Chinese in 406 A.D. has been widely accepted, studied and recited, especially in China, Korea, Japan and Vietnam; and mainly upon this Chinese translation in English, *Scripture of the Lotus Blossom of the Fine Dharma,* by Leon Hurvitz an analysis of its concepts and doctrines will be done here.

I) The Buddhist Philosohical Background of the *Lotus*

A) Vaipulya sūtras:

The *Lotus* is one of the most popular early texts of *Mahāyāna* Buddhism. It is one of the nine *Dharmas,* or 'religious texts', which, were composed at different times and belonged to different sects, which are also called *Vaipulya sūtras*.'[1] *Vaipulya* in general may be taken as the broad school, or *Mahāyāna* in its various forms. The term covers all the specific *Mahāyāna sūtras*. The *sūtras* are also known as scriptures of measureless meaning, i.e.. universalistic or the infinite. The *Vaipulya sūtras* are as follows:

Aṣṭasāhasrikā Prajñāpāramitā

Avataṃsaka

Gaṇḍavyūha

Daśabhūmika

Samādhirāja or *Sūraṅgama*

Saddharmapuṇḍarīka

Lalitavistara

Laṅkāvatāra or *Saddharma Laṅkāvatāra*

Suvarṇaprabhāsa

There are several commentaries and expository works on these *sūtras*. However, a brief account of the contents of these *sūtras* can be given as under:

1) Aṣṭasāhasrikā Prajñāpāramitā

The *Aṣṭasāhasrikā Prajñāpāramitā Sūtra* consists of 8,000 lines and is the earliest and basis of the *Prajñāpāramitā* group of literature, which is the most primitive and fundamental of all those dealing with the idea of Emptiness. This Emptiness develops from the *Pratītyasamutpāda* or causation theory in Primitive Buddhism and is a synthesis of all the ideas of emptiness of the contemporary Buddhist sects. *Prajñāpāramitā Sūtras* are also considered to be among the earliest and most basic texts of the *Mahāyāna* works. The outlook on life and world outlook in all *Mahāyāna sūtras* are established upon the foundation of the *Prajñāpāramitā*. The following *Prajñāpāramitā sūtras* have come down to us in Sanskrit; *Prajñāpāramitā* of 100.000 *'Ślokas' (Śatasāhasrikā)*; of 25,000 *'Ślokas' (Pañca-viṃśatisāhasrikā)*; of 8,000 *'Ślokas' (Aṣṭasāhasrikā)*; of 2,500 *'Ślokas' (Sārdhaḍvaisāhasrikā)*; of 700 *'Ślokas' (Saptaśatikā)*; the *Vajracchedikā Prajñāpāramitā*, "the diamond cutter *Prajñā-Pāramitā* and *Prajñā-Pāramitā hṛdaya-sūtras* which are only used as protecting mystical formulas *(dhāraṇīs)*."

The view of Emptiness in *Prajñāpāramitā sūtras* is not the result of analysis, as in *Hīnayāna*, in which individual elements *(dharmas)* are minutely analysed, but a synthetic view, seen by the intuition, which is called *Prajñāpāramitā* wisdom. This is different from ordinary wisdom, *vijñāna*, for *vijñāna* is the aggregate of experience based on desire *(tṛṣṇā)* while *prajñā* transcends *vijñāna* after overcoming of desire. This emptiness of life and the world is not to be taken in a nihilistic sense. It does not negate the world as fact,but destroys the world as a lower value based upon the notion of egoism or individuality. Thus a free and bright world appears before us, and a new light shines upon the former world of suffering. A new and fundamental alteration of the value of this life is made. Earlier we suffered; now we transcend suffering. This is transvaluation or a shift in value-paradigm.

The *Aṣṭasāhasrikā Prajñāpāramitā* consists of 32 chapters of dialogues between *Buddha* and his disciples *Subhūti*, *Śāriputra* and *Pūrṇa Maitrāyaṇīputra* and frequently *Śakra* the prince of the gods, and sometimes a *bodhisattva* joins them. The work begins with introductory verses, in which the *Prajñāpāramitā*, the perfection of wisdom, is personified and praised as "the sublime producer and the beloved mother of all heroes, she whose mind is fixed firmly on the highest goal", "as the kind grand-mother of all beings" etc. In the very first chapter we see the dialectics and interpretations like this:

> "He leads so many beings to complete *nirvāṇa,* and there is no being which has attained to complete *nirvāṇa,* and there is no one by whom such a being has been led to complete *nirvāṇa.* And why so? That, *Subhūti,* is precisely the true nature of phenomena; they are based upon deceptive appearances. Now, *Subhūti* supposing a skilful magician or magician's apprentice were to conjure up a large crowd of people at a cross road, and after he had conjured up this large crowd of people, he were to cause it to vanish again, - what do you think, *Subhūti* would anyone have been struck down, killed, destroyed, or caused to vanish, by anyone?"[2]

In Chapter II *Subhūti* instructs the gods:

> "O sons of gods, the beings are like an illusion *(māyā),* O sons of gods, the beings are like a dream. No, illusion and beings are not two different things, and do not form a duality; and dreams and beings are not two different things, and do not form a duality. Furthermore, O sons of gods, all objects of thought are like an illusion, like a dream. He, too, who has just entered the stream, (i.e., the new convert) is like an illusion, like a dream.... He, too, who is completely enlightened, is like an illusion, like a dream; the condition, too, of him who is completely enlightened, is like an illusion, like a dream.... O sons of gods, even *nirvāṇa* itself is like an illusion, like a dream, I say, how much more then every other object of thought."[3]

The whole *sūtra* continues in this strain that all phenomena are without self-being *(śūnya),* that even *buddhas, bodhisattvas* and the perfection of wisdom itself have no reality; but, at the same time, the *bodhisattva* ideal is extolled - "O *Subhūti, a Bodhisattva,* a Great Being, who desires to advance to un-surpassable complete enlightenment, must behave alike towards all beings,...in this way he must train himself in being a protector of all beings...he must contemplate the formula of the causally conditioned origination both in regular and in inverted order, he must teach it to others, extol it in their presence, and enable them to take delight in it."[4]

2) Avataṁsaka

The *Avataṁsaka sūtra* is a heterogeneous work, a collection of texts some of which were in circulation separately. Other parts were probably composed at the time of compilation in order to fill obvious gaps in the composite text. Only two sections survive in their entirety in Sanskrit, both of which were without doubt originally separate texts — the *Daśabhūmika sūtra* on the ten stages of the *bodhisattva's* path to enlightenment, and what is now the climax of the *Avataṁsaka* the *Gaṇḍavyūha sūtra.*

This *sūtra* is important because it is considered to be the teaching given out by the *Buddha Śākyamuni* three weeks after his enlightenment when he was still in a state of meditation and in the *Dharmakāya* form; as a result, his enlightenment is made the center of the *sūtra.* Exoterically, the *Buddha* in enlightenment may mean the mendicant under the Bo-tree, but esoterically he is the pervading and permanent *Dharmakāya.*

The *Avataṁsaka Sūtra* stresses the teaching of pure Mind to enlarge the world view on the Absolute Reality. This world is no longer an ordinary world but the universe, *Dharmadhātu (Dharma*-realm*),* in which everything is interpenetrating, everything is mutually conditioned and conditioning. Inside everything is everything else. And yet all things are not confused. All things are one, and that one is the Absolute Reality.[5] This is the universe of the visionary perspective wherein all is empty (and it is only emptiness '*śūnyatā*' — the core and essence of Buddhism, that which is without boundary or obstruction itself, can demolish all obstructions) and therefore is seen as a flow without solid edges. This is described by the *sūtra* as a universe of radiance, luminosity with no shadows. Such is experienced by the meditator. When his mind expands, 'the solid outlines of individuality melt away and the feeling of finiteness no more oppress him.' And the whole of this universe is the embodiment of *Dharmakāya, Vairocana Buddha,* the Great Illumined *Buddha,* who is the *Buddha* of the *Avataṁsaka sūtra,* not *Śākyamuni,* the so-called historical *Buddha* who lived and died in India. It is the particular feature of this world which makes the *Avataṁsaka sūtra* justly famous.

The standpoint of this *sūtra* is Mind-Only "Mind is like a drawer, drawing all five aggregates; everything in this world, none of which is not produced by Mind". According to this *sūtra* the human mind is the universe itself and identical with *Buddha,* and it lays down the famous proposition that *Buddha,* Mind, and beings are one and the same.

* The doctrines of the *Avataṁsaka sūtra* were adapted by the *Hua-yen* school in China. The basic teaching of the *Hua-yen* school centers around the theory of causation by the universal principle or the *Dharmadhātu.* According to this, all the *dharmas* in the universe arose simultaneously; in other words, it is the creation of the universe by the universe itself. The *Hua-yen* teaches that all these *dharmas* are empty. This emptiness has two aspects — the static aspect, as principle or noumenon, and the dynamic aspect, as phenomenon. From this the school proceeds to its basic positions : first, that principle and phenomenon are interfused unimpededly with each other, and second, that all phenomena are mutually identified with one another.

As with the *T'ien T'ai,*[6] the *Hua-yen* also has its classification of the *Buddha's* teachings according to diverse human nature. The *Hua-yen* classification corrects the deficiency with its fivefold division.

1. The teaching of the Small Vehicle *(Hīnayāna)*

This teaching refers to the *Āgamas.* Although they deny the existence of the personal self *(pudgala śūnyatā),* they are realistic and admit the existence of all *dharmas* (separate elements).

2. The Elementary doctrine of the Great Vehicle (Elementary *Mahāyāna*)

Two grades are distinguished in it. First, the elementary doctrine based on the specific character of all elements *(dharma lakṣana),* for example, by *Fa-Hsiang*[7] school. Second, the elementary doctrine based on negation of all elements *(dharma śūnyatā)* by *San-lun*[8] or *Mādhyamika* school.

Since both do not admit the existence of the *Buddhatā* (Buddha nature) in all beings, both are considered to be elementary.

3. The Final doctrine of the Great Vehicle (Final *Mahāyāna*)

This doctrine advocates the Suchness of all elements *(dharma tathatā),* asserting that all living beings have *Buddhatā* and can attain Buddhahood, according to the teaching found in such *sūtras* as the *Laṅkāvatāra, Mahāparinirvāṇa, Saddharmapuṇḍarīka* and the *Mahāyānaśraddhotpāda.* By this teaching, the Ultimate truth of *Mahāyāna* is expounded. Therefore, it is called the doctrine of Maturity, or True Doctrine. The causation theory by *Tathāgatagarbha* (Womb of the *Tathāgata)* is special to this doctrine. It is also called the theory of causation by Suchness.

4. The Supreme doctrine of the Great Vehicle

This doctrine means the training without word(s) or order, directly appealing to one's own insight, by virtue of which one can attain perfect enlightenment all at once. If one's mind is at rest and abides in nonattachment, he is a *Buddha*. This is the doctrine of Ch'an school of *Bodhidharma,*[9] *Hui-neng...*

5. The Round doctrine of the Great Vehicle

The doctrine advocates One Vehicle *(ekāyāna)* instead of three. The three vehicles recognized by *Hua-yen* are : the Small *(Hīnayāna),* the Gradual (Elementary and Final *Mahāyāna)* and the Abrupt *(Ch'an* of *Mahāyāna).*

This doctrine also teaches that the ten thousand things of the phenomenal world represent the absolute mind or the noumenon, so that the all is the one, the one is the all.

The *Hua-yen* differed from other *Mahāyāna* schools such as the *T'ien T'ai* in one important aspect. The latter concentrated its attention on the relationship between the noumenon and phenomenon, whereas the former elucidated the relationship between one phenomenon and another. From the religious point of view everything in the universe, animate and inanimate, are all representations of the same supreme mind, and can perform the work of the Blessed One. This is why the school is called the perfect teaching of the *Buddha.*

3) Gaṇḍavyūha

It is the thirty-ninth and most illuminating chapter of the *Avataṃsaka sūtra* 'Entering into the Universe through the Practice and Vows of *Samantabhadra'* which makes up the *Gaṇḍavyūha sūtra.* It deals with belief, understanding, practice and enlightenment, which are after all nothing but one's own mind, and this one mind enters into universality and becomes enlightenment itself.

The *sūtra* describes the pilgrimage of a youth called *Sudhana* on the advice of *Bodhisattva Mañjuśrī,* and he at last came to *Samantabhadra,* under whose teaching he perfected his vow and entered into the *Dharmadhātu* (Absolute Reality) after an attempt of consulting with fifty-three good friends, of whom there were only five monks and the rest lay people. This shows the *Mahāyāna* tendency to lay stress upon lay people rather than upon monks. During his pilgrimage *Sudhana* was seeking truth without, by asking the help of others, but after passing through many experiences, mental and spiritual, he realised that true knowledge must come from within.

The last volume of the *sūtra* is devoted to *Samantabhadra's* Ten Vows and the desire to be born into *Sukhāvatīvyūha* (the Pure Land). The Ten Vows are: (1) to worship the *Buddhas;* (2) to praise the *Tathāgatas;* (3) to make offerings to all the *Buddhas; (4)* to confess past sins; (5) to rejoice in the virtues and happiness of others; (6) to request *Buddha* to preach the Law; (7) to request *Buddha* to live in this world; (8) to study Buddhism in order to teach it; (9) to benefit all beings; and (10) to turn over the stock of merit to others. These vows are the basis of the *Bodhisattva's* life in *Mahāyāna* Buddhism.

The story of *Sudhana* is an epitome of the entire *Gaṇḍavyūha sūtra.* It is a *sūtra* of enlightenment and emphasies the fact that all beings can be reborn in the house of the *Buddha* if they obtain enlightenment.

4) Daśabhūmika

This *Daśabhūmika Sūtra* is really a part of the *Avataṃsaka,* but has been circulated independently. In it a *bodhisattva* named *Vajragarbha,* explains the ten stages of the development of *bodhisattva.* These are:

1. *Pramuditā* (joyous): joy at having overcome the former difficulties and now entering on the path to Buddhahood.

The *bodhisattva* in this stage practises compassion according to the teaching of the *pāramitā dāna,* giving.

2. *Vimalā* (pure): freedom from all possible defilement, the stage of purity. The *bodhisattva* in this stage has the quality of loving speech and practises according to the *pāramitā sīla,* morality.

3. *Prabhākarī* (brilliant): stage of further enlightenment. The *bodhisattva* in this stage meditates upon the reality of things and seeks to find the Law for suffering beings. In this stage he practises the *pāramitā kṣānti,* patience.

4. *Arciṣmatī* (blazing fire): In this stage the *bodhisattva* exterminates all his false ideas and practises the *pāramitā vīrya,* diligence or energy.

5. *Sudurjayā* (mastery of final difficulties): The *bodhisattva* in this stage perfects his knowledge and practises the *pāramitā dhyāna,* meditation.

6. *Abhimukhī* (to see face to face): The *bodhisattva* in this stage understands the meaning of the Twelvefold Chain of Causation and practises the *pāramitā prajñā,* wisdom.

7. *Dūraṃgamā* (giving up the idea of self in order to save others): In this stage the *bodhisattva* realises and practises the *pāramitā upāya,* skilful means.

8. *Acalā* (immovable): The *bodhisattva* in this stage abides in the condition of neither birth nor death, but enters the *Buddha's* religion, purifies his *Buddha*-land and practises the *pāramitā pariṇāmanā,* transference of merit.

9. *Sādhumatī* (good mind): In this stage the *bodhisattva's* mind is of the finest discriminatory wisdom, knowing where and how to save, and he practises the *pāramitā bala,* power.

10. *Dharmamegha* (law-cloud): In the last stage the *bodhisattva* is seated upon a great lotus and a great light

proceeds from him; he is surrounded by the *Buddhas* of the ten quarters and he himself enters into the centre of the *Buddha*-land; the ten powers are perfected by him and he becomes a *Tathagāta. Jñāna* (wisdom) is the *pāramitā* he practises in this stage.

Beyond the tenth stage is the stage of a *Buddha.*

In this *Daśabhūmika sūtra* we see that *bodhisattva* is praised in contrast to *pratyekabuddhas* and *śrāvakas,* and that compassion is emphasised and placed above all. *Nirvāṇa* appears everywhere; the nature of things is explained; more than one *Buddha* is recognised, and householders or lay *bodhisattvas* are frequently mentioned.

5) Samādhirāja or Śūraṁgama Samādhi

This is a *sūtra* about "King of Meditations," or the *Candrapradīpa-sūtra,* as it is called after the principal speaker. Here, in a dialogue between *Candrapradīpa* and *Buddha,* it is shown how a *bodhisattva* can attain to the highest knowledge by means of the various meditations, especially the highest of all, the "King of Meditations," and preliminary conditions are necessary in order to prepare the spirit for this highest stage of meditation. Such preliminary conditions are the worship of the *Buddhas,* complete renunciation of the world, gentleness and goodness towards all beings, entire indifference as to one's own life and one's own health if there is a question of sacrificing them for others, and lastly the knowledge of the non-reality of the world, the steadfast belief in the unreality *(śūnyatā)* of all phenomena.

The *sūtra* also explains the practice of "King of Meditations," i.e., the meditation on emptiness. *Bodhisattva Sthiramati* questions the *Buddha* as to what *samādhi* should be practised by a *bodhisattva* who wishes to show forth the life of a *bodhisattva,* but does not wish to enter into *nirvāṇa.* According to the *sūtra,* the meditation thereafter explained by *Buddha* is the object of a *bodhisattva* who has reached the tenth stage, and by means of it anyone, lay or priest, man or woman, may enter into *nirvāṇa* without abandoning the life of birth and death.

Passages of moral contents, mostly in verses, are quoted by *Śāntideva* in the *Śikṣā-Samuccaya,* as for instance the beautiful verses about peace of mind *(Śikṣ,* p. 242f.):

"He will never depart from the doctrine of the Blessed Ones *(Sugatas* i.e., *Buddhas),* that hero will never fall into the power of women, he takes a delight in the commandment of the Blessed Ones — he who understands that real peace of mind is the true nature of Religion.

He will soon become a prince of men here, he will be a healing physician, a giver of good fortune, he will pull out completely the thorn (of pain) of the unfortunate, — he who understands that real peace of mind is the true nature of Religion.

He shines forth among the people, like the moon, by the power of his mildness, he is not angered, though he be ill-treated with clods of earth and with sticks, he remains unmoved, though he be pulled to pieces limb by limb, — he who understands that real peace of mind is the true nature of Religion."

In the *Śikṣā-Samuccaya* (p. 134) a verse is cited from the *Jñānavatī* section of the *Samādhirāja,* according to which the eating of meat which is otherwise prohibited, is allowable by way of medicine.

6) Saddharmapuṇḍarīka

The *Saddharmapuṇḍarīka* or *Lotus* declares itself as the 'King of all *sūtras*' and is considered as the most important *sūtra* in China, Korea, Japan and Vietnam and has become an object of reverence, because it is considered to be the last and supreme teaching of the *Buddha.*

At one time the *Buddha* was staying on *Gṛdhrakūṭa* mountain and surrounded by a great assembly. *Buddha* preached the doctrine and then entered into the meditation of the Immeasurable Doctrine *(Anantanirdeśapratiṣṭhāna)*, and delivered from the tuft of white hair between his brows a ray of light which illuminated eighteen thousand worlds in the East. This implies that the phenomenal worlds, though different in forms, but, under the 'eyes of indiscrimination, beyond extremes or Middle-Path' or according to absolute truth, they are simply a united entity in which the individual or ego is demolished. When awakening from his meditation he told *Śāriputra* that it was only 'skilful means' *(upāya-kauśalya)* that caused him to preach different doctrines because of his compassion for beings. His true teaching is that there is only one vehicle *(ekayāna)* of Buddhist teaching, and that it is for all.

The *sūtra* also expounds that the great cause for the appearance of the *Buddhas* is to show the *Buddhajñāna* for the living beings to enter. The *sūtra* also expounds the teaching of the external *Dharmakāya Buddha,* of which *Śākyamuni* was a manifestation. The eternal *Buddha* always dwells on Mount *Gṛdhrakūṭa* and speaks from eternity to eternity, guaranteeing Buddhahood to all beings. The twenty-fifth chapter praises the great compassion through the role of *Bodhisattva Avalokiteśvara* for the sake of serving beings, and of the merit acquired by honouring him and praising him.

All the ideas mentioned above and more things will be analysed in the following chapters of this thesis.

* Besides, the *Saddharmapuṇḍarīka-sūtra* was adapted by the *T'ien T'ai* school in China. The points of view of this school are as follows:

1. According to this school the *Buddha's* teaching is classified into "Five Periods and Eight Doctrines."

a) Five Periods (arranged chronologically):

> The time of Garland: The doctrine taught in this period was what the *Buddha* had conceived in his Enlightenment. His disciples could not understand him at all.

> The time of Deerpark: The *Buddha* preached the early *Āgamas* to suit the people of inferior capacity.

> The time of Development: When the Hinayanistic people were converted to the *Mahāyāna* doctrine. The *Buddha* preached what we call *Vaipulya sūtras*.

> The time of Wisdom: When the *Prajñāpāramitā* was preached and all the ideas of distinction and acquisition were mercilessly rejected.

> The time of the *sūtras* of *Saddharmapuṇḍarīka* and *Nirvāṇa*: Here the analyzing and the uniting of the doctrines are taught. Three vehicles were united into One Vehicle.

The object of the *Buddha's* advent on earth was to save all beings, that object can be accomplished only by practising the teachings of the *Saddharmapuṇḍarīka-sūtra*. Therefore, the *Saddharmapuṇḍarīka-sūtra* is the ultimate doctrine among all the *Buddha's* teachings and is the King of all *sūtras*.

b) Eight Doctrines:

To know properly the nature of the *Buddha's* teachings the *T'ien T'ai* school arranges them in eight doctrines.

i) First, the four doctrines as to the method of teaching:

> Sublime doctrine: The *Buddha* preached what he had conceived without using any *upāya-kauśalya*.

> Gradual doctrine: The *Buddha* induced people gradually into deeper thinking with all sorts of measures.

> Mystic doctrine: It is in reality a mystical indeterminate doctrine. Each listener thinks that the *Buddha* is teaching him alone. Thus all hear separately and variously.

> Indeterminate doctrine: It is a non-mystical indeterminate doctrine. All listeners know that all are hearing together and yet they hear differently, understand variously.

ii) Second, the four doctrines as to the nature of the teaching itself:

> The doctrine of *Piṭakas* (Scriptures).

> The doctrine common to all: It is the elementary doctrine of *Mahāyāna*.

> Distinct doctrine: It is purely *Mahāyāna,* special to *bodhisattva*. This doctrine teaches the Middle Path.

> Round doctrine: This doctrine teaches the Middle Path as noumenon "one is all, and all is one."

2. Threefold Truth and the Absolute Mind

a) Threefold Truth: In order to avoid thinking in terms of a dichotomy — noumenon versus phenomena — the *T'ien T'ai* school established the threefold truth : Void, Temporariness and Mean (Middle). *Hui-Wen* (505-577) is the founder of the *T'ien T'ai* school. He awoke to the truth by a verse concerning the "insight" in the *Mahāprajñāpāramitā śāstra* by *Nāgārjuna* as follows:

"What is produced by causes

That, I say, is identical with void

It is identical with mere name

It is again the purport of the middle path."

b) The Absolute Mind: The identification of phenomena with the absolute is further illustrated by the *T'ien T'ai* doctrine of the Absolute Mind. All things in the world depend on this mind for their existence.

3. Concentration and Insight

It follows that man's view of things in the universe as being large or small, long or short, are due to illusion which can only be destroyed by spiritual cultivation. This cultivation consists of *Chih* (concentration) and *Kuan* (insight).

a) By concentration one realizes that all the *dharmas* do not have any self-nature *(svabhāva)*, hence do not enjoy existence.

b) By insight one realizes that the *dharmas* seem to exist, but in reality they do not.

7) Lalitavistara

Lalitavistara originally contained the description of *Buddha's* life for the *Sarvāstivāda* school of *Hīnayāna*, which is enlarged and added here in the spirit of the *Mahāyāna*. It consists of 27 chapters and describes the *Buddha* as a supernatural being, a god and above all gods. As an exalted, divine being *Buddha* appears in the introductory chapter. As in all the *Vaipulya sūtra* of the *Mahāyāna*, here also the *Buddha* is bathed in the light of divine splendour and is surrounded by a large number of monks and *bodhisattvas*. And after a longwinded introduction that fills a whole big chapter, the actual story, the biography of *Buddha* begins which forms the content of the work. The *bodhisattva* (former life of the *Buddha)* in *Tuṣita* resides in a magnificent divine palace. Under the deafening noise of 84,000 drums he is requested to come down to the earth to begin his work of salvation. The conception and birth of the *bodhisattva* take place to the accompaniment of mighty miracles and omens.

The story is interrupted by a dialogue between *Ānanda* and *Buddha* in which there is a passionate lecture against those infidels who do not want to believe in the miraculous birth of *Buddha*. But belief in *Buddha* is taught as an essential constituent of religion, when *Buddha* says here:

> "To all who believe in me, I do good. Like friends are those to me who seek refuge in me. And many friends has the *Tathāgata*. Those friends of *Tathāgata* however speak always the truth, nothing false...To believe, O *Ānanda*, shall be your endeavour. This I enjoin you."[10]

It is certainly not by chance that this dialogue is added here, but the reason for this is that precisely in respect of the legends of the conception and birth of *Buddha* the *Lalitavistara* differs very much from the reports of other schools through its exaggeration of the miraculous element. Besides, the *Lalitavistara* has something more that is totally missing in the older reports. Two episodes deserve special mention in this context. One of them (chapter 8) tells how the *bodhisattva* is brought by his foster-mother as a boy to the temple and the statues of all gods rise from their pedestals in order to fall at his feet. The other (chapter 10) describes *bodhisattva's* first visit to a school. In this episode the tiny but highly talented *bodhisattva* teaches the schoolmaster and 10,000 boys the alphabets. While learning every letter of the alphabet however the *bodhisattva* gives by himself some saying of wisdom beginning with that particular letter. Also chapters 12 and 13 contain episodes which are missing in the other biographies of *Buddha*. In the next chapters (14-26) however the narrative deviates only very little from the legends known from other sources. And the last chapter (27) is devoted—quite in the manner of the *Mahāyāna sūtras*—to the glorification of the *Lalitavistara* itself and to the enumeration of merits and benefits which one earns by propagating and worshipping it.

Broadly speaking, the *Lalitavistara* is not a good old source for our knowledge of Buddhism, but for the History of Literature it is one of the most important works of Buddhist Literature.

8) Laṅkāvatāra

Laṅkāvatāra is a philosophical discourse attributed to *Śākyamuni* as delivered on the *Laṅkā* mountain in Ceylon. It represents a mature phase of speculation and not only criticizes the *Sāṅkhya, Pāśupata* and other Hindu schools, but is conscious of the growing resemblance of Mahāyānism to Brahmanic philosophy and tries to explain it.

In Buddhism, the *Laṅkāvatāra* teaches principally a modification of the *Śūnyavāda,* the *Vijñānavāda* "Mere Consciousness," which, though it also denies the reality of the external world, does at the same theme recognise that the phenomena of consciousness have a subjective reality. *Laṅkāvatāra* is a very careless compilation and consists of portions which belong to various periods. It includes 10 chapters in which the last *(Sagāthakam)* consists entirely of verse, while the rest of the *sutra* is in prose with occasional *gāthās* interspersed.

Chapter 1 gives a very detailed description of the meeting of Buddha with *Rāvaṇa*, the king of the *Rākṣasas* in *Laṅkā*. Encouraged by the *Bodhisattva Mahāmati*, *Rāvaṇa* asks *Buddha* questions about the difference between true and false doctrine (*Dharma* and *Adharma*). Chapters 2-7 treat of the whole system of the Buddhist doctrine, mainly from the standpoint of the *Vijñānavāda*. In chapter 3, among other things, there is a discussion on the paradoxical utterance of *Buddha*: "the *Buddha* word is a non-word,"[11] there is a remarkable list of names of *Buddha*. This chapter also mentions others : *Anirodhānutpāda*, *Śūnyatā, Tathatā, Dharmadhātu, Nirvāṇa*. Chapter 4 treats of the ten *bhūmis* of bodhisattvahood. Chapter 5 argues the permanency of Tathagatahood in relation to *Buddhajñāna* and *Dharmatā* as follows:

> "However, *Mahāmati*, there is another sense in which the Tathagata can be said to be permanent. How ? Because the knowledge arising from the attainment of enlightenment [=an intuitive understanding] is of a permanent nature, the Tathagata is permanent. *Mahāmati*, this knowledge, as it is attained intuitively by the Tathagatas, Arhats, Fully-Enlightened Ones, is, indeed, permanent. Whether the Tathagatas are born or not, this *Dharmatā*, which is the regulative and sustaining principle to be discoverable in the enlightenment of all the *Śrāvakas*, *Pratyekabuddha,* and philosophers, abides, and this sustaining principle of existence is not like the emptiness of space, which, however, is not understood by the ignorant and simple-minded. *Mahāmati*, this knowledge of enlightenment belonging to the Tathagatas comes forth from transcendental knowledge (*Prajñā*); *Mahāmati*, the Tathagatas, Arhats, Fully-Enlightened Ones do not come forth from the habit-energy of ignorance which is concerned with the *Citta, Manas*, and *Manovijñāna*, and the *Skandhas, Dhātus*, and *Āyatanas*. The triple world originates from the discriminating of unrealities, but the Tathagatas do not originate from the discriminating of unrealities. Where duality obtains, *Mahāmati*, there is permanency and impermanency because of its not being one. *Mahāmati*, [the truth of] absolute solitude is, indeed, non-dualistic (*advayam*) because all things are characterised with non-duality and no-birth. For this reason, *Mahāmati*, the Tathagatas, Arhats, Fully-Enlightened Ones are neither permanent nor impermanent. *Mahāmati*, as long as there is word-discrimination, there follows the faulty notion of permanency and impermanency."[12]

Chapter 8 is on meat-eating. Chapter 9 is on the *Dhāraṇīs,* which protect people against snake-demons and ghosts of all kinds. And the last Chapter 10 is a long philosophical treatise in 884 verses, in which, too, the doctrines put forth, are those of the *Vijñānavāda.* However, it is emphasized again and again that all phenomena are unreal like a *fata morgana,* an illusion, a delusion. In this chapter, *Sāṃkhyas, Vaiśeṣikas,* naked sophists, and the theists, are mentioned as adherents of false doctrines (verse 723); and the speaker in this chapter is not *Śākyamuni,* but one of his predecessors, a *Buddha* of an earlier age.

In ancient China, this *sūtra* was propagated by *Bodhidharma,* and is the recognized text of the *Ch'an* school.

9) Suvarṇaprabhāsa

The last text to be mentioned among the *Vaipulya sūtras* is *Suvarṇaprabhāsa* or 'Splendour of Gold', the contents of which are partly philosophical and ethical, and which also contains many legends, but which, for a great part, already bears the stamp of a Tantra. This *sūtra* consists of 31 chapters, which may be affected from the *Saddharmapuṇḍarīka-sūtra* for it also asserts that not only *Dharmakāya* but also *nirṃāṇakāya* is eternal (chapters 2 and 3) and may be affected from the *Prajñāpāramitā sūtra* for it also deals with *śūnyatā* (chapters 5, 9, 10). This *Suvarṇaprabhāsa sūtra,* however, has its own teachings as follows:

- As other Buddhist *sūtras,* this *Suvarṇaprabhāsa sūtra* also emphasizes the 5-aggregate body. Because from this body the *Dharmakāya* is found and practised. This body depends on *Bhūtatathatā* (the absolute, the ultimate source and character of all phenomena), and it therefore is hard to be exhausted. This body is the great vehicle, the nature of *Tathāgata,* the *Tathāgatagarbha.*

- Repentance for bad *karma* is also emphasised. The original substance of every being is indestructible. It is not subject to birth and death. It is *Bhūtatathatā*. It is luminous and brilliant. Bad *karma* do not destroy it. But bad *karma* are to be removed by repentance. Repentance is, therefore, a must and possibility. Just as moon is ever brilliant and the dark clouds which cover it must be and can be dispelled. So also the original substance has to restore its luminosity by removal of bad *karma*. All *dharmas* are relative; this *dharma* arises, then other *dharma* ceases. Repentance, therefore, arises, then bad *karma* ceases. Because all *dharmas* are *śūnya; Tathāgata* has said no-self, no-*pudgala,* no-beings, no-receiver, no-production, no-cessation, even no-practice-of-repentance.
- From the beginning to the end the *sūtra* mentions the wonderful bliss, particularly the peace and happiness of the world. The *sūtra* speaks of the role of king in using *Dharma* to rule over the country, but if there was a foreign aggression he must fight and fight successfully.
- The *sūtra* also thinks highly of the role of *devas* and good deities in the protection of the nation, people and those who practise this *sūtra*.

B) Some views on Mahāyānism:

Before entering into an analysis of the concepts and doctrines of the *Lotus,* it will be well for us first to consider the views that were held by the Indian Buddhist thinkers concerning the characteristic features of Mahāyānism.

I) *Sthiramati's* conception of Mahāyānism

As mentioned in the text *Outline of Mahayana Buddhism* by D. T. Suzuki, *Sthiramati*[13] in his little but important text *Introduction to Mahāyānism* declares that Mahāyānism is a special doctrine for the *bodhisattvas,* who are to be distinguished from the other two classes, i.e., the *śrāvakas* and the *pratyekabuddhas*. The essential difference of the doctrine consists in the belief that objects of the senses are merely phenomenal and have no reality, that the indestructible *Dharmakāya* which is all-pervading constitutes the norm of existence, that all *bodhisattvas* are incarnations of the *Dharmakāya,* who not by evil *karma* previously accumulated, but by their boundless love for all mankind, assume corporeal existences, and that people who thus appear in the flesh, as embodiments of the *Buddha* supreme, participate themselves with the masses in all possible social relations, in order that they might thus lead them to the goal of enlightenment. Meanwhile this is a short statement of the *Mahāyāna* doctrine, a more elaborate and extended enumeration of its peculiar features in contrast to those of Hīnayānism, is made in the *Miscellanea on Mahāyāna Metaphysics,*[14] *The Spiritual Stages of the Yogācāra,*[15] *An Exposition of the Holy Doctrine,*[16] *A Comprehensive Treatise on* Mahāyānism,[17] and others.

2) Seven Principal Features of Mahāyānism as distinguished from Hīnayānism

According to *Asaṅga,* who lived a little later than *Nāgārjuna,* that is, at the time when Mahāyānism was further divided into two main philosophic schools, *Yogācāra* and *Mādhyamika,* the seven features peculiar to Mahāyānism as distinguished from Hīnayānism as described in his first three texts above-mentioned are as follows:

1. Comprehensiveness: Mahāyānism does not confine itself to the teachings of one *Buddha* alone; but wherever and whenever truth is found, even under the disguise of most absurd superstitions, it makes no hesitation to winnow the grain from the chaff and assimilate it in its own system.
2. Universal love for all living beings: Hīnayānism confines itself to the salvation of individuals only; on the other

hand, Mahāyānism aims at general salvation. All the motives, efforts, and actions of a *bodhisattva* pivot on the furtherance of universal welfare.

3. Greatness in Intellectual Comprehension: Mahāyānism maintains the theory of non-*ātman* not only with regards to living beings but with regards to things in general. Whilst it denies the hypothesis of a metaphysical agent directing our mental operations, it also rejects the view that insists on the noumenal or thingish reality of existences as they appear to our senses.

4. Wonderful Spiritual Energy: *Bodhisattvas* never become tired of working for universal salvation, nor do they despair for the long time required to accomplish this noble object. To try to attain *nirvāṇa* and to be self-sufficient without paying attention to the welfare of the masses, is not the teaching of Mahāyānism.

5. *Upāya*: The term *upāya* means skilful-means. A *bodhisattva* with his altruistic heart full of love and sympathy always thinks of and leads the suffering masses to the final enlightenment according to the disposition and environment of each. And to reach this object he employs innumerable skilful means suggested by his unbiased compassion.

6. Higher Spiritual Attainment: In Hīnayānism the highest fruit attainable does not go beyond Arhatship which is ascetic saintliness. Meanwhile the followers of Mahāyānism attain even to Buddhahood with all its spiritual powers.

7. Greater Activity: When a *bodhisattva* reaches the stage of Buddhahood, he is able to manifest himself everywhere for the benefit of all sentient beings.

These seven features enumerated by *Asaṅga* are considered to be the reasons why the doctrine defended by the progressive

Buddhists is to be called Mahāyānism, or the doctrine of great vehicle, in contrast to Hīnayānism, the doctrine of small vehicle.

3) Ten Essential Features of *Mahāyāna*

The following ten points, which are most essential and enumerated by *Asaṅga* and *Vasubandhu* in their first and foremost comprehensive text *Mahāyānasaṃparigraha* (Comprehensive Treatise on Mahāyānism), are made from their own standpoint of *Yogācāra (Vijñānavāda)*[18] school rather than that of Mahāyānism in general. The analysis and systematisation of the *Buddha's* discourses gave rise to the four schools of Buddhist thought in India. They are — *Vaibhāṣika, Sautrāntika, Yogācāra* and *Mādhyamikas*. The doctrine of *Vijñāptimātratā* or *Cittamātratā* was developed by the *Yogācāra* school of thought as a criticism of contemporary philosophical currents. The two extreme views of the existence of everything by the *Vaibhāṣika* and the voidness of everything by the *Mādhyamikas* were criticised by the doctrine of *vijñāptimātratā*. This doctrine establishes the reality of consciousness or mind only and rejects the existence of external things outside consciousness. The *Yogācāra* claims that this is the True Middle Path taught by the *Buddha*. The text *Mahāyānasaṃparigraha* is a representative compendium of *Vijñānavāda* and dwells chiefly on the ten special characteristics *of Mahāyāna* as follows:

1. *Ālayavijñāna* or Eighth-consciousness : The *ālaya* is the centre of consciousness from which all worldly things and events are projected and manifested due to subjective illusion created by ignorance. All phenomena is originated from pure and impure elements, i.e. "seeds" which are causally combined in the *ālaya*. The *ālaya* is the existence of causal combination, being existent as a transformation of the Absolute *(parinispanna)*. On the basis of three

parināmas (vipāka, manana and *viṣaya-vijñāpti),* the *Yogācāra* accepts three kinds of *vijñāna*, viz. 1. *Ālayavijñāna,* 2. *Manovijñāna* and 3. *Pravṛttivijñāna.* The *vipāka* is called *Ālayavijñāna. Manana* is *Manovijñāna* and the *viṣayavijñapti* is called *Pravṛtti-vijñāna.* In other words, the *Ālaya*-consciousness, *Mano*-consciousness, Eye-consciousness, Ear-consciousness, Nose-consciousness, Tongue-consciousness, Body-consciousness and Mind-consciousness are eight kinds of *vijñāna* in *Yogācāra* system of thought. *Ālayavijñāna* is the place of origin of all kinds of consciousness and working like a flowing stream; but, with the realization of Buddhahood its course stops instantaneously. In addition, the school named *She-lun*[19] admitted the existence of *amalavijñāna* along with the six sense-centered consciousnesses *(pravṛtti-vijñānas),* the seventh thought-centered consciousness *(ādāna),* and the eighth *ālaya.* The *ālaya* appears delusory when all phenomena including seven consciousnesses are originated from "seeds" in the *alaya.* The substance of the *ālaya,* however, is *Tathatā* of pure or taintless nature. This is known as the *amalavijñāna,* the ninth consciousness. Influenced by the defiled seven kinds of consciousness, the *amala-vijñāna* causes the *ālaya* to manifest itself in its delusory aspect. The pure aspect within the *ālaya* eventually purifies the 'tainted' portion of it. In this stage, the *ālaya* as a centre of attachement is dissolved and a pure state of the original mind is realized. This is the state of *Nirvāṇa* of No Abode *(Apratiṣṭhita-Nirvāṇa),* the Suchness or Ultimate Reality *(Tathatā)* beyond conceptions and interpretations.

2. Three kinds of knowledge: The *Yogācāra* school distinguishes three kinds of knowledge: 1) Illusion *(parikalpita),* 2) Discriminative or Relative Knowledge *(para-tantra),* and 3) Perfect Knowledge *(pariniṣpanna),*

According to this school, consciousness actualises itself in dependence on others *(paratantra)*. It is of two kinds — (a) false *(parikalpita),* the defiled aspect of *paratantra* awakened into activity by subjective ignorance, that refers to discrimination *(vikalpa)* divided into the perceiving *(darśanabhāga)* and the perceived *(nimittabhāga)*. This is the characteristics of Mere-consciousness *(vijñaptimātratā)*; and (b) the absolute *(pariniṣpanna),* i.e., the pure or real aspect of *paratantra* that refers to True Thusness. This is the nature of the *Vijñaptimātratā*. It is this clear insight into the nature of things, i.e., into their non-realness as *ātman* or the emptiness of all *dharmas* that constitutes perfect knowledge.

3. The attainment of the insight of mere ideation: When we attain to the perfect knowledge, we recognise the ideality of the universe. There is no an objective world, which is really an illusive manifestation of the mind called *Ālayavijñāna*. And even this supposedly real existence of the *Ālayavijñāna* is a product of particularisation called forth by the ignorant *Manovijñāna* (or Sixth consciousness). The *Manovijñāna,* or empirical ego, as it might be called, having no adequate knowledge as to the true nature of the *Ālaya,* takes the latter for a metaphysical agent, that like the master of a puppet-show manages all mental operations following its humour. Like the silkworm imprisons itself in the cocoon created by itself, the *Manovijñāna,* entangling itself in ignorance and confusion, takes its own illusory creations for real realities *(dharmas)*.

4. Six Perfections (*pāramitās*): For the regulation of moral life, the *Yogācāra* school as well as the other *Mahāyāna* schools, advocates the practising of the six *Pāramitās,* i.e., 1. *Dāna* (giving), 2. *Śīla* (moral precept), 3. *Kṣānti* (patience), 4. *Vīrya* (effort), 5. *Dhyāna* (meditation), and 6. *Prajñā* (knowledge or wisdom). These Six *pāramitās*

are explained by *Asaṅga* respectively, by not clinging to wealth or pleasures (1), by not cherishing any thoughts to violate the precepts (2), by not feeling dejected in the face of evils (3), by not awakening any thought of indolence while practising goodness (4), by maintaining serenity of mind in the midst of disturbance and confusion of this world (5), and finally by always practising *ekacitta* (One mind) and by truthfully comprehending the nature of things (6), the *bodhisattvas* recognise the truth of *Vijñaptimātra,*- the truth that there is nothing that is not of ideal or subjective creation.

5. Ten *Bhūmis:* Mahāyānism asserts that there are ten spiritual stages of bodhisattvahood, viz., (1) *Pramuditā,* joy at having overcome the former difficulties and now entering on the path to Buddhahood; (2) *Vimalā,* freedom from all possible defilement, the stage of purity; (3) *Prabhākari,* stage of further enlightenment; (4) *Arciṣmatī,* of glowing wisdom; (5) *Sudurjayā,* mastery of utmost or final difficulties; (6) *Abhimukhī,* the open way of wisdom above definitions of impurity and purity; (7) *Dūraṃgamā,* proceeding afar, getting above ideas of self in order to save others; (8) *Acalā,* attainment of calm unperturbedness; (9) *Sādhumatī,* of the finest discriminatory wisdom, knowing where and how to save, and possessed of the ten powers; and (10) *Dharma-megha,* attaining to the fertilizing powers of the law-cloud. By passing through all these ten stages one after another, an aspirant is believed to reach the oneness of *Dharma-kāya.*

6. *Śīla* (Moral precepts): The Yogācārists claim that the precepts practised by the Mahāyānists are far superior to those of Hīnayānists. The latter tend to externalism and formalism, and do not go deep into our spiritual, subjective motives. As for the physical, verbal, and spiritual precepts observed by the *Buddha,* the Hīnayānists observe the first

two neglecting the last which is more important than the rest. For instance, the *śrāvakas* follow the ten *śikṣās*[20] because they wish to attain *Nirvāṇa* for their own sake, and not for other's. Conversely, due to aiming at an universal emancipation of mankind the *bodhisattva* even violates the ten *śikṣās,* if necessary, provided his action is right and beneficient to humanity at large.

7. *Samādhi* (Meditation): *Mahāyāna* emphasises the purification of the inner life. Its teaching applies not to things outward and its principles are not of the ascetic and exclusive class. The Mahāyānists do not shun to commingle themselves with the 'dust of worldliness' for the spiritual benefits of the masses; even so, having immovable faith in the *Mahāyāna,* they never become contaminated by vanity and worldly pleasures with which they may constantly be in touch. They aim at the realisation of the *Bodhi* and have a clear insight into the doctrine of non-*ātman*. Being free from all spiritual faults, they live in perfect accord with the laws of Suchness and discharge their duties without the least conceit.

8. *Prajñā* (Perfect wisdom): The intellectual superiority of a *bodhisattva* is shown by his possession of knowledge of non-particularisation *(anānārtha)*. This knowledge, philosophically considered, is the knowledge of the absolute, or the knowledge of the universal in which the *bodhisattva's* mind is free from the dualism, namely *saṃsāra* (birth-and-death) — *nirvāṇa,* being — non-being, object — subject, ego — non-ego.

9. The higher knowledge without discrimination: In consequence of the intellectual elevation, a *bodhisattva* perceives the identity of the two extremes. He sees the 'ever-changing many' in the 'never-changing one' and vice versa, *saṃsāra* in *nirvāṇa* and vice versa. His inward life is in accord at once with the laws of transitory phenomena

and with those of transcendental Suchness. He lives in the world like unto the lotus flower, the emblem of immaculacy, which grows out of the mire and yet does not share its defilement.

10. *Trikāya* (The threefold body of the *Buddha)*: The last characteristic to be mentioned as distinctly Mahāyānistic is the doctrine of *Trikāya.* There is, it is asserted, the highest being which is the ultimate cause of the universe and in which all existences find their essential origin and significance. This is called by the Mahāyānists *Dharmakāya.* The *Dharmakāya,* however, does not remain in its absoluteness, it reveals itself in the realm of cause and effect and manifests in concrete forms after the people' inner needs. This is called *Nirmānakāya,* that is, the Body of Transformation, that of which *Gautama Buddha* is an example. But when *Dharmakāya* responds to the needs of the *bodhisattvas* whose spiritual life is on a much higher plane than that of ordinary mortals, it takes on itself the Body of Bliss or *Sambhogakāya.* This third Body is a supernatural existence.

The above-mentioned seven or ten peculiarly Mahayánistic characteristics are what the Indian Buddhist philosophers of the first century down to the fifth or sixth century A.D. thought to be the most essential points of their faith and what they thought to be called 'Great Vehicle' *(Mahāyāna)* of deliverance, in contrast to the faith of their conservative brethren.

4) *Gotra*: The foundation of *Mahāyāna*

Philosophy in India, generally, is considered as consisting in the interpretation of experiences in order to search for the underlying principle so that people may guide their life. The term referred to the underlying principle or force which causes transformations in the substratum is *Gotra.* The *Uttaratantra,* one of the five works[21] attributed to *Maitreya* discusses the philosophy comprised in *Gotra.* The importance of the *Uttaratantra* lies in the fact that it discusses those notions of Buddhism prior understanding of which is essential to understand the *Mahāyāna,* especially the *Mādhyamika,* spiritual discipline. The most important of them is the notion of *Gotra,* which has a history of its development. The main concern of the *Uttaratantra* is to discuss and elaborate the concept of *Gotra* which is the basis and source of various *Mahāyāna* notions, such as *Dhātu,*[22] *Dharmadhātu,*[23] *Buddhatā,*[24] *Tathāgata-garbha,*[25] *Tathatā,*[26] *Dharmatā,*[27] *Niḥsvabhāvatā,*[28] *Śūnyatā,*[29] *Pudgalanairātmya,*[30] *Samatā,*[31] *Trikāya,*[32] and *Ekayāna.*[33] The word *'Gotra'* is variously translated as family, clan, spiritual lineage, germ, seed, class, category, mine and matrix.

The *Gotra* is considered by D.T. Suzuki as Suchness, he puts it:

> "Suchness *(Bhūtatathatā),* the ultimate principle of existence, is known by so many different names, as it is viewed in so many different phases of its manifestation. Suchness is the Essence of *Buddhas,* as it constitutes the reason of Buddhahood: it is the *Dharma,* when it is considered the norm of existence; it is the *Bodhi* when it is the source of intelligence; *Nirvāṇa,* when it brings eternal peace to a heart troubled with egoism and its vile passions; *Prajñā* (wisdom), when it intelligently directs the course of nature; the *Dharmakāya,* when it is religiously considered as the fountainhead of love and wisdom; the *Bodhicitta* (intelligence-heart), when it is the awakener of religious consciousness; *Śūnyatā* (vacuity), when viewed as transcending all particular forms; the *summum bonum (kuśalam),* when its ethical phase is emphasise; the Highest Truth *(Paramārtha),* when its epistemological

feature is put forward; the Middle Path *(mādhyamārga)*, when it is considered above the onesidedness and limitation of individual existence; the Essence of Being *(Bhūtakoti)*, when its ontological aspect is taken into account; the *Tathāgata-garbha* (the Womb of *Tathāgata)* when it is thought of in analogy to mother earth, where all the germs of life are stored, and where all precious stones and metals are concealed under the cover of filth."[34]

Gotra possesses ten characteristics, discussed by the *Uttaratantra*, as follows: 1) Essence (*svabhāva*), 2) Cause (*hetu*), 3) Effect (*phala*), 4) Function (*karma*), 5) Relation (*yoga*), 6) Manifestation (*vṛtti*), 7) State (*avasthā*), 8) All-pervasive (*sarvatrānugata*), 9) Unmodifiable essence (*avikāritva*), and Unitedness (*asambheda*).[35]

II) Language and Style of the *Lotus*

The *Lotus* underwent several revision and was completed after some additions. It is composed in a language which represents the mixture of both Prakrit and Sanskrit, popularly known as *Gāthā* Sanskrit, or Mixed Sanskrit, or Buddhist Sanskrit, or Buddhist Hybrid Sanskrit (BHS) and so on. F. Edgerton says:

> "The SP shows itself as a well-planned systematic introduction to the special dogmas of the *Mahāyāna*. From the literary point of view, too, it is one of the best in all BHS literature; only the Lalitavistara can be said to rival it in literary merit."[36]

The whole structure of the *Lotus* is dramatic; scenes change often and suddenly; *Buddhas, bodhisattvas*, and living beings behave themselves very actively and lively. Some scholars took it as the influence of Indian dramas.[37] Some aspects of its style may not appeal to many moderns. It is leisurely, formulaic, and repetitious; it does not try to be concise or economical in style.[38]

III) Date of Compilation and Spread of the *Lotus*

The prototype of the *Lotus* now existing was produced in the first century A.D. and the original consisting of 27 chapters was already existent in 150 A.D.[39] This *sūtra* had at least four periods to pass through before it was completed. The approximate dates of the four periods as assigned by Fuse are as follows:[40]

I: chapters 1-9 and 17, (verse);	1st century B.C.
II: chapters 1-9 and 17, (prose);	1st century A.D.
III: chapters 10-20 and 27 (except the chapters Devadatta and 17);	circa 100 A.D.
IV: chapters 21-26;	circa 150 A.D.

If we presume that *Nāgārjuna* lived about the end of the second century, we might conclude that the central part of the *Lotus* had already been in existence at the end of the first century A.D.,[41] and the *Lotus* was completed about the end of the second century A.D. in *Gandhāra* or somewhere in the neighbourhood of *Kapiśa.*[42]

The above-mentioned presumption advanced by various scholars is further confirmed by the facts relating to the social background of the coming into existence of *Mahāyāna* Buddhism. The parable of a son of the money-lender who had amassed a huge fortune by collecting exorbitant interest from his clients, is given in the fourth chapter *(Adhimukti-parivarta)* of the *Lotus.*

> *Bahu-dhana-dhānya-hiraṇya-kośa-koṣṭhāgāś cabhaved bahusurvar-ṇarūpya-maṇi-muktā-vaiḍūrya-śaṅkha-śilā-pravāḍa-jātarūpa-rajata-samanvāgataś ca bhaved bahu-dāsi-dāsa-karmakara-pauruṣeyaś ca bhaved bahu-hasty-aśva-ratha-gaveḍa-kasamanvāgataś ca bhavet. Mahāparivāraś ca bhaven mahājanapadeṣu ca dhanikaḥ syād āyoga-prayoga-kṛṣi-vaṇijya-prabhūtaś ca.*[43]

On his death-bed, the parable runs, he ordered his son to call his relatives for a conference, to which the king and his ministers came.

Sagṛhapatis...maraṇakālasamaye pratyapasthite taṃ daridrapuruṣam ānayya mahato jñātisaṃghasyopanāmaitvā rājṇo vā rājamātrasya vā purato naigama-jānapadānāṃ casaṃmukham evaṃ saṃśrāvayet.[44]

The account of this capitalist, who was so powerful that he could call to his death-bed even the king and his ministers, tells how highly developed was the monetary economy during this age.

As a matter of fact, India's monetary economy made a precipitous advance in the period of Wema Kadphises (after about 37 A.D.).[45] It is therefore thinkable that the *a quo* of the period of the appearance of the *Lotus* was about 40 A.D. Many *stūpas* remaining in North-West and other parts of India are those built in the period of King *Vāsudeva*. In fact, those built during his period are overwhelmingly large in number. And after his death the erection of *stūpas* abruptly went out of fashion, as is evidenced from archaeological relics of the age.[46] Now, since King *Vāsudeva* reigned during 202-229 A.D., it is certain that the portion of the *Lotus* up to the XXII chapter came into being some time between 40 and 220 AD.

An inscription referring to the Three Vehicles (55 A.D.) was found.[47] This may indicate the date of the formation of the *Lotus*, because the *sūtra* did mention Three-Vehicles, i.e., *Śrāvakayāna*, *Pratyekabuddhayāna* and *Bodhisattvayāna*. According to the *Buddha* in the *Lotus* there is only One Vehicle, but not any of the above-mentioned Three-Vehicles, which is the real path or real goal for the deliverance.

The *Lotus* was completed in India about the time of *Nāgārjuna* and of the two Indian Buddhist philosophical schools of *Mādhyamika* and *Yogācāra* (or *Vijñaptimātratā*).[48] It became popular and centrally philosophic first in China in the 6th century A.D. and later in some Eastern countries in the early phase of the expansion of Buddhism there. It is the most sacred text of the *T'ien T'ai* sect of China as well as *Tendai* and *Nichiren*[49] sects of Japan and is the favourite, the best known and most universally authoritative, text of the Buddhists in China, Japan, Korea and Vietnam, till the present day.

IV) Meaning of the Title:

The title of the *Saddharmapuṇḍarīka-sūtra* or *Lotus* implies the basic Buddhist concepts discussed in the text such as *Ekayāna, Buddhajñāna, Buddhatā*... On which some Vietnamese scholars explain:

-"In the *Saddharmapuṇḍarīka, Saddharma* refers to One-Vehicle (to confirm everybody is *Buddha*-to-be). The One-Vehicle is compared to *pùṇḍarīka.*"

(Diệu-pháp Liên-hoa có gốc từ tiếng Phạn *Saddharmapuṇḍarīka.* Diệu-pháp là chỉ cho Nhất thừa (xác quyết ai cũng làm Phật). Nhất hthừa ấy ví dụ như hoa sen.)[50]

-"The inconceivably ultimate *Dharma* is called *Saddharma*. *Saddharma* is the cause of the path of One-Vehicle, is the effect of the path of One-Vehicle. The first half 14 chapters speaks of the cause of One-Vehicle, the last half 14 chapters of the effect of One-Vehicle. Naming the cause-effect of the One-Vehicle as Fine *Dharma* aims against at the inferior *Dharma* of Three-Vehicles. *Puṇḍarīka* is simile. The lotus petals and lotus seed-pots existing simultaneously represent the simultaneity of the cause and effect of One-Vehicle."

(*Saddharma:* Pháp thù thắng dệ nhất không thể nghĩ bàn thì gọi là Diệu-pháp... Diệu-Pháp là nhân của dạo Nhất-thừa, là quả của dạo Nhất-thừa. Mười bốn phẩm dầu nói về nhân của Nhất-thừâ, mười bốn phẩm cuối nói về quả của Nhất-thứa. Gọi nhân quả Nhất-thừa là diệu pháp dể dối lại với thô pháp của Tam-thừa. Liên-hoa(hoa sen) là thí dụ, cánh sen và hạt sen đồng thời tồn tại biểu trưng cho nhân và quả của Nhất-thừa.)[51]

-"In India there have been 4 kinds of lotus: 1) *utpala;* 2) *kumuda; 3) padma;* 4) *pundarīka.* They have the colour of blue, yellow, red, white respectively and plus nilotpala, the fifth. All these five kinds were translated into lotus. But the usually so-called lotus is the white *pundarīka.* This lotus has 3 periods *mukula,* when not yet blossom; *kamala,* when blossomed and nearly crumble; and *pundarīka,* during blossoming beautifully."

(Padma: *Ở thiên trúc có 4 loại hoa sen* :1) utpala; 2) kumuda; 3) padma; 4) *pundarīka. Theo thứ tự là: xanh, vàng, dỏ, trắng và thêm loại nilotpala là năm. Năm loại này dịch chung là hoa sen. Nhưng thông thường gọi hoa sen là chỉ loại hoa sen pundarīka màu trắng. Loại hoa này có 3 thời: Khi chưa nở gọi là Mukula, khi nở rồi và khi sắp tàn gọi là Kamala. Đang dộ nở dẹp ghì gọi là pundarīka.*)[52]

"The Lotus is compared to the relation of falseness, means and realness: The lotus petals are falseness, means and lotus seed-pots are realness."

(*Hoa sen ví với quan hệ giữa quyền và thực : cánh sen là quyền, hạt sen là thực.*)[53]

Besides, one more explanation giving the detailed meaning of the title of the *Saddharmapuṇḍarīka-sūtra* is as follows:

"The title of the text in its full name in Chinese is *"Diệu-pháp Liên-hoa giáo Bồ-tát Phật sở hộ-niệm*

(The *Saddharmapuṇḍarīka,* a *Dharma* to be taught to *bodhisattvas, a Dharma* which the *Buddha* keeps ever in mind), in its shorter *"Diệu-pháp Lêin-hoa"* (The *Saddharmapuṇḍarīka),* and in its shortest *"Pháp- Hoa"* (The *Dharma*-Flower). The title is a compound noun belonging to the style of *"Pháp dụ" (Dharma*-simile), *"Diệu-pháp"* is *Dharma, "Liên-hoa"* is simile. According to the text *Pháp-Hoa, Diệu-pháp (Saddharma)* is *Buddhajñāna* available in every living being, which is also called *"Pháp-thân thanh-tịnh"* (Pure *Dharmakāya)* or *"Phật-tánh" (Buddhatā)...* If one realizes the *Buddhajñāna,* he will not be stuck in the dual things as an ordinary man is. *Liên-hoa (puṇḍarīka)* is simile. *Buddhajñāna* is compared to lotus because the lotus bears the following characteristics:

1) Simultaneous cause-effect: It means that the lotus petals and lotus seed-pots exist simultaneously. Unlike other flowers, when blossoming the petals fall and the flower buds develop into fruits. But in the lotus the seed-pod is available in the flower. Since the petals have not fallen the seed-pods have not displayed. If the petals all fall, then the seed-pods would display completely. Just so, *Buddha's* wisdom is available in every living being. For being covered by ignorance the *Buddha's* wisdom does not come out. If one cultivated perfectly, his *Buddha's* wisdom would come out brilliantly. That is simultaneous cause-effect.

2) Although coming out from the filthy mud, the lotus still keeps its perfume and pureness. Many people have a taste for the lotus not for its beauty, fragrance like other flowers but for its keeping pure, perfume having grown from the filthy mud. Likewise, the body of five aggregates *(pañcaskandha),* if viewed from the enlightened eyes, it is very foul, impure. For all that, it possesses an

eternally brilliant and pure thing, which the text *Lotus* calls *Buddha's* wisdom.

3) Lotuses exist in their various states: some come out of the surface of water and display the buds, blossoming and showing the seed-pods; some are still in the water; and some have just come out of mud. Likewise, all human beings, *devas, śrāvakas, pratyekabuddhas,* and *bodhisattvas,* though possessing various levels of understanding, do possess their own immanent Buddha's wisdom. If they cultivated perfectly they would become *Buddhas.*

4) Lotuses are neither touched by bees and butterflies, not being used to make up by women. Likewise, *Buddha's* wisdom is a transcendental, wonderful *Dharma* which cannot be made impure by any worldly things."

(Tên kinh, bản chữ Hán nói dủ là "Diệu-Pháp Liên-Hoa Giáo Bồ-Tát Pháp Phật Sở Hộ Niệm"', gọi tắt là Diệu-Pháp Liên-Hoa, nói gọn nữa là Kinh Pháp-Hoa. Tên kinh được cấu tạo theo đề ghép, thộc loại pháp dụ. Diệu-pháp, là pháp, Liên-hoa là dụ. Theo kinh Pháp-Hoa. Diệu-pháp lá Tri kiến- phật có sẵn nơi mỗi chúng sanh, còn gọi là Pháp thân thanh tịnh hay Phật tánh... Nếu người nhận ra Tri- kiến- Phật thì không còn kẹt trong pháp đối đãi hai bên của phàm phu. Liên-hoa là dụ, sở dĩ dụ Tri- kiến- phật như hoa sen, vì hoa sen có những đặc điểm sau:

1) *Nhán quả dồng thới, nghĩa là hoa sen, gương sen có đồng một lúc, không giống như những hoa khác khi nở, cánh hoa tàn rồi mởi tượng nụ thành trái. Gương sen đã có sẵn trong hoa, vì cánh hoa chưa rụng nên gươnbg chưa lộ ra. Nếu cánh hoa rụng hết thì gương sẽ lộ ra đầy dặn. Cũng vậy, Tri- kiến- phật có sẵn nơi mỗi chúng sanh, vì vộ minh phủ che nên nó không hiện. Nếu ngươi biết tu hành, công phu viên mãn thì Tri- kiến- phật hiện tròn sáng. Đó là ý nghĩa nhân quả dồng thời.*

2) *Hoa sen mọc trong bùn lầy nhơ nhớp mà không bị hôi tanh, vẫn đẹp thơm thanh khiết. Hoa sen được người ưa quí, không phải ở sắc đẹp, mùi thơm như những hoa khác, mà quí ở chỗ : Hoa mọc từ nơi bùn lầy như nhớp mà vẫn giữ được sắc hương thanh khiết. Cũng giống như thân năm uẩn này, nếu nhìn với con mắt giác ngộ thì nó rất ô uế bất tịnh. Tuy nó ô uế bất tịnh nhưng có cái hằng thanh tịnh sáng suốt, kinh Pháp-hoa gọi đo là Tri kiến Phật.*

3) *Hoa sen có nhūng hoa vượt lên khỏi mặt nụước hé nụ, trổ hoa, bày gương, hạt; lại có những hoe còn đang ở trong nước, và cũng có những hoa vừa nhú lên khỏi bùn. Tất cả những hoa sen ấy, trươc sen đều nở hoa sắc hương thanh khiết. Cũng vậy, Người. Trời, Thanh văn, Duyên giác. Bồ tát căn cơ tuy cơ sai biệt; nhưng ai cũng có Tri-kiến- phật, nếu tu hánh viên mãn thì thành Phật.*

4) *Hoa sen không bị ong bướm bu đậu và không bị phụ nữ dùng để trang điểm. Cũng vậy, Tri- kiến- phật la pháp vi diệu nhiệm mầu, không bị bất cứ pháp thế gian nào làm ô nhiễm.*[54]

V) Structure of the Lotus:

The *Lotus* consists of 28 chapters in English translation[55] but of 27 chapters in extant Sanskrit. The following is a comparative catalogue of the chapter titles in the two versions.[56]

Chinese translation by Kumarajiva	Extant Sanskrit
1. Introduction *(hsu)*	1.Introduction *(nidānaparivarta)*
2. Expedient devices *(fang pien)*	2. Skill in means *(upāyakauśalya)*
3. Parable (p'i *yu)*	3. Parable *(anupamya)*

4. Belief and understanding *(hsin chieh)*	4. Strong inclination, attachment *(adhimukti)*
5. Parable of medicinal herbs *(yao ts' ao yu)*	5. Medicinal herbs *(auṣadhī)*
6. Bestowal of prophecy *(shou Chi)*	6. Prophecy *(vyākaraṇa)*
7. Parable of the conjured *(hua ch'eng yu)*	7. Former connection city *(pūrvayoga)*
8. Receipt of prophecy by five hundred disciples *(wu pai ti tzu shou chi)*	8.Prophecy to five hundred mendicant Monks *(Pañacabhiksuśatsa-vyākarana)*
9. Prophecies conferred on *(shou hsueh wu hsueh jen chi)*	9.Prophecy to *Ānanda* and learners and adepts others *(Ānandādivyākaraṇa)*
10. Preachers of *Dharma* *(fa shih)*	10. Preachers of *Dharma* *(dharmabhāṇaka)*
11. Apparition of the jeweled *stūpa (hsien pao t'a)*	11. Apparition of the *stūpa* *(stūpasaṃdarśana)*
12. Devadatta *(T'i-p'o-ta-to)*	12. Blank
13. Fortitude *(ch'uan ch'ih)*	13. Fortitude *(utsāha)*
14. Comfortable conduct *(an lo hsing)*	14. Pleasant conduct *(sukhavihāra)*
15. Welling up out of the *(ts'ung ti yung ch'u)*	15. Rise of *bodhisattvas* out earth of an aperture in the earth *(bodhisattva Pṛthivīvivarasamudgama)*
16. The life span of the Thus Come One *(Ju lai shou liang)*	16. The life span of the Thus Gone One *(Tathāgatāyuṣpramāṇa)*

17. Discrimination of merits *(fen pieh kung te)*	17. Circuit of merits *(puṇyaparyāya)*
18. The merits of appropriate joy *(sui hsi kung te)*	18. Exposition of the merits of Appropriate joy *(anumodanāpuṇyanirdeśa)*
19. The merits of the *Dharma-preachers (fa shik kung te)*	19. Praise of the *Dharma-preachers (dharmabhāṇakānusamsa)*
20.The *Bodhisattva* Never Disparaging *(ch'ang pu chi'ing p'u-sa)*	20. *Sadāparibhūta*
21. The supernatural powers of the Thus Come One *(ju lai shen li)*	21.The constituents of magic of the Thus Gone One *(Tathāsgataddhy-abhisaṃskāra)*
22. Entrustment *(chu lei)*	22. Entrustment *(aṇuparīndanā)*
23.The former affairs of the *Bodhisattva* Medicine King *(yao wang p'u-sa pen shih)*	23. The former connection of *Bhaiṣajyarāja (Bhaiṣajyarājapūrvayoga)*
24.The *Bodhisattva* Fine Sound *(miao yin p'u-sa)*	24. *Gadgadasvara*
25. The gateway to every where of the *Bodhisattva* He Who Observes the sounds of the World *(Kuan shik yin p'u-sa p'u men)*	25. entitled the Chapter *Samantamukha* of *Avalokiteśvara,* entitled the Chapter of *Samantamukha (Samantamukhapa-rivarto nāmāvalokiteśavara-Vikurvaṇa-nirdeśaḥ)*
26. *Dhāraṇī (t'o-lo-ni)*	26. Magic formulas *(Dhāraṇī)*
27. The former affairs of the King Fine Adornment	27. The former connection of *Śubhavyūharāja*

(miao chuang yen wang	*Śubhavyūharājapūrvayoga)* *pen shih)*
28. The encouragements of the *Bodhisattva* Universally Worthy *(p'u hsien p'u-sa chu,an fa)*	28. The encouragements *of Samantabhadra (Samanatabhadro-tsāhana-parivarta)*

VI) Philosophy of the Lotus **in General:**

The *Lotus* owes various ideas to works prior to it.[57] It was produced with materials obtained from various *sūtras,* e. g. the Diamond *sūtras,*[58] some of its special features being derived from the *Paravaradevaaparipṛcchā.*[59] It has been asserted that even the influence by the *Chāndogya-upaniṣad* can be found in this *sūtra.*[60] The *sūtra* reflects some events of the life of the *Buddha* and his disciples.[61] The followers of the *Lotus* extolled the practice of reciting *sūtras.*[62] The custom of copying manuscripts of the *Lotus* as a meritorious act did not exist from the earliest times when the earlier portion of the *sūtra* was composed, but it occurred in the process of enlarging and developing the *sūtra.*[63] *Dhāraṇis* were inserted later in the *sūtra.*[64]

The historical *Sākyamunibuddha*, in this *sūtra*, is no longer a man, the mendicant of the *sūtras*, but a god above all gods, who has lived for countless ages and will live for ever. His doctrine is that everyone who has heard the preaching of *Buddha*, performed meritorious works, and led a moral life can become a *Buddha*. Even those who adore relics, erect stūpas, make *Buddha* images and even *icchantikas*[65] obtain the highest enlightenment.

After having given the requisite background the philosophy of the Lotus may be given in short. As aforesaid, the *Lotus* exists in its Indian philosophical background. Therefore, it is affected by those philosophical doctrines. However, it calls itself the 'King of all *sūtras*.' For this reason it certainly has its own specific features, which maybe summarised as below:

Firstly, the *Lotus* puts forth the Ultimate Reality or the *Ekayāna,* Oneness *(Ekatva Advayatā),* the complete symbiosis of the extremes, such as theory and practice, cause and effect, noumenon and phenomena, *ad infinitum*; in other words, there is no dichotomy, duality from the standpoint of Absolute. *Gotra,* an underlying principle of *Mahāyāna,* is here identical with *Ekāyāna* or *Buddhajñāna* when it is viewed from the subjective phase.

In the sense of the complete symbiosis the *Lotus gives* us a right world outlook as well as a right outlook on life. For instance, how is the relation between *samsāra* and *nirvāṇa* ? The thinking may be like this : *Nirvāṇa* is the reality of *samsāra;* conversely, *samsāra* is the falsity *(samvṛti)* of *nirvāṇa. Nirvāṇa* is *samsāra* without birth and decay. The difference between them is in our way of looking at them; it is epistemic, not metaphysical. For this reason the *Lotus* extols the *Buddhajñāna,* which is an intuitive perception of the real *(tattva)* as non dual *(advaya).* Here is the central philosophy of the *Lotus.* Thus, the doctrine of *Trikayāna,* i.e., *śrāvakāyāna, pratyekabuddhayāna* and *bodhisattvayāna* is considered by the *Lotus* as an *upāya-kauśalya,* and the *Lotus* replaces them with the doctrine of *Ekāyāna,* in which all *dharmas* are seen as the sameness (*samatā*), which is not substance *(svabhāva)* in the *Sarvastivadins,* or self (*ātman*) in the *Upaniṣadic* sense. In the sense of the sameness the *Lotus* now means quite different from other *Mahāyāna sūtras,* for it is the course of enlightenment open to everybody, *śrāvakas, pratyekabuddhas* and even to *icchantikas* without discrimination. And following are some among the messages of the *Buddha* or of the *Lotus* to us:

> "*Sāriputra,* the Thus Come One by resort to the One *Buddha* Vehicle alone preaches the *Dharma* to beings. There are no other vehicles, whether two or three."[66]

"*Sāriputra,* I do this only in order that they may gain the One *Buddha* Vehicle and knowledge of all modes."[67]

"The *Buddhas,* the Most Venerable of 'Two-Legged Beings,
Know that the *Dharmas* are ever without a nature of their own.
By virtue of conditions is the *Buddha*-seed realized:
For this reason they preach the One Vehicle."[68]

Realizing that the notions of *ātman* and *pañca-skandhas* (five aggregates) are dangerous products of ignorance which obliterate the noble path of the aspirants as well as of the great fountain of loving kindness, the *Lotus* arranges some chapters in its latter part for the elimination of these notions and for the raising of the great compassion *(karuṇā)* of *bodhisattvas.*

Secondly, the *Lotus* higlights the knowledge *(prajñā)* and the practice *(śīla* and *karuṇā)* of the Ultimate Reality, which the two Buddhist philosophical schools, i.e., the *Mādhyamika* and the *Yogācāra* (or *Vijñānavāda)* call *Paramārtha-satya* (Absolute Truth) and *Parinispanna* (Absolute Knowledge or Absolute Reality) respectively.

Thirdly, as far as the literature aspect is concerned, the *Lotus* makes use of many personifications, similies, symbols for the illustration of the qualities, attributes, concepts and doctrines. Besides, it also uses *dhāraṇī* as a particular method of *Mahāyāna* requiring the help of the *Buddha's* supernatural powers for the attainment of the supreme goal, Buddhahood.

Lastly, as far as the philosophical structure of the *Lotus* is concerned, through all its 28 chapters translated by *Kumārajīva,* this *sūtra* may be systematically divided as follows:

- The former 14 chapters speak of the historical or phenomenon *Buddha* and the doctrine of One-Vehicle. To start, the *Buddha* entered into the *sāmadhi* of the Abode of the Immeasurable Doctrine *(Anantanirdeśa)* ; his body, speech and mind were motionless. This implies that the Ultimate Reality is inxpressible. Then he performed the miracles (chapter 1). A ray of light emitting from the white curls between his eyebrows that illuminates eighteen thousand worlds in the east. This implies that with the middle-path vision of *Buddhajñāna,* there is the realisation that many is one and one is many, nothing obliterates one another; because, all the *dharmas* do not have any self-nature *(niḥsvabhāva)*.

  From chapter 2 onwards the *Buddha* stopped meditation and began to preach (by means of language, and due to this, the term *Upāya-kauśalya* appears) to human beings. He preached the doctrine of One Vehicle directly (chapter 2). He preached the doctrine of One Vehicle by similes (chapters 3, 4, 5, 7, 11) and by predicting the Buddhahood (chapter 3, 6, 7, 8, 9, 12, 13). He also mentioned the four conditions to practise the doctrine One Vehicle (chapters 10, 14).

- The latter 14 chapters speak of the supernatural or noumenon *Buddha* (chapter 16), the meritorious deeds of *bodhisattvas* (chapters 15, 20, 23, 24, 25, 27, 28), the great benefits for the followers of the doctrine of One Vehicle (chapters 16, 17, 18, 19) and the spiritual dissemination of the One Vehicle doctrine (chapters 21, 22, 26).

And, an intensive study of the *Lotus* reveals that underlying the highly symbolic expressions of this *sūtra* is a philosophical system, which contains the concepts and doctrines as under:

- *Ekayāna* (One-Vehicle),
- *Upāya-kauśalya* (Skilfull means),

- *Bodhisattva,*
- *Buddhahood,* and
- *Dhāraṇī.*

References

1. Encyclopedia of Religion and Ethics. Vol. 8, p. 88.
2. *Aṣṭasāhasrikā,* in Bibliotheca Indica (Calcutta), 1888, p. 20f.
3. Ibid., p. 39f.
4. Ibid., p. 32ff.
5. See *"Buddhistic Foundations of Global Ethics"* by Prof. S. R. Bhatt, paper presented in Indo-Korean International Seminar, Indian Council of Philosophical Research, New Delhi, 2001.
6. A Buddhist school in China depends on the *Saddharmapuṇḍarīka-sūtra* as its Lodestar.
7. Also a Buddhist school in China depends on the doctrine of the *Yogācāra (Vijñaptimātratā).*
8. Also a Buddhist school in China.
9. He is the founder of Ch'an school in China.
10. *Lalitavistara,* Ch. 7, ed. Lefmann, 1908, pp. 87-91.
11. *Laṅkāvatāra*, ed. Bunyiu Nanjio, Kyoto, 1923 (Bibliotheca Otaniensis, Vol. 1), p. 142ff.
12. The Lankavatara Sutra, tr. D.T.Suzuki, Colorado, 1978, p. 188.
13. It seems that he lived later than *Aśvaghosa,* but prior to, or simultaneously with, *Nāgārjuna.* His little text occupies a very important position in the development of Mahāyānism in India.
14. *Mahāyāna-abhidharma-sangīti-sāstra,* by Asanga, Nanjio, No. 1199.
15. *Yogācārya-bhūmi-śāstra,* Nanjio, No. 1170. The text is supposed to have been dictated to *Asaṅga* by a mythical bodhisattva.

16. By Asaṅga, Nanjio, 1177.

17. *Mahāyāna-samparigraha-śāstra,* by *Asaṅga,* Nanjio, 1183.

18. The first founder of the school was *Asaṅga-* an elder brother of *Vasubandhu-* who was the author of the text *Yogācāra-bhūmi*. In India the school was formerly called the *Yogācāra,* which means the practice of self-concentration. *Vasubandhu,* when he was convened to *Mahāyāna* by his brother and succeeded in systematizing the philosophical views of the *Yogācāra* school, designated the tenet of the school as *Vijñaptimātra* (Mere consciousness), attributing the existence of all the outer world to inner consciousness -in short, holding that nothing but consciousness exists.

19. A School founded by *Paramārtha* on the basis of the *Mahāyānasaṃgrahaśāstra,* a comprehensive work on the *vijñaptimātratā.*

20. The ten precepts of the Buddha are: (1) Kill no living being; (2) Take nothing that is not given; (3) Keep matrimonial sanctity; (4) Do not lie; (5) Do not slander; (6) Do not insult; (7) Do not chatter; (8) Be not greedy; (9) Bear no malice; (10) Harbor no scepticism.

21. According to the Tibetan sources, the five works of Maitreya are: *Mahāyānasūtālaṃkāra, Madhyāntavibhāga, Abhisamayālaṃkāra, Dharmadharmatāvibhāga* and *Uttaratrantra.* But according to the Chinese sources, his works are : *Yogācāra-bhūmi, Yogavibhāga* (now lost), *Mahāyāna-sūtrālaṃkāra, Madhyāntavibhāga* and *Vrjtacchedikavyākhyā.* In the Chinese sources, the *Uttara-tantra* is attributed to *Sāramati* (350-450 A.D.).

22. The eighteen phenomenal elements of existence in the *Abhidharma.* In *Mahāyāna,* they lack independent ontological status. Their existence is epistemic only but their appearances are grounded in the ultimate essence (*gotra*).

23. The underlying substance and root cause of the *dharmas*; identified with the Absolute. Its other synonyms are 'non-duality,' 'the realm of non-discrimination,' 'non-production.' 'the true nature of *Dharma*, 'inexpressible,' 'the

unconditioned,' 'the unimpeded,' 'the actual fact,' 'that which realty is' (*yathābhūta*), '*Nirvāṇa*,' 'truth' (*satya*), 'the true reality,' 'cessation,' 'Buddhahood' and also 'wisdom,' 'enlightenment, 'the cognition which one must realize within oneself,' the 'Dharmabody of the Buddha' etc.

24. Its synonyms are *Buddhatva, Buddhabhāva, Buddhasvabhāva*, etc. "When of *Buddhatā* results. Thus to the Buddhists the true state of reality is the state without any specific nature (*mādhyamika*). When this view is negatively expressed it indicates the true negation, the void (*śūnya*). But, positively it is called *Buddhatā, Dharmakāya, Buddhasvabhāva, Tathāgata-garbha, Tathatā* etc. As void (*śūnya*) it is not nothingness but the unconditioned. This state of Buddha-nature, unlimited in time and in space, is attainable by man, is the great message of Buddhism to the suffering humanity." *Encyclopedia of Buddhism*, Vo. III, p. 442.

25. Here are some of the significant passages on *tathāgatagarbha* from Takasaki: P. 25, fn. 44: The word is interpreted in the *Ratnagotravibhāga* in three ways, namely: 1) *tathā-gatasya ime garbhāh sarvasattvāḥ*. [p.70..17]; 2) *tathāgatasyatathatāesām garbaḥ sarva-sattvānām* [p.71.11]; 3) *tathāgatadhātur esām garbhaḥ sarvasattvānām* [p. 72.89]. They correspond to *dharma-kāya, tathatā and tathāgatagotra*, respectively.

26. *Tathatā* is actually the non-qualificative mode of expressing the Absolute.

27. *Dharmatā* is used mainly for the underlying essence or principle of all *dharmas*. There is a reality (*dharmatā*) that endures, it is the realm beyond the ken of discrimination (*vikalpa*); it is the mind itself but free from the entanglements of speculation and imagination; it reveals itself through our empirical consciousness when our empirical consciousness goes beyond itself, that is, when it transcends dualism. *Dharmatā* or reality, then is there no other than the supreme wisdom *āryajñāna* realised inwardly by an in oneself *(pratyātmādhigama)*. When this realisation comes to one, no proofs are now needed for the doctrine of 'Mind-only.'

28. See *Madhyamakakārikā*, XV: *Svabhāvaparīkṣā* and *Vṛtti* on it.

29. Here *śūnyatā* means *sarvadṛṣṭiśūnyatā* as well as *bāhyārthaśunyatā*.

30. The *Mahāyāna* schools maintain *pudgala naitātmya* as well as *dharmanairātmya*. The *Mahāyāna* systems clearly recognise this dialectical necessity when they speak of the *pudgalanaitātmya* — the denial of substance — as intended to pave the way for Absolutism. *Śūnyatā* is the unreality of the elements as well *(dharmanairātmya)*.

31. The concept of *'samatā'* is derived from the cosmic principle immanent in all beings. The whole *tathāgatagarbha* theory, as found in the *Uttaratantra* (The *Ratnagotravibhāga)* and the *Srīmālā-siṃhanāda-sūtra* (Alex Wayman, 1990), shows this pantheistic state of the Absolute. This realization, says *Asanṅga,* is the source of social emotions such as compassion toward fellow beings. He also discusses the process of change in one's attitude to work for the welfare of humanity.

32. "The dual nature of Buddha, as shown with the Absolute *(śūnyatā)* and at once actively pursuing the welfare of beings, supplies the philosophical basis for the theological conception of the *Trikāya* of Buddha. The three bodes or aspects of Buddha are: 1. The *Dharmakāya* — The Cosmic body in his essential nature; it is one with the Absolute; 2. *Sambhogakāya* — The body of bliss; and the 3. *Nirmānakāya* — Assumed body." —Murti. p. 284.

33. *Mahāyāna* and *ekayāna* are used synonymously. But we must remember that the *Ekayāna* has really nothing to do with the number of *Yānas* though *eka* means 'one', *eka* in this case rather means oneness', and *Ekayāna* is the designation of the doctrine teaching the transcendental oneness of things, by which all beings inclusive of the Hīnayānists and Mahāyānists are saved from bondage of existence. Therefore, "*ekayāna*" should not be taken in literal sense. The concept of *ekayāna* ensues from the highest Wisdom in which one identifies himself with the Absolute. The *Laṅkāvatārasūtra,* III. 1-2 emphasizes this point. The talk of different *yānas* is

only for those who are at lower level of consciousness. At the highest level such differentiation is simply not needed: The *ekayāna* theory is a corollary of the *tathāgatagarbha* theory.

34. D. T. Suzuki, *Outline of Mahayana Buddhism*, NY, 1963, pp. 125-126.
35. See *Vijñāna (Yogācāra) and Its Tradition*, ed. K. K. Mittal, Delhi, 1993, pp. 109-112.
36. Franklin Edgerton, *Buddhist Hybrid Sanskrit Language and Literature*, Banaras Hindu University, Banaras, 1954. p. 36.
37. Indian theatre in all its various aspects is essentially genuine. It evolved from a tiny seed into a glorious flower without outside influences. (Andrej Gawronski: *The Beginnings of Indian Drama and the Problem of Greek Influence*, Varanasi: Banaras Hindu University, 1965.)
38. Franklin Edgerton, op. cit., p. 36.
39. K. Fuse Hokekyò Seishinshi, p. 263.
40. Michael Pye, *Skilful Means, A Concept in Mahayana Buddhism*, LD, 1978, p. 179.
41. Winternitz, vol. II, p. 304, On the compilation of the *Saddharmapuṇḍarīka-sūtra*.
42. G. Ono: Bukkyò no Bijutsu to Reikishi, p. 47.
43. the *Saddharmapuṇḍarīka-sūtra*, ed. by Kern and Nanjio, p. 102.
44. Ibid., p. 180.
45. H. Nakamura in *IBK.*, IV. *Indo Kodaishi* (History of Ancient India), Vol. II, Tokyo, Shunjùsha, 1964.
46. H. Nakamura in Miyamoto: Daijò Seritsu, p. 369.
47. Sten Konow: A New Charsadda Inscription, *Bhandarkar Vol.*, p. 305 f.
48. *Śūnyavāda* (or *Mādhyamika*) and *Vijñānavāda* originated about 200 B.C., continued to develop probably till the eight century A.D. See S. Dasgupta, *A History of Indian Philosophy*, Vol.1, Motilal Banarsidass, Delhi, 1975, p. 167.

49. The Tendai school is in some ways a further development of the *Mādhyamika* school, the Kegon of the *Yogācāra*, but both are synthetic philosophies, and have borrowed largely from all available sources. The doctrines of the two schools closely resemble each other, differing chiefly on points of emphasis, so that for the time being they may be considered together.

50. Trí Quang, *Pháp Hoa Lược Giải* HCMC, 1998, p. 30.

51. Giáo-hội Phật-giáo Việt-nam, *Tù-điển Phật-học Hán-việt*, HN, 1992, pp. 338-339.

52. Ibid., p.748.

53. Ibid., 339.

54. Thích Thanh Từ, *Kinh Diệu Pháp Liên Hoa Giảng Giải Tp.* Hồ Chí Minh: Thành hội Phật giáo 1993, pp. 10-11.

55. translated from the Chinese of *Kumārajīva* by Leon Hurtvitz in 1976, *Scripture of the Lotus Blossom of the Fine Dharma*, the latest translation in English on which the writer is depending on for his Ph.D. thesis.

56. *Scripture of the Lotus Blossom of the Fine Dharma*, trans. by Leon Hurtvitz from the Chinese, NY, 1976, pp. xxiv-xxv.

57. G. Shioda in Osaki Gakuhò No. 97, p. 23ff.

58. Kazuyoshi Kino (in Engi.) in *IBK.*, Vol. 10, No. 2, Jan. 1962, pp. 380f.

59. B. Watanabe: *Buttan*, p. 581f.; S. Mochizuki: *Bukkyō Daijiten*, p. 2698.

60. Kazuyoshi Kino in Miyamoto: *Daijō Seiritsu*, p. 323f.

61. Enichi Ochò in *IBK.*, Vol. 11, No. 1, Jan. 1963, pp. 10-19.

62. Ṭsugunari Kubo, *IBK.*, Vol. 16. No. 1, March 1968, pp. 148-153.

63. Jakuun Kiyota in *Ohyama Comm.* Vol. 2, pp. 160-171.

64. *Dhāraṇīs* in the *Lotus* were discussed by Bunpo Kojima, *Nihon Chibetto Gakkai Kaihò* No. 14, Oct. 1967, pp. 3-4.

65. Those who have cut off their roots of goodness.
66. Op.cit., trans. by Leon Hurvitz, p. 30.
67. Ibid., p. 31.
68. Ibid., p. 41.

Chapter II

The *Lotus* in Brief

In this chapter a synoptic and analytical account will be given of all the twenty eight chapters of the *Lotus* pointing out their philosophical implications in the Buddhist theory and practice.

As mentioned earlier, with a complete vision of the Reality, in which there are no longer any dichotomy, *vikalpas* (mental constructions), no discrimination of subject and object, and this also means the Ultimate Reality is identical with the *Buddhajñāna* and vice versa, the *Lotus* wishes to show this complete vision to all living beings. That is why in the *Lotus* the *Buddha* says:

> "*Śāriputra,* what do I mean by 'The *Buddhas,* the World-Honored Ones, for one great cause alone appear in the world?' The *Buddhas,* the World-Honored Ones appear in the world because they wish to cause the beings to ***hear*** of the *Buddha's* knowledge and insight and thus enable them to gain purity. They appear in the world because they wish to ***demonstrate*** the *Buddha's* knowledge and insight to the beings. They appear in the world because they wish to cause the beings to ***understand***. They appear in the world because they wish to cause the beings to ***enter into*** *the path* of the *Buddha's* knowledge and insight. *Śāriputra,* this is the one great cause for which the *Buddhas* appear in the world."[1]

Through its all 28 chapters translated by *Kumārjīva*, the *Lotus* may be systematically divided chapter-wise as follows:

a) As far as concepts and doctrines in the *Lotus* are concerned, the *Lotus* can be viewed as mentioned in the previous chapter:

- The first 14 chapters speak of the historical or phenomenon *Buddha* and the doctrine of One Vehicle. To start, the *Buddha* entered into the *samādhi* of the Abode of the Immeasurable Doctrine *(Anantanirdeśa)*; his body, speech and mind were motionless. This implies that the Ultimate Reality is inexpressible.

Then he performed miracles (chapter 1). A ray of light emitting from the white curls between his eyebrows that illuminated eighteen thousand worlds in the east. This implies that the Ultimate Reality when it is seen by the *Buddhajñāna* it is of the nature of 'many' in 'one' and 'one' in 'many', nothing obliterates one another; because, all the *dharmas* do not have their self-nature (*niḥ-svabhāva*).

From chapter 2 onwards the *Buddha* stopped meditation and began to preach (by means of language, and due to this, the term *Upāya-kauśalya* appears) to human beings. He preached the doctrine of One Vehicle directly (chapter 2). He preached the doctrine One Vehicle by similes (chapters 3, 4, 5, 7 and 11), by prediction of the Buddhahood (chapters 3, 6, 7, 8, 9, 12 and 13). He also mentioned the four conditions to practise the doctrine of One Vehicle (chapters 10 and 14).

- The latter 14 chapters speak of the supernatural or noumenon *Buddha* (chapter16), the meritorious deeds of *bodhisattvas* (chapters 15, 20, 23, 24, 25, 27 and 28), the great benefits for those who practise the doctrine of One Vehicle (chapters 16, 17, 18 and 19) and the spiritual dissemination of the One Vehicle doctrine (chapters 21, 22 and 26).

b) As far as the process of four periods of hearing, demonstrating, understanding and entering the path of *Buddhajñāna* is concerned, the *Lotus* can be viewed as this:

- Chapter 1: Manifesting the Ultimate Reality or *Buddhajñāna*.
- Chapters 2-10 Hearing of the *Buddhajñāna*.
- Chapters 11-22 : Both demonstrating and understanding the *Buddhajñāna*.
- Chapters 23-27 : Entering the path of *Buddhajñāna*.
- Chapter 28 : Mixing with the world to enlighten others.

Now we come into the philosophical implications in each chapter of the *Lotus*.

Chapter 1: Introduction *(Nidāna)*

The *Lotus* starts with the homage to all the *Buddhas* and *badhisattvas*[2] and six perfections to certify that the *Lotus* was expounded by the *Buddha:* 1) 'Thus' implies perfect faith; 2) 'have I heard,' perfect hearing; 3) 'at one time,' the perfect time; 4) 'the *Buddha*,' the perfect Lord or master; 5) 'on *Gṛdhrakūta* mountain,' the perfect place; and 6) 'together with twelve thousand great *bhikṣu*,' the perfect assembly.

Next is the preaching of the scripture of the *Mahāyāna* named *Anantanirdeśa* (Immeasurable Doctrine) and the entering into its *samādhi* by the *Buddha*. This implies that the Ultimate Reality is inexpressible. Then in this state of *samādhi* the *Buddha* emits from the white curls between his eyebrows a ray of light that illuminates eighteen thousand worlds in the east. The cause of this wonder is explained by *Mañjuśri* to *Maitreya* that the *Buddha* is about to preach the Great Dharma (the *Lotus)*. This denotes that this *sūtra* is preached by the 'middle-path' vision, according to which many is in one and vice versa.

Then, this chapter continues to describe the Oneness of Truth for all the times through the images of twenty thousand continuous *Buddhas* having the same name, powers, and the same way of preaching of the True Dharma suitable to the different levels of beings: Firstly, the Four Noble Truth to *śrāvakas*; secondly, the *pratītyasamutpāda* to the *pratyekabuddhas*; thirdly, the six *pāramitās* to the *bodhisattvas*; and lastly, the highest *Mahāyāna Saddharmapuṇḍarīka-sūtra* to *Varaprabha* (the *bodhisattva* who has the light of wisdom). At that time the multitude sit in the same place for a period of sixty minor kalpas listening the *Lotus* as for a small duration of a meal. Why ? because the *Lotus*, a *sūtra* of the Ultimate Reality, in which there is no concept of time. Then, the *Buddha* foretells *Śrīgarbha* (the *bodhisattva* who stores the merits) about his attainment of Buddhahood. Finally, the *Buddha* enters *nirvāṇa*.

After the *Buddha's* passage into extinction, *Bodhisattva Varaprabha* continues to expound the *Lotus* to others. All eight princes, placing themselves, under the tutelage of this *bodhisattva*, achieved their *anuttarasaṃyaksambodhi* and even finally the *Buddha* path, a position the Hīnayānists never think of. Here, the eight consciousnesses of the *Vijñaptimātratā* are introduced through the images of these eight princes. Eight consciousnesses, which are illuminated by the *Lotus*, become the *Buddhajñāna*.

Among the eight hundred disciples was one named *Yaśaskāma*, who craved advantage and profit, though reading lots of scriptures but forgetting most, for which reason he was called Seeker of Fame. *Buddha Śākyamuni* said that *Bodhisattva Varaprabha* was he himself and *Bodhisattva Yaśaskāma* was *Maitreya*.

Furthermore, the locale of *Śākyamunibuddha* to preach the *Lotus* is *Gṛdhrakūta* mountain, which is symbolic. *Gṛdhrakūta* is a high mountain, from its peak one can spread his heart and mind to the limitless space, and in this state the subject and object coalesce into one another, or in other words, no-duality is experienced. By virue of this the peak is used as a symbol of *sūnyāta* (emptiness) and *Mahākaruṇā* (great compassion) in *Mahāyāna* Buddhism. The Mahāyānists first placed the *Buddha* in the *Tuṣita* heaven before his birth, (as was done by the Hīnayānists,) then made him feel pity for the distressed world below, made him resolve to deliver it from the 'ocean of misery', and after his *Parinirvāṇa*, they made him abide forever on the peak of *Gṛdhrakūta* delivering the sermon of immortality to a great assembly of spiritual beings. In this way, they explained the significance of the appearance of *Śākyamuni* on earth, which was nothing but a practical demonstration of *Mahākaruṇā*.

Chapter 2: Expedient devices (*Upāyakauśalya*)

From this chapter onwards the *Buddha* begins to express the nature of Ultimate Reality by means of language. In this chapter the *Buddha* speaks of the *Tathāgatajñāna*, *Niḥsvabhāvata, Upāya-kauśalya, Tathatā* and *Ekayāna*.

Emerging from his *samādhi* the *Buddha* says that the *Tathāgatajñāna* is profound and incalculable, and no *śrāvakas* or *pratyekabuddhas* could know it; as a result, he must use a variety of means like parables and other skilfulness to enlighten low creatures who were attached to the existence of *dharmas*. But in fact, all the *dharmas* have no separate reality of their own (*niḥsvabhāva*). So what the *Buddha* taught before, such as the *nirvāṇas* of the *śrāvakas* and *pratyekabuddhas,* or *śrāvakayāna, pratyekabuddhayāna, bodhisattvayāna,* etc., are simply his *upāya-kauśalyas.*

> "For their sake I established an expedient device,
> Preaching ways that put an end to woe
> And showing them *nirvāṇa.*

Though I preach *nirvāṇa,*
This is no true extinction.
The *dharmas* from their very origin
Are themselves eternally characterized by the marks of quiet extinction."[3]

Instead, the *Buddha* introduces the manifestations of the Ultimate Reality, which are *Tathāgatajñāna*, *Tathatā*, *Ekayāna.*

The *Buddha* says all the *Buddhas* appear in the world only because they wish the worldly beings to hear, to be demonstrated, to understand, and to enter into the path of the *Tathāgatajñāna.*[4] And the beings, after hearing the *Dharma* from the *Buddhas*, shall attain complete knowledge of the total realities.[5]

Tathatā, or Suchness of the *dharmas*, has been said to be tenfold as under:

> "The Suchness of their marks, the Suchness of their nature, the Suchness of their substance, the Suchness of their powers, the Suchness of their functions, the Suchness of their causes, the Suchness of their conditions, the Suchness of their effects, the Suchness of their retributions, and the absolute identity of their beginning and end."[6]

Ekayāna is an important concept or doctrine of the *Lotus*:

> "The *Buddhas*, the Most Venerable of Two-Legged Beings, Know that the *dharmas* are ever without a nature of their own By virtue of conditions is the *Buddha*-seed realized: For this reason they preach the One Vehicle."[7]

However, as to those who possess wrong views (here sixty-two wrong views are mentioned) are hard to be saved.

"That men of slight virtue and little merit
Were attacked by multitudinous woes;
That, entering into the luxuriant forest of wrong views,
Whether of existence, or of nonexistence, or the like,
And relying on these views,
They fulfill sixty-two[8] of them;
That, profoundly attached to vain and arbitrary *dharmas,*
...
That men the likes of these are hard to save;"[9]

When hearing the above words from the *Buddha,* in the assembly about five thousand *bhikṣus, bhikṣunīs, upāsakas,* and *upāsikās,* straightway rose from their seats and withdrew. The *Buddha* did not restrain them and said to *Śāriputra*: "My assembly has no more branches and leaves, it has only firm fruit."[10]

From this chapter onwards the *Buddha* borrows language, parables, tales of the past times as expedients to lead beings to the true goal. This chapter, with chapter 16, "The Life Span of the Thus Come One" has long been regarded as the heart of the *Lotus*.

Chapter 3: Parable *(Aupamya)*

This chapter clarifies further the doctrine of One Vehicle through the parable of 'Burning House' and from the doctrine of One Vehicle considered as an object to the doctrine of One *Buddha* Vehicle as a subject. Here, a more philosophical implication is taken : object is identical to subject and vice versa.

> There are three sons of a rich man playing and trapped inside a burning house, which has been in ruins and in danger of one's life. So absorbed are they in their games that they are unaware of the fire. The father, resolves to

save them by seducing them to come out with goat carriages, deer carriages, and ox carriages, which they like. Immediately, they rush to their father. Then the father gives them each a wonderful carriage, the best, drawn by a white ox.

This parable says,

- The rich man refers to the *Buddha* and his children, steeped in their games in the burning house, refer to the *śrāvakas, pratyekabuddhas* and *bodhisattvas.*
- Rotting halls, crumbling walls, decayed pillars, malignant demons, poisonous insects, disastrous fire... refer to the suffering of beings in the triple world *(triloka).* [11]
- Three carriages refer to the Three Vehicles or three levels of discipline, i.e. *śrāvakas, pratyekabuddhas* and *bodhisattvas.* The first two who save themselves only are compared to the goat-drawn and deer-drawn carriages of which the power only can carry one person. But the last one who self-forget for the sake of others are compared to the oxen-drawn carriage.
- The rich man seduced his children getting out of the burning house with the carriages they desired. But, after that, he gave to all of them the equally precious white oxen carriages, which refer to the Buddhahood.

And the *Buddha,* by resort to this parable, preached the One *Buddha* Vehicle, which is the highest:

"For the beings' sake, I,
By resort to this parable,
Preach the One *Buddha* Vehicle;"[12]

"This vehicle is fine,
Supremely pure,
In all the worlds
Having not its master."[13]

Just as the father in the parable of "Burning House" cannot be accused of having deceived his children because he brings the benefits to them, so the *Buddha* cannot be accused of deceiving the beings with the doctrine of the Three Vehicles.

In this chapter the *Buddha* assured *Śāriputra* of his future *Buddha* named *Padmaprabha* (Flower Glow).

Chapter 4: Belief and understanding (*Adhimukti*)

Just like in previous chapter, in this chapter the *Lotus* clarifies further the nature of Ultimate Reality by another simile of 'the Poor Son' through the words of the four great *śrāvaka* disciples of the *Buddha*, namely, *Subhūti*, *Mahākatyāyana*, *Mahākāśyapa* and *Mahāmaudgalyāyana*, who had just received a prophecy of *anuttarasamyaksaṃbodhi* from the Buddha.

There were a young man forsaking his father and running off. After scores of years with old age and destitution in quest of food and clothing, at length, he accidentally came back to his native land. His father was a millionaire, now very old and seeking for his lost son to hand down his riches. One day the father saw and recognized the son but the son did not. The father immediately ordered his attendant to catch the son. Being arrested, the poor son was very frightened. Although imploring but not getting released the poor son fell to the ground in a dead faint. The father knew that his son's ambitions were mean, and he knew that he himself, being rich and powerful, would be a source of trouble to his son. Then the father released the son but devised an expedient to seduce him.

The father secretly dispatched two men who disguised as the poor, approached and invited the poor son for sweeping away dung in the father's house with a good pay; and he agreed. After that, the father also disguised as a poor man who approached, made the acquaintance of the son and called him his son. The poor son, though delighted by this treatment, continued as before to call himself a lowly workman as from elsewhere.

Then, when some time had passed, the father knew that his son had at length became more at ease and confident, that, having achieved a great ambition, he was ashamed of his former state of mind. When facing to his end, the old man commanded his son to gather all his kinsmen, the nobles and householders. Then the old man proclaimed that the poor son was his real son and all his treasure now belonged to him. At that time, the poor son, hearing his father's words, straightway rejoiced greatly. He gained something he had never had before.

In this parable, the rich father (*Buddha*) devised an expedient means of reducing his wisdom to the low level of his son (*śrāvaka* or *pratyekabuddha*) who dare not think of the richness (Buddhahood). But when the son received all treasure (*Buddhajñāna*) from his dying father, he knew that he was also a rich man (Buddhahood).

Here, the *Buddha's* expedient teachings are all for the sole purpose of helping beings discover and awaken to their own *Buddhajñān,* which is the true one and which is different from the other two knowledges of *śrāvaka* and *pratyekabuddha*.

Chapter 5: Parable of medicinal herbs (*auṣadhī*)

In this chapter the *Lotus* presents the Ultimate Reality as *Dharma* which manifests the *Ekatva* (Oneness), *Samatā*, *Ekayāna* or *Buddhayāna, Buddhajñāna* through three parables, viz., 'rain,' 'sun and moon light,' and 'pots.'

1) Parable of the rain:

There are various kinds of plants receiving the rain and they all derive the full benefit of the moisture. Similarly, the

Dharma has a single flavor of 'deliverance and *nirvāṇa;*' because, the *Buddha* realizes that all *dharmas,* such as *Trikāya* or *nirvāṇas* of *śrāvakas* and *pratyekabuddhas* being due to the different levels of beings, have no separate reality (*svabhāva*) of their own.

"Just as that great cloud rains down on all grasses and trees, shrubs and forests, and medicinal herbs, and just as they all, in accord with their nature and kind, derive the full benefit of the moisture, each gaining in growth, just so is the *Dharma* preached by the Thus Come One of a single mark and a single flavor, namely, the mark of deliverance, the mark of disenchantment, the mark of extinction, arriving completely at knowledge of all modes."[14]

"With discrimination he sets forth
The reality of the *dharmas*."[15]

"The *Dharma* having a single flavor,
That of deliverance and *nirvāṇa*."[16]

2) Parable of the sun and moon light:

The *Samatā* (sameness of *Dharma* towards the living beings) is also compared to the light of the sun and moon illuminating the world equally. And the discriminated *dharmas* such as *Triyāna,* if any, are only an expsedient.

"Again, O *Kāśyapa* the Thus Gone One, in his guidance of the beings, is equitable, not inequitable. O *Kāśyapa*, just as the light of the sun and the moon illuminates the whole world,. . . ,just as that light falls everywhere equally, not unequally, in just that way, O *Kāśyapa,* does the light of the thought of the knowledge of the All-Knowing, of the Thus Gone Ones,. . ,the demonstration of the True Dharma, function equally among all beings in the five destinies according to their predispositions, be the persons of the Great Vehicle, persons of the Vehicle of the Individually Enlightened, or persons of the Vehicle of the Auditors... O *Kāśyapa*, there are not three vehicles. There are only beings of severally different modes of conduct and for that reason three vehicles are designated."[17]

3) Parable of the pots:

The *Samatā* is again compared to the clay of the pots. And just so, there is only *Ekayāna* i.e. the *Buddhayāna*.

"It is just as the potter, O *Kāśyapa,* makes pots with the same clay. Among them, some become pots for sugar lumps, some pots for clarified butter, some pots for curds or milk, while some become pots for inferior and filthy things; and just as there is no difference in the clay, but rather a supposed difference in the pots based solely on the things put into them, in just this way, O *Kāśyapa,* is there this one and only one vehicle, to wit, the *Buddha* Vehicle. There exists neither a second nor a third vehicle."[18]

In these three parables the *Lotus* reaffirms that there is only One Vehicle, the *Buddha* Vehicle, and only One *nirvāṇa,* not two and not three. *Nirvāṇa* comes from an understanding of the Oneness or Sameness of all *dharmas* (things).

Chapter 6: Bestowal of prophecy (*Vyākaraṇa*)

The *Buddha* prophesies the future Buddhahood to four other *śrāvakas,* namely, *Mahākāśyapa, Subhūti, Mahākātyāyana,* and *Mahāmaudgalyāyana.* And in the lands of those to-be *Buddhas* there are incalculable *bodhisattvas* and *śrāvakas.*

In other *Mahāyāna sūtras* the *Buddha* only conferred the prophecies upon the *badhisattvas,* but in the *Saddharmapuṇḍarīka-sūtra,* the *śrāvakas, pratyekabuddhas,* and even the evil human beings, female human beings, and animals as seen in the latter chapters are all granted prophecies. Why ? Because the *Saddharmapuṇḍarīka* is a *sūtra* of the Ultimate Reality where there is no place for discrimination.

Chapter 7: Parable of the Conjured city (*Pūrvayoga*)

The *Buddha* clarifies and reaffirms *Ekayāna* through the parable of the 'conjured city,' and reaffirms that among the three doctrines of Fourfold Truth *(Catvāri ārya-satyāni)*, Dependent Origination *(Pratītyasamutpāda)* and *Saddharmapuṇḍarīka-sūtra,* the last one is true.

> "Just as there is a steep, difficult, very bad road, long, empty and devoid of human beings, which leads to a cache of precious jewels. The multitude being led in the midway by a guide — perceptive and wise, and of many skilful devices — are exhausted, frightened and wish to turn back. Then, the guide, with his compassion and his power of devising expedients, conjures upon the road, three hundred *yojanas* away, a city; and asks the multitude to enter the city for refreshment and composure. The multitude, then, overjoy and proceed to enter the conjured city. After that, the guide, knowing that the multitude have rested and are no longer fatigued, straightway dissolves the conjured city and says to the multitude, 'Come away ! The jewel cache is near. The great city of a while ago was conjured up by me for the purpose of giving you a rest, nothing more.'[19]
>
> Just so, the *Buddha,* as a Great Guide, knowing the state of mind of the beings to be cowardly and mean when hearing of the difficult and far-reaching of the *Buddha* Vehicle, by resort to his power to devise expedients, preaches two *nirvāṇas* midway for the purpose of giving them a rest. When the beings take up residence in these two lands, then the Thus Come One preaches to them,

'what you had to do is not yet done. The lands in which you dwell are near to *Buddha*-knowledge. You must observe and consider, weigh and measure. The *nirvāṇa* you have gained is not the real one.' This is simply the Thus Come One's power to device expedients : within the One *Buddha* Vehicle he speaks of a threefold distinction."[20]

The two *nirvāṇas* of *śrāvakas* and *pratyekabuddhas* are not the real ones and "It is only with the *Buddha* Vehicle that one can gain extinction; that there is no other vehicle, except for the *dharmas* preached by the Thus Come One as a matter of expedient device."[21]

Chapter 8: Receipt of prophecy by five hundred disciples (*Pañcabhikṣuśatavyā-karana*)

The *Buddha* continues to assure of Buddhahood to five hundred *śrāvakas* such as *Pūrṇa, Kauṇḍinya..,* who relate the parable of 'the priceless jewel in the interior of the garment.'

> "Just as a drunk man, given and put a priceless jewel into the interior of his garment by his friend, is unaware of anything. Then he goes to another country, where he seeks for food and clothing. He suffers such hardship that he is content with however little he may get. 'The *Buddha* is also thus. When he was a *bodhisattva,* he taught and converted us, inspiring in us the thought of All-Knowledge, but later we forgot, and thus neither understood nor were aware of anything. Having achieved the way of the *arhant,* we said to ourselves that this was passage into extinction. We were so hard-pressed to support life that we were satisfied with what little we got, though the vow concerning All-Knowledge, still there, had never lost its effect.'"[22]

In this chapter, the *Buddhajñāna* is reaffirmed by the *Buddha* to be the true form of *nirvāṇa* and available to all living beings, even though they are unaware of it, or do not avail of it.

Chapter 9: Prophecies conferred on learners and adepts (*Ānandadivākaraṇa*)

More prophecies of future Buddhahood are given to such *śrāvakas* as *Ānanda* and *Rāhula* and two thousand others. The *Buddha* relates a tale of the pastimes to imply that the *śrāvakas* have their own seeds of *Mahāyāna*.

> The *Buddha* explained the reason why *Ānanda,* a *śrāvaka* not a *bodhisattva,* can get such a prophecy. In the past, the *Buddha* shared a place with *Ānanda* in the presence of the *Buddha* King of Emptiness,[23] and at the same time [as *Ānanda*] experienced the thought of *anuttarasamyuaksaṃbodhi*. [However,] *Ānanda* constantly wished to be a hearer of much [*bahuśruta,* very learned person], while the *Buddha* constantly strove with vigor [for the enlightenment of all]. This is why the *Buddha* has already contrived to achieve *anuttarasamyaksaṃbodhi,* while *Ānanda* guards and keeps the *Buddha's Dharma,* teaching, converting, and perfecting a multitude of *bodhisattvas.* Such having been his former wish [i.e., to guard the *Dharma*], he has now received this prophecy [as his reward].

Chapter 10: Preachers of Dharma (*dharmabhāṇaka*)

The *Buddha* praises the *Lotus,* the practitioners and propagators of it and points out three conditions for the preachers of it, i.e., compassion, patience, and the understanding of the emptiness of all *dharmas.*

> "When this man preaches Dharma with joy, anyone who hears it for a moment shall straightway achieve ultimate

anuttarasamyaksaṃbodhi,"[24] and it is that "the *anuttarasamyaksaṃbodhi* of all *bodhisattvas* in every case belongs to this scripture. This scripture opens the door of expedient devices; it shows the marks of reality."[25] "This scripture is the treasure house of the *Buddhas'* secret essentials."[26]

Those who propagate the *Saddharmapuṇḍarīka-sūtra* will be covered with garments, will be caressed at their heads by the *Tathāgata*. They shall have dwelt together with the *Tathāgata* and shall also benefit from the protective mindfulness of *Buddhas* now in their quarters. And, wherever this *sūtra* may be preached, or read, or recited, or written, or whatever place or roll of this scripture may occupy, in all those places one is to erect a *stūpa* of the seven jewels. There is no need even to lodge *śarīra*[27] in it.

"O Medicine King ! If a good man or good woman after the extinction of the Thus Come One wishes to preach this Scripture of the Dharma Blossom to the fourfold assembly, how is he or she to preach it ? This good man or good woman is to enter the room of the Thus Come One, don the cloak of the Thus Come One, sit on the throne of the Thus Come One, and only then preach this scripture broadly to the fourfold assembly. The room of the Thus Come One is the thought of great compassion toward all living beings. The cloak of the Thus Come One is the thought of tender forbearance and the bearing of insult with equanimity. The throne of the Thus Come One is the emptiness of all *dharmas*. It is only by dwelling securely among these that he or she can with unabating thought broadly preach this Scripture of the Dharma Blossom to the *bodhisattvas* and the fourfold assembly."[28]

Chapter 11: Apparition of the Jeweled Stūpa (*Stūpa-saṇdarśana*)

In this chapter, the *Lotus* implies the manifestations of the Ultimate Reality, i.e., *Trikāya* and *Śūnyatā*.

> An immense jeweled *stūpa* arises out of the earth, and the *Buddha* tells his listeners that it contains the body of a *Buddha* named *Prabhūtaratna,* who in the distant past preached the *Lotus,* vowing to produce his reliquary, after his *nirvāṇa,* wherever and whenever the *Lotus,* should happen to be preached and on condition that the emanations of that *Buddha* must gather in one place. All requirements are done. Then the *stūpa* opens up, and *Prabhūtaratna,* seated within it, offers half his seat to the *Buddha.* A number of beings salute both Buddhas. The whole scene happens in open space.

Implications in the scene are: (1) *Trikāya,* i.e., *Dharmakāya* (illustrated with the *Buddha* named *Prabhūtaratna*), *Sambhogakāya* (illustrated with the emanations of the *Buddha*), *Nirmāṇkāya* (the *Buddha),* and (2) *Śūnyatā* (illustrated with the open space). Although Three bodies (*Trikāya*) of the *Buddhas* are separately but they have the same nature, i.e., gathering together in the open space (*Śūnyatā*).

The locale of the sermon so far has been in Mount *Gṛdhrakūṭa,* but here it shifts to the sky, where it remains until the end of chapter 22, "Entrustment," after which the sermon is resumed on earth. After *hearing, demonstrating,* and *understanding* the *Buddhajñāna* is the *entering into the path of* it, which is taken from chapter 23 onwards. It pertains to eradicating the notion *of ātman or pañcaskandhas.*

Chapter 12: Devadatta

The *Lotus* again speaks of itself as the most important *sūtra* and clarifies further the manifestations of the Ultimate

Reality such as *Ekayāna, Tathatā,* and *Śūnyatā.* More prophecies of future Buddhahood, in this chapter, not to *śrāvakas* but to an evil man and a dragon girl.

According to the viewpoint of Hīnayānists those who commit the five grave sins[29] and those who are women cannot attain the Buddhahood, which is contrary to that of the *Lotus. Devadatta* is the *Buddha's* cousin making the *Buddha* hurt physically and disuniting the *saṅgha* (assembly); but, *Śākyamunibuddha* confers upon *Davadatta* the prophecy of the future *Buddha* named *Devarāja. Śāriputra* does not believe that the dragon girl can attain unexcelled *bodhi* because of her filthy body;[30] but, this eight-year-old daughter of the dragon king *Sāgara* puts the *Lotus* into practice by the strenuous application of vigor, and speedily attains Buddhahood. Besides, there are numberless *badhisattvas* welling up out of the great sea, from the dragon palace of *Sāgara,* and resting in mid-air, "who had formerly been voice-hearers...but now all were putting into practice the Great Vehicle' doctrine of emptiness."[31]

Chapter 13: Fortitude (*Utsāha*)

The *Lotus* is again extolled and the manifestations of the Ultimate Reality such as *Ekayāna* and *Tathatā* are reaffirmed by more prophecies of the future Buddhahood to six thousand *bhikṣuṇīs, Bhikṣuṇīs Mahāprajāpatī* (the *Buddha's* maternal aunt) and *Yaśodharā* (the *Buddha's* former wife).

Chapter 14: Comfortable Conduct (*Sukhavihāra*)

This chapter highlights the *prajñā* and the practice of *sīla* and *karuṇā* of the Ultimate Reality through the following four *dharmas* or conditions:

1) By dwelling in the place where the *bodhisattva* acts : it asks the *bodhisattva* to be patient, gentle, not frightened, viewing the *dharmas* (things) with their true marks,

performing no-selfish act and committing no discrimination.

2) Avoiding somebody and dwelling in *Prajñā:*

- Not approaching all the following people : kings, officials, heretical monks, dancers, actors, those who raise cattle, or do hunting, or fishing, or cultivating other evil practices; those who seek to be *śrāvakas;* little girl, or maidens, or widows.

- Viewing "all *dharmas* as empty, in accord with their true marks, not inverted, nor moving, nor receding, nor revolving, devoid of character as empty space, inaccessible of approach by any words, not born, nor coming out, nor arising, nameless, signless [markless ?], having in truth no being, incalculable and unlimited, unimpeded and unobstructed, existing solely by virtue of causes and conditions, [their "reality"] born of inverted notions.,"[32]

3) Dwelling in comfortable activity : It means not wishing to mention the faults of men or of the scriptural canon, non despising other *Dharma*-masters, nor giving rise to a heart of resentment and suspicion. If there are objections or queries, one is to explain only in terms of the Great Vehicle, causing persons to gain knowledge of all modes.

4) Thinking with great good will of persons in the household and of those gone forth from the household, with great compassion of those who are not *bodhisattvas.* "Although those persons do not inquire into, nor believe, nor understand this scripture, when I attain *anuttarasamyaksaṃbodhi,* then wherever they may happen to be, with my power of supernatural penetration and my power of wisdom I will draw them to me, enabling them to dwell in this *Dharma.*"[33]

Chapter 15: Welling up out of the earth (*Bodhisattvapṛthivīvivarasamudgama*)

This chapter implies the *Buddhajñāna* or *Buddhatā* which is simply awakened by practice.

The *bodhisattvas* from the other worlds wanted to spread the *Saddharmapuṇḍarīka-sūtra* in this *sahā* world after the *Buddha's* extinction; but the *Buddha* assures them that there is no need for their help, for from the past there were countless *bodhtsattvas* in this world whose duty was to preach the *Saddharmapuṇḍarīka-sūtra*. At that moment innumerable *bodhisattvas* who had bodies of golden hue, the thirty two marks and illuminative rays of light were welling up out of the earth in an open space belonging to this sphere.They all had been under this *sahā* world. Those *bodhisattvas* were led by four leaders : Superior Conduct (*Viśiṣ-ṭacārita*), Limitless Conduct (*Ananta-cārita*), Pure Conduct (*Viśuddhacārita*), and Conduct Standing Firm (*Supratiṣṭhita-cārita*). However, although it was in a short time of his life, the *Buddha* could teach and convert incalculable, limitless *asaṃkhyeyas* of great *bohisattvas,* causing them to dwell in *anuttara-samyak-saṃbodhi*. Such a thing as this the world finds hard to believe: "It is as if there were a man, his natural color fair and his hair black, twenty five years of age, who pointed to men a hundred years of age and said, 'these are my sons'."[34]

In this account the *Buddhajñāna* or *Buddhatā* (Buddha nature) is not from outside (which is illustrated with the *bodhisattvas* from the other world) but immanent in the living beings (which is illustrated with the golden-body *bodhisattvas* welling out of this *sahā* world). This *Buddhajñāna* or *Buddhatā,* however, is simpy awaken by the practice or conduct of the living beings (which is illustrated with the *bodhisattvas* led by four leaders who have the same name - conduct '*cārita*').

This wonderful account will be clarified further in chapter 16, which reveals the Absolute Truth by explaining the question of 'a twenty-five year old father and his one hundred year old children.'

This chapter 15 together with the whole chapter 16 and the first half of chapter 17 give us the essence of the latter half of the *Lotus*.

Chapter 16: The life span of the Thus Come One (*Tathāgatāyuṣpramāṇa*)

In this chapter the *Lotus* speaks of the doctrine of two truths : *Paramārtha satya* (Absolute Truth, Noumenon, which is illustrated with the countless life-span of the *Tathāgata*) and *Saṃvṛti Satya* (Relative Truth, Phenomena, which is illustrated with a historical *Śākyamunibuddha*). The Absolute is known as the reality of the appearances, which is in fact the inexpressible. Phenomena are utilised as devices (*upāya*) to reach the unconditioned (*Paramārtha*) which is their end (*upeya*).

In order to explain the question 'that the father is young and the sons old' in chapter 15, the *Buddha* shows the life-span of *Tathāgata*. The *Buddha* said that since his attainment of Buddhahood it has been a very great interval of time; his life-span was incalculable *asaṃkhyeya-kalpas*[15],ever enduring, never perishing; he was in fact limitless in both time and space, assuring various forms in different ages and under circumstances but all for one and the same purpose, namely, the salvation of the beings.

But, if the *Buddha* lived long in the world, men of thin qualities would not plant wholesome roots; while the lowly and the poor would crave the objects of the five desires and enter into the net of recollections, notions, and false views. So the *Buddha* by resort to expedient devices manifested himself a historical *Śākyamunibuddha* having birth and death. And the *Buddha* gave a parable of "Physician's ill sons,"

"Suppose there is a good physician, wise, who intelligently refines medical herbs and skillfully heals many sickness. Returning home from afar the father saw his sons getting unintentional poisoning, some serious and some light. The light sons took the medicine from their father, but the serious sons did not. Then the father devised an expedient with which to induce them to take the medicine. Straightway he spoke to his sons that he was now aged and infirm, and that his time of death was already at hand; the fine and good medicine he now left there for them to take; no worry about not recovering. When he had given these instructions, he went again to another country and sent a messenger back to declare to his sons that he was dead. The sons thought themselves from now on forsaken and exposed, having nothing further on which to rely, they harbored feelings of sadness. It is only when at length their thoughts were awakened that they understood that the medicine was colorful, fragrant, and tasty. Then straightway they took it, and the poisons and the sickness were all healed."[36]

The death of *Śākyamunibuddha* and physician in this parable is an expedient. In fact they are alive. The death of these two is an illustration of the Empirical Truth and their being alive the Trans-empirical truth. The latter is experienced only in *prajñā* which is the non-dual intuition.

Since the level of beings was still inferior, the *Buddha* by resort to expedient devices, spoke to the beings of the Relative Truth, viz., the Three-Vehicles. In fact, the One Vehicle or *Buddha* Vehicle is the real, which is identical with the Absolute truth, the real mark of things.

This chapter is the most important one of the latter fourteen chapters of the *Lotus*. *Nāgārjuna* says "Those that are unaware of the distinction between these two truths are incapable of grasping the deep signigicance of the teaching of *Buddha*." (M.K. XXIV, 9). And the *Mādhyamika* holds that the Absolute is cognised in a non-dual intuition (*prajñā*).

Chapter 17: Discrimination of merits (*Puṇyaparyāya*)

The *Buddha* narrates the incalculable merit which shall accrue to those who venerate the foregoing chapter of the *Lotus,* which tells about the unlimited nature of the *Buddha's* life-span, the illustration of the Absolute Truth.

> After the great assembly had heard the *Buddha* speak of the great length of his life-span, incalculable living beings gained acceptance of the doctrine of the unborn *dharmas;* heard and were enabled to take hold of the gateway of the *dhāraṇīs;* gained joy in preaching and unimpeded eloquence; gained the *dhāraṇīs* that can be turned to a hundred thousand myriads of millions of incalculable uses; were enabled to turn the unreceding wheel of the *Dharma;* were enabled to turn the pure wheel of the *Dharma;* and would be gained *anuttarasamyaksaṃbodhi*.
>
> And, whatever living beings, hearing that the *Buddha's* life-span is as long as this, can produce as much as a single moment of faith and understanding shall gain merit that shall have no limit, no measure. Further, if there is anyone who, hearing of the great length of the *Buddha's* life-span, understands the import of the words, the merit gained by that man shall have no limit or measure, for he shall be able to produce the unexcelled knowledge of the *Tathāgata*. And the highest merit that one can gain is believing and understanding the doctrine of the life-span of the *Tathāgata,* and at the same time practising the Six *pāramitās,* i.e., spreading of gifts, the keeping of the

prohibitions, forbearance, energy, single-mindedness, and wisdom; and again, erecting *stūpas,* building *saṃgha*-cell, spreading the *Saddharmapuṇḍarīka-sūtra.*

Chapter 18: The merits of appropriate joy (*Anumodanāpuṇyanirdeśa*)

In this chapter more details are mentioned on the merit accruing to those who extol the *Lotus.*

Chapter 19: The merits of the Dharma-Preacher (*Dharmabhāṇakānu-śaṃsā*)

This chapter dwells on the Dharma-preacher's six faculties of cognition and the merits acquired by him or her by teaching the Dharma.

Chapter 20: The *Bodhisattva* Never Disparaging (*Sadāparibhūta*)

Gotra in the *Lotus* is identical with the *Buddhajñāna* or *Buddhatā* which is immanent in all creatures.

In the *Buddha's* narration of his own behavior in a previous era, in which, he is the *Bodhisattva Sadāparibhūta* (Never Disparaging) and is the object of much contempt and violence; but he responds wit love and patience for he wishes to remind people to awaken their own *Buddhajñāna.*

Chapter 21: The supernatural powers of the Tathāgata (*Tathāgatarddhyabhi-saṃskāra*)

Absolute Truth or the *Buddhajñāna* in the *Lotus* is true and is simply known by intuition. And in this Truth there is no obstruction among things.

Before *Mañjuśrī* and many others, the *Buddha* and his replicas displayed great supernatural powers, putting forth their long, broad tongues, which reached upward as far as the *Brahmā*—world, while their pores emitted rays in incalculable, numberless colors, all universally illuminating the world-spheres in all ten quarters. After a hundred thousand years all the *Buddhas* withdrew their tongues and at once both coughed and snapped their fingers. These two sounds reached throughout the world-spheres of the *Buddhas* in all ten quarters. Straightway in open space the gods with a loud voice said that now in the *Sahā* world-sphere the *Śānkyamunibuddha* was preaching a scripture of the Great Vehicle named *Saddharmapuṇḍarīka-sūtra* to *bodhisattvas*. At that time, beings in all ten quarters faced the *Sahā* world-sphere and scattered many offerings on it. And, through the world-spheres in all ten quarters passage was unobstructed, as if they had been one *Buddha*-land.[37]

All the supernatural events mentioned above are beyond the limit of cognition and it is in this context the *Lotus* appears. This gives an implication that all the *Tathāgata's* dharmas, supernatural powers of mastery, secrets and profound affairs are included in the *Lotus*.

Chapter 22: Entrustment (*Anuparīndanā*)

The *Buddha* then hands down the *Lotus,* an embodiment of his wisdom, to his followers for spreading and asks all of them and *Buddha Prabhūtaratna* to go back to their home lands.

Śākyamunibuddha rose from his seat and entrusted the Dharma of *anuttarasamyaksaṃbodhi* he had obtained incalculable time ago to all the *bodhisattvas* and asked them to spread it to all beings. This Dharma is the *Saddharmapuṇḍarīka-sūtra,* the wisdom of the *Buddha,* the wisdom of the *Tathāgata,* the wisdom that is so of itself. All the *bodhisattvas* expressed their great joy and obedience. Then he told them and *Buddha Prabhūtaratna* to return back to their home worlds.

This chapter ends the portions pertaining to hearing, demonstrating, understanding of the *Lotus* and from the next chapter till the last one constitute the portion of 'practice' or 'entering the path of *Buddhajñāna*.'

Chapter 23 : The former affairs of the *Bodhisattva* Medicine King (*Bhaiṣajya-rājapūrvayoga*)

Ātman as a personal ego, which is in fact a combination of *pañcaskandhas*. It is the main obstacle on the way to the final goal of enlightenment. Thus to destroy it is a must. And this chapter is to eliminate the first out of the *pañcaskandhas*, i.e., *rūpaskandha*.

The *Buddha* narrates an incident from a former incarnation of *Badhisattva Bhaiṣajyarāja*.

> *Bodhisattva Sarvasattvapriyadarśana*, the former life of *Bhaiṣajyarāja*, desiring to cultivate painful practices and hearing the *Lotus* from the *Buddha Candrasūrupavimalaprabhāśrī*, obtained the *samādhi* that displays all manner of physical bodies *(sarvarūpasandarsana)*.
>
> Then *Bodhisattva Sarvasattvapriyadarśana* burnt his own body for making offerings to this *Buddha*. But, after his life had ended he was born again in the realm of this *Buddha*. Before entering *nirvāṇa*, *Buddha Candrasūrupavimalaprabhāśrī* entrusted the *Buddha's Dharma* to this *bodhisattva* on the purpose of spreading it. One more strange thing happens when this *bodhisattva* makes another offering to the relics of this *Buddha* by burning his forearm—these arms were restored as before, and this *bodhisattva* gained the *Buddhas* gold-colored body.

This chapter implies that in order to obtain the *Buddhajñāna*, both self (illustrated with the body) and wrong views of grasping (illustrated with the forearm) should be destroyed (illustrated with 'burnt'). This conduct is considered as the 'King of all kinds of medicine,' which is the name of *Bodhisattva Bhaiṣajyarāja*.

Chapter 24 The *Bodhisattva* Fine Sound (*Gadgadasvara*)

It aims at ruling out *vedanāskandha,* which are the feelings towards the six *guṇas,* i.e. sight, sound, smell, taste, touch, and idea. Out of these the 'sight' and 'sound' attract the living beings most. But, when disregarding the two (here, in the story of this chapter, illustrated with the *Bodhisattva Gadgadasvara* who does not despise and who comes to the ugly *Sahā* world and makes offerings of music and jeweled alms bowls), the mind returns back to the *Buddhajñāna* (illustrated with the *Bodhisattva Gadgadasvara* who comes to see *Buddha Prabhūtaratna*). This is an implication of the story in this chapter.

Chapter 25 The Gateway to Everywhere of the *Bodhisattva* He Who Observes the Sounds of the World (*Samantamukhaparivarto nāmāvalokiteśvaravikurvaṇa-nirdeśaḥ*)

This chapter teaches us how to rule out *samjñā-skandha,* the third of *pañca-skandhas*. When entering into the path of *Buddhajñāna,* one eradicates *samjñāskandha,* ends sufferings, and is possessed of the supernatural powers of self-mastery in this suffering world. Suffering originates from the mental constructions. That is why *Bodhisattva Akṣayamati* (Inexhaustible Mind) advised the living beings to be mindful of and bow down their heads before *Boddhisattva Avalokiteśvara,* an incarnation of *Buddha's* wisdom and compassion, for free from pain.

"Therefore one must ever be mindful of them.

From moment to moment conceive no doubts,

For the pure saint Who Observes the Sounds of the World

In the discomforts of pain, agony, and death

Can be a point of reliance.

Fully endowed with all the merits,

His benevolent eye beholding the beings,

He is happiness accumulated, a sea incalculable.

For this reason one must bow one's head to him."

Chapter 26: Dhāraṇi

This chapter is to destroy *saṃskāra-skandha,* the fourth of *pañcaskandhas*. To eliminate this *skandha* it must need the help of the *Buddha's* supernatural power. Thus there is no any role of *bodhisattvas* here. The role of the *bodhisattvas* is confined to the eradication of the first three *skandhas*. The fourth one, however, can be eradicated only by the Buddha's supernatural powers. In this chapter, the role of the *Bodhisattvas, Bhaiṣajyarāja* and *Pradānasūtra*, two god kings, the ten daughters of *rākṣasas*, with the mother of the ghosts' children, who pronounced *dhāraṇīs*, is only to protect those who accept and keep, read and recite, put into practice and preach the *Lotus*.

Saṃskāra-skandha is the action of mind which is very fine, not as easily knowable as *sañjnāskandha.* When destroying completely *sañjnā-skandha*, there remain no illusions. At this state the *śrāvakas* and *pratyekabuddhas* mistakenly think that their minds are pure, and they think that they have realised *nirvāṇa* and dwell in it. The Chinese *Ch 'an* school portrays this step as the eighth painting of "ox-pictures."[38] Here both man and ox dissappear. This step should be overcome, ortherwise the aspirant will be stuck here. Similarly, the *Laṅkāvatāra-sūtra* describes this step as the eighth *bhūmi* of *bodhisattvas*, which is simply overcome by the *Buddha's* supernatural power.[39] When recited with an aware-mindfulness, *dhāraṇīs* of the *Buddha* can rule out the *saṃskāra-skandha*.

Chapter 27: The former affairs of the King Fine Adornment (*Śubhavyūharāja-pūrvayoga*)

This chapter is to destroy *vijñānaskandha,* the last of five aggregates. According to the *Vijñānavāda,*[40] *vijñānaskandha* here does not only mean the six kinds of consciousness produced by the objects and six sense organs and the seventh consciousness, but also the *Ālayavijñāna,* which contains good and evil seeds. When all these seeds dissappear, the *Ālayavijñāna* becomes pure, this is called *Tathāgatagardbha,* i.e. Buddhahood.

King *Śubhavyūha* represents the *Ālayavijñāna,* King's lady *Vimaladattā* represents *kliṣṭa-mano-vijñāna* (the seventh consciousness), the two princes, *Vimalagarbha* represents *manovijñāna* (the sixth or mind consciousness) and *Vimalanetra* represents the five senses of seeing, hearing, smelling, tasting, and touch. *Manovijñāna* is the most active and clever and is also the main agent which produces and changes *karmas*. When the first six kinds of consciousness accumulate sufficient merits, they will change the *Ālayavijñāna* into *Tathāgatagardbha*. Thus, in this chapter, after ordination, by their magic powers, the two princes converted the King and King's lady into the Path (*Dharma*). But, at last, the *Buddha* conferred Buddhahood on the King, not on the two princes. This indicates that *Ālayavijñāna* is the main consciousness to become *Buddha,* not the remaining seven. Everything is included in the *Ālayavijñāna*.

Chapter 28: The encouragements of the *Bodhisattva* Universally Worthy (*Samantabhadrotsāhanaparivarta*)

This chapter describes the entering the world of *Bodhisattva Samantabhadra* to save or enlighten living beings.

Here the *bodhisattva* vows to enter in the midst of a muddied, evil age in order to guard and protect those who receive and keep this *Lotus*. Replying the question of this *bodhisattva,* the *Buddha* shows the living beings to practise four *dharmas* for the penetration of the profound meaning of the *Lotus* or *Buddhajñāna*. The four *dharmas* are as follows:

- First, man must be the object of the protectively mindful thoughts of the *Buddha* (It means that the living beings should live up to the *Buddhajñāna*).
- Second, man must plant the roots of a multitude of excellence (It implies the self-enlightenment and the enlightening others).
- Third, man must enter the right concentration (to stop the wrong views and tricky illusions).
- Fourth, man must launch the thought of rescuing all living beings.

The white elephant-king with six tusks that *Bodhisattva Samantabhadra* mounted on represents the 'firm great conduct and pureness;' six tusks refer to the six *pāramitās*. After eradicating the *pañcaskandha* and attaining the tenth *bhūmi* a *bodhisattva* must enter the *Sahā* world to save living beings. If he attains enlightenment (chapter 27) but not yet to enlighten others (chapter 28), he does not have sufficient merits to attain Buddhahood.

In most of *Mahāyāna-sūtras, Bodhisattva Mañjuśrī* usually appears in the first chapter, and in the last chapter is *Bodhisattva Samantabhadra*. In chapter 1 of the *Lotus, Bodhisattva Mañjuśrī* terminates the doubt of *Bodhisattva*

Maitreya and of the fourfold multitude; and in chapter 28 the conduct and vow of *Bodhisattva Samantabhadra* are described. *Bodhisattva Mañjuśrī* stands for wisdom and *Bodhisattva Samantabhadra* for great conduct or practice. Both wisdom and practice have to be in a unity.

Through the philosophical implications in 28 chapters of the *Lotus* one can derive from them such basic concepts and doctrines as *Ekayāna, Upāya-kauśalya, Bodhisattva, Buddhahood, Dhāraṇī,* and even the doctrines of the *Śūnyavāda* and *Vijñapatimātratā* as well.

References

1. Leon Hurvitz, *Scripture of the Lotus Blossom of the Fine Dharma,* New York: Columbia University Press, 1976, p. 30.
2. The *Saddharmapuṇḍarīka,* tr. H. Kern, Delhi, 1994, p. 1.
3. Leon Hurvitz, Op. cit., pp. 36-37.
4. Ibid., p. 30.
5. Ibid.
6. Ibid., pp. 22-23.
7. Ibid., p. 41.
8. Sixty-two are enumerated in the *Brahmajālasūtra* and in the *Dīghnikāya* and consisted all views other than the "right view" of selflessness. All sixty-two fall into either one of the two categories known as the "two extremisms" — "eternalism" (*sāśvatavāda*) and "nihilism" (*ucchedvāda*).
9. Leon Hurvitz, Op. cit., pp. 35-36.
10. Ibid. p. 29.
11. *Triloka* consist of: a) *Kāmadhātu* is the realm of sensuous desire: it includes the six heavens of desire, the human world, and the hells, b) *Rūpadhātu* is the realm of form, it is above the lust world and contains bodies, palaces, thing; it is represented in the four *dhyāna* heavens, i.e. the division of

the eighteen *brahmalokas* into four *dhyānas,* c) *Arūpadhātu,* is the formless realm of pure spirit, where there are no bodies, palaces, things, where the mind dwells in mystic contemplation: its extent is indefinable, but it is conceived of in four stages, i.e. the four formless realms.

12. Leon Hurvitz, Op.cit., p. 73.
13. Ibid.
14. Ibid., p. 102.
15. Ibid., p. 105.
16. Ibid., p. 106.
17. Ibid., p. 110.
18. Ibid.
19. Ibid., p. 149.
20. Ibid.
21. Ibid., pp. 147-148.
22. Ibid., p. 165.
23. named in Sanskrit *Tathāgata Dharmagahanābhyudgatarāga,* The *Saddharmapundarika,* tr. H. Kern, Op.cit., p. 208.
24. L. Hurvitz. Op.cit., p. 176.
25. Ibid., p. 179.
26. Ibid., p. 178.
27. Relics.
28. L. Hurvitz. Op.cit., p. 180.
29. Killing father, killing mother, killing *Arhant,* disuniting the *saṅgha,* and making the Buddha's body bloody.
30. The body of a female has five obstacles as follows : It cannot become first a *Brahmā* god king, second the god *Śakra,* third King *Māra,* fourth a sage-king turning the wheel, fifth a Buddha-body.
31. L. Hurvitz. Op.cit., p. 198.

32. Ibid., p. 210.

33. Ibid., p. 217.

34. Ibid., p. 234.

35. or countless kalpas showing the period of destruction, the period of continued destruction or emptiness, the period of reproduction or formation; and the period of continued reproduction or settlement. Each of these *asaṃkhyeyakalpas* is subdivided into 20 small kalpas.

36. See Hurvitz, Op.cit, pp. 240-241.

37. See Hurvitz, Op.cit, pp. 287-288.

38. Ten *Ch'an* ox-pictures are as follows: 1) a man looking for an ox, 2) seeing its tracks, 3) seeing the ox, 4) catching it, 5) feeding it, 6) riding it home, 7) ox dies man lives, 8) both dead, 9) return whence they came, and 10) enter the dust.

39. See The Lankavatara Sutra, trans. D. T. Suzuki, Boulder, 1978, p. 183.

40. A Buddhist school advocates Mind Only, and this Mind consists of eight *parijñāna,* or kinds of cognition, perception, or consciousness. They are the five senses of *cakṣur-vijñāna, śrota-v., ghrāṇa-v., jihvā-v.,* and *kāya-v.,* i.e. seeing, hearing, smelling, tasting, and touch. The sixth is *mano-vijñāna,* the mental sense, or intellect. The seventh is styled *kliṣṭa-mano-vijñāna* which is the discriminating and constructive sense, as infected by the *ālaya-v.,* or receiving "seeds" from it, it is considered as the cause of all egoism and individually. The eighth is the *ālaya-vijñāna,* which is the store house (or basis from which come all "seeds"—wholesome and unwholesome-of consciousness).

Chapter III

One Vehicle (*Ekayāna*)

Nāgārjuna has been the foremost of the Buddhist tinkers and exponents. In him Buddhist thought reaches great sophistication.

According to *Nāgārjuna* there are two kinds of truths: *Samvṛti satya* (Empirical Truth or Phenomena) and *Paramārtha satya* (Absolute Reality). *Paramārtha* is identified by the *Lotus* with *Ekayāna*. Besides, *Ekayāna* is identical with *śūnyatā, Tathatā, Samatā, Dharmakāya, Nirvāṇa, Madhyamā Pratipad*. Also, the *Lotus* expresses the *Ekayāna* through similes and predictions. In order to understand and appreciate properly these fundamental concepts and doctrines, first of all, the evolution of Buddhist thought should be known.

I) The Evolution of Buddhist Thought

In the 1st and 2nd centuries A.D., around 500 years after the passing away of the *Buddha*, a major revolution in Buddhist thought took place. The movement with its mobility, adaptability and progressive spirit arose out of ideas that had been evolving over a long period in a number of sects in southern and northwestern India. The new Buddhist thinkers called their system, *Bodhisattva*-career (*Bodhisattvayāna*), and later on, the *Mahāyāna*, the 'great vehicle' or 'ferryboat', and they sometimes described the older Buddhist schools, pejoratively, as *Hīnayāna* or the 'lesser, inferior, low vehicle.' The *Mahāyāna* seemed great for many reasons — chiefly because of the all-embracing nature of the compassion, and emptiness which it taught, and because of the greatness of the goal it advocated, Buddhahood.

The doctrine of the *Mahāyāna sūtras* was developed in a systematic and philosophical form by the *Mādhyamikas*. *Madhyama* means middle, and the *Mādhyamikas* are those who take the Middle Way, avoiding the two extremes: affirmation and denial. The school was founded, probably about 150 A.D., by *Nāgārjuna* and his disciple, *Āryadeva*. *Nāgārjuna* was one of the most subtle dialecticians of all times. His theory is called *Śūnyavāda,* or emptiness doctrine. He was considered as the systematizer of the *Mahāyāna* philosophic system. *Mahāyāna* thought developed partly as a response to the demands of Indian lay Buddhists. Buddhism up to this time, in the first centuries up to about 400 A.D., had been largely the preserve of monks. Lay people were excluded from full participation in religious activity, and the *arhat* (enlightened person) came increasingly to be regarded as a spiritual aristocrat on the path to a purely personal deliverance. And during this time, we hear a great deal about the *śrāvakas* and *pratyekabuddhas*. However, according to the Buddhist thought, no one could truly become an *arhat* if he/she had not, with insight and compassion, burned the notion of *ātman* away. Thus, the central ideal of the new *Mahāyāna* movement was a shift of focus from *arhat* to *bodhisattva* (enlightened being). In earlier Buddhism, *bodhisattva* denoted a previous incarnation of the *Buddha*. The term was taken up by the Mahayanists in its literal sense: a person made of, or for, enlightenment. *Bodhisattvas* were those who vowed they would be enlightened. But this enlightenment was not for themselves alone: it was pursued for the deliverance of others. The *bodhisattvas* would refuse entry into *nirvāṇa* until they had led all other beings there before them. And a *bodhisattva* is a being compounded of the two different forces of wisdom and compassion. In his wisdom, he sees no separate persons; in his compassion he is resolved to save them:

> "And yet, although innumerable beings have thus been led to *Nirvāṇa,* no being at all has been led to *Nirvāṇa.* And why? If in a *Bodhisattva* the perception of a 'being' should take place, he would not be called an 'enlightenment-being' *(bodhisattva)*"[1]

His ability to combine these different attitudes is the source of his greatness, and of his ability to save himself and others.

Two things are most needful to the *bodhisattva,* and to his practice of wisdom: 'Never to abandon all beings and to see into the truth that all things are empty.' Here, we should make an effort to understand this very important idea of emptiness.

What we call emptiness in English is *śūnyatā* in sanskrit. The sanskrit word *śūnyatā* is derived from the root SVI, to swell. *Śūnya* means literally: relating to the swollen. The root SVI seems to have expressed the idea that something which looks 'swollen' from the outside is 'hollow' inside. Our personality is swollen by the five *skandhas,* but it is hollow inside, because it is devoid of a central self. In Buddhist art emptiness is usually symbolised by an empty circle, but one must not regard the Buddhist emptiness as a mere nought, or a blank like turtle's hairs or rabbit's horns. It is a term showing the absence of self nature *(svabhāva).*

In Buddhist literature we see that the Abhidharmists knew the term empty, but used it very sparingly. In the Pali canon it occurs only on a few occasions. But in the new *Mahāyāna* movement treats the term as the sesame which open all doors to *nirvāṇa,* and *Nāgārjuna* worked out its epistemological and spiritual implications. Emptiness here means the identity of the two extremes: yes and no, affirmation and negation, existence and non-existence, eternity and annihilation. According to *Nāgārjuna*, *śūnyatā* means nothing acquirable.[2] Everything exists temporarily and nothing is permanent under the law of Dependent Origination.[3] Existence is temporary and not fixed. Even non-existence is temporary and not fixed. So there is neither a real existence nor a real void. Negation of wrong views of attachment to anything inclusive of extremes is the middle path. Negation and negation only can lead to the Ultimate Truth. And it is the theory of the eightfold negation set forth by *Nāgārjuna* in his dedicatory verse of the *Mūlamadhyamakakārikā,* which runs as follows:

> "*Anirodhamanutpādamanucchedamaśāśvataṃ*
>
> *Anekārthamanānārthamanāgamamanirgamaṃ.*
>
> *Yah pratītyasamutpādaṃ prapañcopasamaṃ śivaṃ*
>
> *Deśayāmāsa saṃbuddhastaṃ vande vadatāṃ varaṃ.*"
>
> I pay homage to the Fully Awakened One,
>
> the supreme teacher who has taught
>
> the doctrine of relational origination,
>
> the blissful cessation of all phenomenal thought constructions
>
> [Therein, every event is "marked" by]:
>
> non-origination, non-extinction,
>
> non-destruction, non-permanence,
>
> non-identity, non-differentiation
>
> non-coming (into being), non-going (out of being).[4]

Here, we can see that the *Nāgārjuna's* viewpoints are not much different from those of the *Buddha's* discourse to *Kaccāyana,* a Pali discourse whose authority was recognized by almost all the major philosophical schools of Buddhism. Following is the complete text of the discourse as reported by *Ānanda:*

"Thus have I heard: The Blessed One was once living at *Sāvatthi,* in the monastery of *Anāthapiṇḍika,* in Jeta's Grove. At that time the venerable *Kaccāyana* of that clan came to visit him, and saluting him, sat down at one side. So seated, he questioned the Exalted One: "Sir [people] speak of 'right view, right view.' To what extent is there a right view?

This world, *Kaccāyana,* is generally inclined towards two [views]: existence and non-existence.

To him who perceives with right wisdom the uprising of the world as it has come to be, the notion of non-existence in the world does not occur. *Kaccāyana,* to him who perceives with right wisdom the ceasing of the world as it has come to be, the notion of existence in the world does not occur.

The world, for the most part, *Kaccāyana,* is bound by approach, grasping and inclination. And he who does not follow that approach and grasping, that determination of mind, that inclination and disposition, who does not cling to or adhere to a view: 'This is my self,' who thinks: 'suffering that is subject to arising arises; suffering that is subject to ceasing, ceases,' such a person does not doubt, is not perplexed. Herein, his knowledge is not other-dependent. Thus far, *Kaccāyana,* there is 'right view.'

'Everything exists,'—this, *Kaccāyana,* is one extreme.

'Everything does not exist,'—this, *Kaccāyana,* is the second extreme.

Kaccāyana, without approaching either extreme, the *Tathāgata* teaches you a doctrine by the middle.

Dependent upon ignorance arise dispositions; dependent upon dispositions arise consciousness; dependent upon consciousness arises the psychophysical personality; dependent upon the psychophysical personality arise the six senses; dependent upon the six senses arises contact; dependent upon contact arises feeling; dependent upon feeling arises craving; dependent upon craving arises grasping; dependent upon grasping arises becoming; dependent upon becoming arises birth; dependent upon birth arises old age and death, grief, lamentation, suffering, dejection and despair. Thus arises this entire mass of suffering. However, from the utter fading away and ceasing of ignorance, there is ceasing of dispositions; from the ceasing of dispositions, there is ceasing of consciousness; from the ceasing of consciousness, there is ceasing of the psychophysical personality; from the ceasing of the psychophysical personality, there is ceasing of the six senses; from the ceasing of the six senses, there is ceasing of contact; from the ceasing of contact, there is ceasing of feeling; from the ceasing of feeling, there is ceasing craving; from the ceasing of craving, there is ceasing of grasping; from the ceasing of grasping, there is ceasing of becoming; from the ceasing of becoming, there is ceasing of birth; from the ceasing of birth, there is ceasing of old age and death, grief, lamentation, suffering, dejection and despair. And thus there is the ceasing of this entire mass of suffering."[5]

The *Buddha* says to *Kātyāyana* that the world usually bases its views on two things, existence and non-existence. 'It is' is one extreme; 'it is not' is another. Attaching to them the world is imprisoned. The holy men transcend this limitation of attachement. Avoiding both extremes, the *Tathāgata* teaches a *Dharma* by the middle, where alone the truth can be found. This *Dharma* is now, in *Nāgārjuna's* viewpoint, called emptiness. The Absolute is emptiness and all things also are empty. However, it is unjust to regard emptiness as a kind of Absolute behind the conditioned world, as a kind of basis for it, for *'Nirvāṇa* is not in the least distinct from birth-and-death.' It is not a separate reality at all.

The Hīnayānists admit two kinds of truth: Ultimate Truth of *Dharmas,* and Conventional Truth of persons and things. The *Dharmas* of this school have very much the same function as atoms, cells and similar entities. Meanwhile the Mahāyānists take the concept of Ultimate Truth a step further. It is now found exclusively in relation to the one Ultimate Reality, which is the Absolute in its emptiness. Thus we cannot get at it in thoughts and words, and even if we could, we should not identify it as this or that since it has no distinctive marks. All doctrines, even the Four Noble Truths, are ultimately false. The Absolute alone is not dependent on anything else; it is ultimately real. Any relative thing is functionally dependent on other things, and can exist, and be conceived, only in and through its relations with other things. By itself it is nothing, it has no separate intrinsic reality: "Know that the *Dharmas* are ever without a nature of their own."[6] But if each and every thing is 'devoid of self-nature' and does not really exist, like "tortoise's hair," how is it that we can see, hear and feel the things around us which are really just emptiness? The similes of a dream, etc., are intended to answer that question. One sees a magical show, one experiences a dream, and yet we all know that the magical appearance is merely deceptive, that the objects one saw, loved, hated and feared in one's dream did not really exist.

Thus, the doctrine of emptiness is frequently expressed by way of similes for both schools *Hīnayāna* and *Mahāyāna,* specially in the *Lotus*. The similes had the purpose of implying that the world is relatively unimportant, worthless, deceptive and unsubstantial.

One of the most frequent synonyms of emptiness is Non-duality (*advayatā*). In the perfect gnosis, all dualities are abolished, the object does not differ from the subject, *nirvāṇa* is not distinguished from the world, existence is no longer something apart from non-existence. Discrimination and multiplicity are the hallmarks of ignorance. From another point of view emptiness is called Suchness (*Tathatā*), because one takes reality such as it is, without superimposing any ideas upon it.

One more point of differentiation between the two schools is understanding the nature of *nirvāṇa*. According to the Sarvāstivādins there are three different ways to *nirvāṇa*: There are the *śrāvakas,* who attain *nirvāṇa* through arhatship. There is the *pratyekabuddha,* who is 'one enlightened by himself, i.e. one who has attained full enlightenment, but who passes away without proclaiming the truth to the world.' There are the Supreme *Buddhas,* who win perfect enlightenment, and teach the *Dharma* to others. Each individual, by his past life, by character and temperament, belongs to one of these three groups, and he must use the means which suit his make-up. Some Mahāyānists agree to this point. Others, however, insist that there is but one way to final *nirvāṇa* —the *Buddha* Vehicle, or the Great Vehicle, which is true and others are false: "It is only with the *Buddha* Vehicle that one can gain extinction; that there is no other vehicle, except for the *Dharmas* preached by the Thus come One as a matter of expedient device."[7] The *Lotus,* for instance, says: "All Disciples fancy they have attained *nirvāṇa*. But the *Jina* instructs them, and says: 'This is a temporary repose, no final rest.' It is a device of the *Buddha* when he taught this method. There is no real *nirvāṇa* without omniscience. Strive to reach this!" The *arhats* are told that they had not 'accomplished their tasks,' they had not 'finished what they had to do'. They had to strive on, until they gained the *Buddhajñāna*.

II) Meaning and Significance of One Vehicle (*Ekayāna*)

1) *One Vehicle and Triple Vehicle*

One of the principles of the *Lotus* is the One Vehicle. At the time of the *Lotus* was compiled it was accepted on all accounts that there were *arhats, pratyekabuddhas,* and *Buddhas*. Most were following the path to arhatship. Somewhere, sometimes, perhaps, there were *pratyekabuddhas,* while certain rare beings such as *Siddhārtha Gautama* became *Buddhas*. It was agreed that the attributes of these were different, the *Buddha* was in certain respects superior, but all were truly enlightened — after death none would be reborn. We have seen in the *Lotus,* however, and indeed in texts belonging to certain non-*Mahāyāna* traditions, a gradual devaluation of *arhats* and *pratyekabuddhas,* and an elevation of the *Buddha* and his attainment. The *Lotus* marks the culmination of this process. There is in reality only One Vehicle, only one path conducive to the final goal of Buddhahood, not three; if any, they are beings of severally different modes of conduct "O *Kāśyapa,* there are not three vehicles. There are only beings of severally different modes of conduct and for that reason three vehicles are designated."[8] This One Vehicle is the Supreme *Buddha* Vehicle. Just as the *Buddha* is infinitely superior to the *arhat* and the *pratyekabuddha*, so the only final vehicle is the One Vehicle to Perfect Buddhahood. All will eventually become *Buddhas* — the doctrine of the three vehicles was in reality nothing more than the *Buddha's* skilful means (*upāya-kauśalya*):

> "*Śāriputra*, I, too, am like this. Knowing that the beings have various desires and objects to which their thoughts are profoundly attached, following their basic natures, by resort to the expedient power of various means, parables, and phrases, I preach the *Dharma* to them. *Śāriputra*, I do this only in order that they may gain the One *Buddha*

Vehicle and knowledge of all modes. *Śāriputra*, in the worlds of the ten directions there are not even two vehicles. How much the less can there be three!"[9]

The One Vehicle and Triple Vehicle are also mentioned in the *Laṅkāvatāra-sūtra.* According to this *sūtra,* in reality there is only One Vehicle; but to lead the ignorant the *Buddha* talks of some more. And the One Vehicle characterizes the inner attainment of noble wisdom, discarding erroneous views and discriminations and abiding in the reality of Suchness:

"There is really no establishment of various vehicles, and so I speak of the one vehicle; but in order to carry the ignorant I talk of a variety of vehicles."[10]

"As they have not yet destroyed the habit-energy (memory) of karma and the hindrance of knowledge, all the *śrāvakas* and *pratyekabuddhas* are unable to realise the egolessness of things and have not attained the inconceivale transformation-death, I preach to the *śrāvakas* [and *pratyekabuddhas*] the triple vehicle and not the one vehicle."[11]

"How is this path of the one vehicle to be recognised and realised? The recognition of the one vehicle is obtained when there is no rising of discrimination by doing away with the notion of grasped and grasping and by abiding in the reality of suchness (*yathābūta*). *Mahāmati,* this recognition of the one vehicle, except by the *Tathāgata* himself, has never been obtained before by anybody else — the philosophers, *śrāvakas, pratyekabuddhas, Brahmans,* etc. For this reason, *Mahāmati,* this is known as the one vehicle."[12]

2) One Vehicle and Śūnyatā

Śūnyatā is the central idea of the *Mādhyamaka* philosophy. It is so important that this system is generally known as *Śūnyavāda* i.e., the philosophy that asserts *śūnyatā* as the characterization of Reality. Consequently, a right understanding of *śūnyatā* helps us very much in understanding the *Lotus,* which has been worked out on the basis of *śūnyatā.*

Śūnyatā is a most perplexing word in Buddhist philosophy. Non-Buddhists have interpreted it only as nihilism. But that is not the case. The import of *śūnyatā* may be understood in many ways:

i. **In the ontological sense:** According to some scholars *śūnyatā* has no ontological signification. But it is obviously used in an ontological sense with an axiological implication and soteriological background.

In reference to ontological sense *śūnyatā* is the essencelessness which also implies fulness. Because it is nothing in particular, it can be identified with everything. It has been identified with *Nirvāṇa,* with the Absolute, with *Paramārtha-sat* (the Absolute Reality), with *Tattva* (Reality). The *Buddha* is said to be seated in *śūnyā tattva,* in the *śūnyā* principle. The word *śūnyā* seems to have been used in an ontological sense in such contexts. What is the *śūnyā tattva? Nāgārjuna* says:

"Aparapratyayam śāntam prapañcair aprapañcitaṃ
Nirvikalpam anānārtham etat tattvasya lakṣaṇaṃ."

(M.K., 18, 9)

1. It is *aparapratyayam.* It is that experience which cannot be imparted to any one by another.

2. It is *śāntam* It is quiescent, unaffected by the empirical mind.

3. It is *prapañcair aprapañcitam* i.e. inexpressible by the verbalising mind. It is non-determinate, free of thought construction. That is', 'not is', 'both is and not is', 'neither is nor not is' — no thought category or predicate can be applied to it. It is transcendent to thought.

4. It is *nirvikalpam* i.e. it is transcendent to discursive thought.

5. It is *anānārtham.* It is non-dual, devoid of plurality, that it is a Whole or Oneness which cannot be sundered into parts.

ii. In the axiological sense: All empirical things are devoid of independent, substantial reality. Therefore they are ultimately worthless. It is because of our ignorance that we attach so much value to worldly things. Once *śūnyatā* is properly understood, the inordinate craving for a thing will stop, and we experience the blessing of peace.

iii. In the soteriological sense: *Śūnyatā* is not merely an intellectual concept. Its realization is a means to *nirvāṇa. Nāgārjuna* puts it as follows:

"Karmakleśa-kṣayān-mokṣaḥ, karma kleśā vikalpataḥ

Te prapañcāt prapañcastu śūnyatāyām nirudhyate."

(M.K. 18, *5)*

(Emancipation is obtained by the dissolution of selfish deeds and passions. All selfish deeds and passions are caused by imaginative constructs which value that worthless things are full of worth. The *vikalpas* or imaginative constructs are born of *prapañca,* the verbalizing, imaging activity of the mind. This activity of the mind ceases when *śūnyatā,* emptiness or hollowness of things is realized).

iv. Śūnyatā - the symbol of the inexpressible

In *Mādhyamika* philosophy *śūnyatā* is used as a symbol of the inexpressible. In calling Reality *śūnya,* the *Mādhyamika* connotes it *avācya, anabhilāpya* i.e inexpressible. In the *Mādhymakakārikā, Nāgārjuna* makes the stand-point of *Śūnyavāda* luminously prominent. The standpoint consists of the eight 'Nos'

"Anirodham anutpādam anucchedam aśāśvataṃ,

anekārtham anānārtham anāgamam' anirgamaṃ"

It is (1) *anirodham,* no-ceasing; (2) *anutpādam,* no-arising; (3) *anucehedam,* no-dissolution; (4) *aśāśvataṃ,* no-eternity; *(5) anekārtham,* no-oneness; (6) *anānārtham,* no-plurality; (7) *anāgamam,* no-ingress; (8) *anirgamaṃ,* no-egress.

v. Śūnyatā — not a theory

The original and important contribution of *Nāgārjuna* in the Buddhist philosophy is the dialectic (originated from the silence of *Buddha* on the Truth or Reality), formulated into the *catuṣkoṭi,* which shows up the inevitable conflict in which Reason gets involved when it goes beyond its confined ability of comprehending phenomena, and enters the forbidden land of noumenon. By the use of his dialectic, he comes to the conclusion that all views are conflicted and all the *dharmas* are *śūnya* or *niḥsvabhāva,* i.e. devoid of any independent, substantial reality. Therefore, it may be thought that *śūnyatā* itself is a theory. But *śūnyatā* is not a theory. *Nāgārjuna* says:

"Atra brūmaḥ śūnyatāyām na tvam vetsi prayojanam

Śūnyatām śūnyatārtharn ca tat evam vihanyase."

(M.K. 24, 7)

(You do not know the purpose of *śūnyatā*. *Śūnyatā* is not used as a theory just for the sake of *śūnyatā*).

Nāgārjuna also says that *śūnyatā* is meant to destroy the incessant cogitation of the verbalizing mind (*prapañcastu śūnyatāyām nirudh-yate*).

So, *śūnyatā* is used not for its own sake, but for leading the mind to Reality by restraining its conceptualizing tendency. It is an expression of aspiration, not of theory.

vi. Śūnyatā - not nihilism

It is misunderstood by some that *śūnyatā* is complete negativism, rejects everything, has no positive suggestion to offer, and leads us nowhere. It is rank nihilism. *Nāgārjuna's* dialectic leading to *śūnyatā* is not mere negativism. It does not only negate all affirmations about Reality; but it also negates all negations about Reality. It says Reality is neither *sat* (existent) nor *asat* (non-existent). It just asserts that the Absolute is inaccessible to thought; it does not say that the Absolute is a non-entity like tortoise's hair, rabbit's horn. It only maintains that the Absolute is realized in non-dual, transcendental wisdom. It even pleads for the realization of the Absolute Truth. *Nāgārjuna* says *"Paramātham anāgamya Nirvāṇam nādhigam-yate"*, to wit, "without realizing the Absolute Truth, one cannot attain *Nirvāṇa*".

Nāgārjuna only negates all views about Reality; he does not negate Reality itself. *Śūnyatā* cannot, therefore, be called nihilism.

vii. Śūnyatā — not a goal in itself

Nāgārjuna warns that one should not make a fetish of *śūnyatā*. It is not a goal in itself. It is only a means to lead the mind up to *prajñā* (transcendental insight). *Nāgārjuna* says:

> *"Śūnyatā sarvadṛṣṭīnām proktā nihsaraṇam jinaih.*
>
> *Yeśām tu śūnyatā drṣṭistan asādhyān babhāṣire."*
>
> (M.K. 13, 8)

(*Śūnyatā* was declared by the *Buddha* for dispensing with all views or 'isms'. Those who convert *śūnyatā* itself into another 'ism' are verily beyond hope or help).

In reference to this the *Buddha* is said to have remarked that *śūnyatā* is to be treated like a ladder for mounting up to the roof of *prajñā*. When the roof is reached, the ladder should be discarded.

viii. Meditation on śūnyatā

It has been mentioned that *śūnyatā* is not simply an intellectual concept but an aspiration. In order to complete this aspiration one has to meditate on *śūnyatā*. This leads to *prajñā* (transcendental wisdom), which brings about the emancipation of the aspirant from spiritual darkness.

The sole purpose of the *Lotus* is to reveal the *Buddhajñāna* or *Ekayāna* and to put an end to the discrimination of all *Dharmas* for they are *nairātmya* (no self), *niḥsva-bhāvatā* (no self-nature), *śūnyatā* (emptiness).

"The *Buddhas,* the Most Venerable of Two-Legged Beings,
Know that the *Dharmas* are ever without a nature of their own.
By virtue of conditions is the *Buddha*-seed realized:
For this reason they preach the One Vehicle."[13]

One of three necessary conditions to be a preacher of the *Lotus,* which emphasizes the One Vehicle, is to sit on the throne of the *Tathāgata.* But "the throne of the Thus Come One is the emptiness of all *Dharmas.*"[14]

The emptiness in the *Lotus* is also expressed by the symbol of 'open air', 'mid-air'. In chapter 11, *Apparition of the Jeweled stūpa,* when the *Śākyamunibuddha,* with his power of supernatural penetration, touched the great multitude so that they were all in open space and hence could see both *Buddhas* - *Śākyamuni* and *Prabhūtaratna* in the Jeweled *stūpa*. Then and only then the *Śākyamunibuddha* said : "Who can broadly preach the Scripture of the Blossom of the Fine *Dharma* in this *Sahā* land ? Now is the very time!"[15] Yes, only when one realizes the emptiness of all *Dharmas* does he exhaust the meaning of the *Lotus* or of the One-Vehicle.

It is also noticeable that the emptiness of the *Lotus* is that of *Mahāyāna* not of *Hīnayāna*.

"Those who had formerly been voice-hearers were in mid-air preaching the conduct of the voice-hearer... But now all were putting into practice the Great Vehicle's doctrine of emptiness."[16]

Another feature of the *Lotus* is that of burning body (the illustration of no-self, *nairātmya*). Chapter 23 of the *Lotus* recounts how the *Bodhisattva Sarvasattvapriyadarśana* in a previous life wished to make the most perfect offering to the *Buddha Candrasūrupavimalaprabhāśrī*. He accordingly offered his body by setting fire to it. The body burned for a very longtime, and he was eventually reborn in the realm of this *Buddha*. Again, he burnt his forearm to make an offering to the relics of this *Buddha* when this *Buddha* passed away. But both arms were restored completely and he gained the *Buddha's* gold-colored body. This chapter gives an implication that in order to obtain the *Buddhajñāna* or Buddhahood one must destroy one's self (body) and wrong views of attachment (forearm).

3) One Vehicle and *Tathatā*

Tathatā is Suchness, i.e. such as is its nature. It is the reality as contrasted with unreality, or appearance, and unchanging or immutable as contrasted with form and phenomena. It resembes the ocean in contrast with the waves. It is the eternal, impersonal, unchangeable reality behind all phenomena. The word is fundamental to philosophy, implying the absolute, the ultimate source and character of all phenomena. It is the All. It is also called *Nirvikalpajñāna* (the self-existent pure Mind), *Buddhatā* (Buddha nature), *Dharmakāya* (Dharma body), *Tathāgatagarbha* (the womb of the *Tathāgata*), *Buddha-ratna* (Buddha treasury), *Tattva* (Reality), *Dharmaviśaya* (Dharma realm), or *Dharmatā* (Dharma nature).

Tathatā or *Dharmatā* is the word used in the *Mādhyamaka* philosophy for the Absolute. *Candrakīrti* says, "*Yā sa dharmāṇāṃ dharmatā nāma saiva tatsva-rūpam*" (P. P. p. 116) (That which is the essential being of all elements of existence is the nature of Reality). It is *Tathatā,* it is Reality such as it is. According to *Candrakīrti,* "*tathā-bhāvo 'vikāritvam sadaiva sthāyitā*" (P. P. p. 116) (The thatness of Reality consists in its invariability, in its remaining for ever as it is).

Tathatā is the Truth, but it is impersonal. In order to reveal itself, it requires a medium. *Tathāgata* is that medium. *Tathāgata* is the embodiment of Reality. He is Reality personalized. *Tathāgata* is an amphibious being partaking both of the Absolute and phenomena. He is identical with *Tathatā,* but embodied in a human form. That is why *Tathatā* is also called *Tathāgatagarbha* (the womb of *Tathāgata*).

The word *Tathāgata* is interpreted as *Tathā* + *gata* or *Tathā* + *āgata* i.e. 'thus gone' or 'thus come'. *Tathāgata* is used for those who realize Truth and are untraceable. The word 'untraceable' is used for *Tathāgata* in *Majjhima Nikāya* Vol. 1, p. 140 P. T. S. ed. "*Tathāgatam ananuvejjoti vadāmi*" (I declare that *Tathāgata* is *annuvejya,* i.e., whose track is untraceable, who is above all the dichotomies of thought).

Tathatā is the same in all manifestation, therefore all beings are potential *Tathāgatas*. It is the *Tathāgata* within us who makes us long for the goal *nirvāṇa* and finally sets us free.

In the *Lotus,* it is the *Buddha* who could exhaust the reality of all *Dharmas*: "Concerning the prime, rare, hard-to-understand *Dharmas*, which the *Buddha* has perfected, only a *Buddha* and a *Buddha* could exhaust their reality, namely, the Suchness of the *Dharmas*, the Suchness of their marks, the Suchness of their nature, the Suchness of their substance, the Suchness of their powers, the Suchness of their functions, the Suchness of their causes, the Suchness of their conditions, the Suchness of their effects, the Suchness of their retributions, and the absolute identity of their beginning and end."[17]

In the world there are only two things to be known: people and things. One who is able to penetrate these two [kinds of] emptiness eternally realizes the true pinnacle of Suchness. With the realization of Suchness, one can see the image of the lotus flower in the mud. This realization is characterized by non-attachement to extremes, such as *nirvāṇa* and *saṃsāra* due to the realization of their intrinsic nondifference. Nonobstruction is described as the *Tathāgata's* all-knowledge; it is knowledge of all realms and all *Dharmas*, on both the worldly and the ultimate levels.

As Buddhism does not separate being from thought nor thought from being, what is Suchness in the objective world is Transcendental truth or Absolute knowledge in the subjective world, and vice versa. Thus, from the ontological point of view, *Paramārtha-satya* (Transcendental truth) of the *Mādhyamika* or *Pariniṣpanna* (Absolute knowledge) of the *Yogācāra* is called *Bhūtatathatā*, which literally means "Suchness of existence". It marks the consummation of all our mental efforts to reach the highest principle, which unifies all possible contradictions and spontaneously directs the course of world-events. In short, it is the ultimate postulate of existence. Like *Paramārtha-satya*, it does not belong to the domain of demonstrative knowledge or sensuous experience; it is unknowable by the ordinary process of intellection, which the natural sciences use in the formulation of general laws. *Bhūtatathatā,* thus absolutely viewed, does not fall under the category of being and non-being, of contrasts; and it is grasped, declare the Buddhists, only by the minds that are capable of exercising what might be called religious intuition. *Nāgārjuna* puts it:

"*Astīti śāśvatagrāho nāstītyucchedadarśanaṃ*
Tasmādastitvanāstitve nāśrīyeta vicakṣaṇaḥ."
(M.K., 15, 10)

(To think 'it is', is eternalism,
To think 'it is not', is nihilism:
Being and non-being,
The wise cling not to either.)

Aśvaghoṣa argues in his text *Śradhotpādaśāstra* (Awakening of Faith) for the indefinability of this first principle, i.c., *Tathatā*. He wishes to eschew all definite statements concerning the ultimate nature of being, but as language is the only mode with which we mortals can express our ideas and communicate them to others, he thinks the best expression that can be given to it is *Bhūta-tathatā*, i.e., "Suchness of existence," or simply, *Tathatā*, i.e., "Suchness". And in the *Lotus*, *Tathatā* or *Bhūta-tathatā* is described into the *tenfold Suchness* as mentioned on the previous page.

4) One Vehicle and *Samatā*

Samatā means sameness, feeling of Oneness with all, without partiality, equality, tranquility. It especially refers to the *Buddha* in his universal, impartial, and equal attitude towards all beings.

According to *Mahāyāna*, the *dharmas* are not ultimate realities at all, but only phenomenal. *Nāgārjuna* pointed out that even the so-called ultimate *saṃskṛta* (*dharmas* with signs) and *asaṃskṛta* (*dharmas* without signs) are dependent upon conditions and so relative. Being relative, they are *śūnya* (essenceless), hence all are of the same nature (*samatā*). The sameness of the *dharmas* in the *Lotus* is compared to the same clay of the multiple pots. And that is the *Dharmakāya, Ekayāna* or *Buddhayāna*:

"It is just as the potter, O *Kāśyapa*, makes pots with the same clay. Among them, some become pots for sugar lumps, some pots for clarified butter, some pots for curds or milk, while some become pots for inferior and filthy things; and just as there is no difference in the clay, but rather a supposed difference in the pots based solely on the things put into them, in just this way, O *Kāśyapa*, is there this one and only one vehicle, to wit, the *Buddha* Vehicle. There exists neither a second nor a third vehicle."[18]

The sameness is also expressed in disposition, sex (chapter 12), etc. This chapter explains the doctrine of One-Vehicle in the sense of looking the dual things in the world, i.e. good-evil, men-women...with the vision of the sameness and indiscrimination, because the nature of all things is *śūnya*. As mentioned earlier, according to the viewpoint of the *Hīnayāna*, those who commit the five grave sins, and those who are women cannot attain the Buddhahood. But in the *Mahāyāna*, specially in the *Lotus*, all of them can attain the Buddhahood. In a previous life the *Buddha* offers himself as lifelong servant to anyone who can preach to him the *Mahāyāna*. Eventually a hermit offers to preach the *Lotus*. That hermit is in the present life none other than *Devadatta*, who is the *Buddha's* cousin, who makes the *Buddha* suffering physically and, who disunites the *Saṅgha*. The evil-some *Devadatta* is in reality the *Buddha's* best friend. Thanks to *Devadatta* the *Buddha* has been able to practise throughout his lifetimes the various virtues, especially, perhaps, the virtue of patience. That is why *Devadatta* is foretold about his attainment of Buddhahood !

Not only are the wicked greatly encouraged by the *Lotus*, but also the other group so often discriminated against in early Buddhism such as women due to their filthy bodies as mentioned earlier. A *Nāga* princess appears, only 8 years old. She has become an advanced *bodhisattva* in a moment due to the preaching of *Mañjuśrī*, another celestial *bodhisattva*. With her supernatural power the princess before *Śāriputra's* very eyes is instantly transformed into a male and attains Buddhahood.

Abhayākaragupta, one of the last of the great Indian Buddhist masters, puts it as, "The *Ekayāna* theory is in fact founded on the oneness of the knowledge of reality (*tattvajñāna*), which has its 'object' the single undifferentiated reality (*tattva*) or *dharmadhātu*."[19]

The sameness or identification, non-dualism, non difference of all *dharmas* is also expressed by *Nāgārjuna* when mentioning the relation of *nirvāṇa* and *saṁsāra.*

"*Na saṁsārasya Nirvāṇāt kimcid asti viśeṣaṇaṃ*

Na Nirvāṇasya saṁsārāt kimcid asti viśeṣaṇam"

(M.K. 25, 19)

[Nothing of phenomenal existence (*saṁsāra*) is different from *nirvāṇa*, nothing of *nirvāṇa* is different from phenomenal existence]

5) One Vehicle and Similes

The purpose of the *Lotus* is to show the Absolute Truth, *Ekayāna* or *Buddhajñāna* to the beings. The *Buddhajñāna*, however, was profound and incalculable. The gateway of their wisdom is hard to understand and hard to enter, so no *śrāvaka* or *pratyekabuddha* could know it. According to *Candrakīrti*, the Absolute is inexpressible "*Paramārtho hi āyāṇām tūṣṇīmbhāvaḥ*" (P. P. p,19) (To the saints, the Absolute is just silence, i.e., it is inexpressible). If the Absolute is inexpressible, how can the Absolute be described ? The answer is — Phenomena do not completely cut us off from Reality. Phenomena are appearances, and appearances point to their Reality. The veil gives a hint of that which is veiled. And parable is a kind of veil.

Candrakīrti quotes a saying of the *Buddha*,

"*Anakṣarasya dharmasya śrutiḥ kā deśanā ca kā*
Śrūyate deśyate cāpi samāropādanakṣaraḥ"

[How can there be any understanding or teaching of that which is wordless (i.e. inexpressible) ? That can be understood and taught only by *samāropa* - an ascribed mark]. Parable serves as the 'ascribed mark' of Reality.

Thus the *Buddhas* had to make use of similes or parables as a skilful means for understanding the Absolute and One Vehicle. In the *Lotus* there are eight parables as follows:

i. **The parable of burning house** (Chapter 3): It tells how three sons of a rich man are trapped inside a burning house while playing. So absorbed are they in their games that they are unaware of the fire. The father, resolves to save them by seducing them to come out with goat carriages, deer carriages, and ox carriages, which they like. Immediately, they rush to their father. And the father gives them each a wonderful carriage, the best, drawn by a white ox.

   In this parable, the father is the *Buddha*. The burning house is the house of *saṃsāra*, within which sentient beings directed by their ignorance are trapped. The *Buddha* with his compassion using skilful means offers various vehicles as bribes, suitable to the tastes of sentient beings, but when they have taken up the practices and are saved from *saṃsāra* he gives them all the only One Vehicle of Buddhahood.

ii. **The parable of the Poor Son** (Chapter 4): A man's son has left home, wandered away, and fallen into extreme poverty. Meanwhile his father's business by contrast has prospered in another city and has become a very rich man. One day the son arrives at his father's house. While the son no longer recognizes his father or his new mansion, the father instantly recognizes his son and sends a servant to fetch him. Alas, the son is terrified. Thus the father realizes that he must introduce him in gradual stages to the truth that he is the son of the father and heir to all this wealth. The father offers his son very menial and dirty work (Arhatship!). He does the job well, and the father gradually promotes him. Eventually the father starts to treat him like a son. At long last the father, about to die, announces to all that this man really is his son and natural heir. The son is, of course, overjoyed.

In this chapter, the *Buddha* (the father) devises an expedient of reducing his wisdom to the low level of knowledge of his son (*śrāvaka* and *pratyekabuddha*). But when the son receives all treasure (*Buddhajñāna*) from his dying father, he knows that he is also a rich man (Buddhahood).

iii. **The parable of the rain (Chapter 5)**: The *Buddha's* teaching is likened to the rain which pours down equally on various kinds of plants and is of a single mark and a single flavor. This rain is nevertheless absorbed and used by each plant in accord with its nature and kind.

This parable gives an implication that the *Buddha Dharma* is the Sameness, Oneness, One Vehicle or *Buddha* Vehicle.

iv. **The parable of the sun and moon light** (Chapter 5): The *Buddha Dharma* is also likened to the light of sun and moon which illuminates the whole world equally.

v. **The parable of the pots** (Chapter 5): A potter makes various kinds of pots for various kinds of things to be put into them but with the same clay. Just so, there is this One and only this One Vehicle, to wit, the *Buddha* Vehicle. There exists neither a second nor a third vehicle.

vi. **The parable of the Conjured city** (Chapter 7): Among the *Buddha Dharma*, only One Vehicle or *Buddha* Vehicle is true and others (*śrāvaka* vehicle and *pratyekabuddha* vehicle) are false.

While heading for a cache of precious jewels the multitude in the midway are exhausted, frightened and wish to turn back. Then, the guide with his compassion and his power of devising expedients conjures upon a city for them to take a rest. After that, the guide tells them the cache (*Buddhajñāna*) is near and the city (two *nirvāṇas* of *śrāvaka* and *pratyekabuddha*) is conjured up by him for the purpose of giving them a rest, nothing more.

vii. **The parable** of **the priceless jewel in the interior of the garment** (Chapter 8): The *Buddha's* teaching of the universal Buddhahood is illustrated with the case of a poor man who fell asleep while drinking with a wealthy friend. The friend, having to leave, sews a jewel into his poor friend's garment. The poor man eventually wanders off without knowing the jewel in his garment. When the two meet again the rich man is astonished. Why is his friend so poor with the available jewel ? He can have all that he ever wishes for ! Likewise is the joy of discovering that one is really destined for Buddhahood.

viii. **The parable of the *Buddha's* life-span** (Chapter 16): In this chapter the *Buddha* explains that although he is usually thought of as coming from the *Śākya* clan and renouncing his palace life, taking up a place of meditation not far from the city of *Gayā* and there attaining to enlightenment, the reality is that innumerable world-systems have come to be and passed away since he originally became a *Buddha*. Ever since an inconceivably long time ago he has been constantly teaching both in this world and in innumerable others.

In chapter 16, the *Lotus* implies the two truths as mentioned earlier: a) Relative truth or phenomena (illustrated with a historical *Śākyamuni*), and b) Ultimate truth or noumenon (illustrated with the countless life-span of the *Tathāgata*). Since the level of beings was still low, the *Buddha* by resort to expedient devices, spoke to the beings of the Relative truth, viz., the Three-Vehicles. In fact, the One Vehicle or *Buddha* Vehicle is the real, the Ultimate truth, the real mark of things. The Ultimate truth (*Buddhajñāna, Buddhatā,* or the real aspect of the Universe, of the human beings) is forever and eternal.

ix. **The parable of the physician's ill Sons** (in the same Chapter 16): A physician is travelling abroad and in the meantime his sons drink some poisonous medicines and become delirious. When he returns he prepares good medicine for them. The ones who take the good medicine recover, but the others have quite lost their senses and refuse to take the good medicine. The father reflects, and decides upon a skilful means to make them take it. He warns them that he is very old and approaching death, then leaves for another country from where he sends a messenger back to report that he has died. The sons are overcome with grief, come to their senses and take the medicine. The poisons and sickness are all healed.

This parable has the same philosophical implications as in the previous one (viii).

6) One-Vehicle and *Trikāya*

In *Mahāyāna, Trikāya* is the threefold body or nature of a *Buddha*, i.e., *Dharmakāya*, *Saṁbhogakāya* and *Nirmāṇakāya*. (1) *Dharmakāya* in its earliest conception was that of the body of the *Dharma*, or truth, as preached by *Śākyamuni*; later it became his mind or soul in contrast with his material body. In *Mādhyamika*, the *Dharmakāya* was the only reality, the ground of all phenomena. According to the *Hua-yen* (*Kegon*) School it is the noumenon, while the other two *Sambhogakāya* and *Nirmāṇakāya* are phenomenal aspects. (2) *Sambhogakāya*, a *Buddha's* reward body, or body of enjoyment of the merits he attained as a *bodhisattva*; in other words, a *Buddha* in glory in his heaven. This is the form of *Buddha* as an object of worship. (3) *Nirmāṇakāya,* a *Buddha's* transformation, or miraculous body, in which he appeas at will and in any form outside his heaven, e.g. as *Śākyamuni* among them. *Trikāya* is not divided, for a *Buddha* in his *Nirmāṇakāya* is still one with his *Dharmakāya* and *Sambhogakāya*, all three bodies being co-existent. And not only has every *Buddha* all the three bodies or aspects, but as all men are of the same essence, or nature, as *Buddhas*, they are therefore potential *Buddhas* and are in and of the *Trikāya*.

Chapter 11 of the *Lotus* explains the *Ekayāna* and *Trikāya* through a lively scene of a seven-jeweled *stūpa*, which wells up out of the earth and resting in mid-air. In the *stūpa* is the whole body of *Buddha Prabhūtaratna* who had a vow in the distant past that after his passage into extinction, in any of the lands of the ten directions there is a place in which the *Lotus* is preached, in order that that scripture may be heard, his *stūpa*—shrine will well up before it, praising it, saying 'Excellent!'...,if there is anyone who wished to show the body of *Buddha Prabhūtaratna* to the fourfold assembly, then may the *Buddhas* who are emanations of that *Buddha's* body, when they have finished preaching the *Dharma* in the world-spheres of the ten directions, again gather in one place. And at the request to see the *Buddha Prabhātaratna* in the open air by the fourfold assembly the *Śākyamunibuddha* emits a single glow from his white hair-turf to all directions, then his emanations from the ten directions gather in the *Sahā* world. After that, *Śākyamunibuddha* with his supernatural power, touches the great multitudes, so that they are all in open space.

The above event gives an implication of the *Trikāya* or Threefold body of the *Buddha*: (1) *Buddha Prabhūtaratna* (*Dharmakāya*), (2) the emanations of *Śākyamunibuddha* (*Sambhogakāya*), and (3) *Śākyamunibuddha* (*Nirmāṇakāya*). When there appears wisdom (illustrated with the emission of the glow from the *Śākyamunibuddha's* white hair-turf), the false thoughts will stop (illustrated with all the emanations of the *Śākyamunibuddha* from all directions gathering in the *Ṣahā* world). At that very moment the Absolute truth appears (illustrated with the body of *Buddha Prabhūtaratna* appears to be seen by the fourfold assemblies). And through the event we realize that although the three bodies of the *Buddha* are different but they have the same nature (*śūyatā,* illustrated with the gathering of three bodies of the Buddha in the same 'open air'); hence, three are in one and one is in three. Besides, when the fourfold asemblies have the *śūnya* mind (illustrated with being put in mid-air), they can see the *Dharmakāya* (illustration of the Absolute truth). Again, from this point leads to the realization of the identification of subject (the fourfold assemblies) and object (*Dharmakāya*); for both of them have the same nature — *śūnyatā* (in the mid-air). Everyone can attain the Buddhahood. This is the doctrine of One Vehicle.

7) One Vehicle and predictions

The doctrine of One Vehicle or *Buddha* Vehicle in the *Lotus* is also expressed by the predictions of future Buddhahood. Unlike other *Mahāyāna sūtras*, the *śrāvakas* and *pratyekabuddhas* (of the Hīnayānists) in the *Lotus* are foretold about their attainment of Buddhahood. Not only that, even female beings or *icchantikas* and animals are assured of obtaining the highest enlightenment. In other words, all beings have their own *Buddha's* seed or *Buddhatā*. Following are the accounts concerning to the predictions of Buddhahood:

i. **Chapter 3** : The *Buddha* foretells *Śāriputra*, the wisest disciple, about his being a future *Buddha* named *Padmaprabha*.

ii. **Chapter 6 :** In this chapter the *Buddha* foretells the four other *śrāvakas* about their attainment of Buddhahood with their names as follows: *Mahākāśyapa* becoming a *Buddha* named *Raśmiprabhāsa*, *Subhūti* becoming a *Buddha* named *Śaśiketu*, *Mahākātyāyana* becoming a *Buddha* named *Jāmbūnadaprabhāsa*, and *Mahāmaudgalyāyana* becoming a *Buddha* named *Tamālapatracandanagandha*.

iii. **Chapter 8** Other five hundred *śrāvakas* are assured of their attainment of *anuttarasamyaksaṃbodhi* or the *Buddhajñāna*.

iv. **Chapter 9** *Ānanda* and *Rāhula*, two learners[20], together with two thousand other *learners* and adepts are foretold about their attainment of the Buddhahood.

v. **Chapter 12** This chapter mentions the becoming of *Buddhas* of the two persons: *Devadatta* and a dragon girl. *Śākyamunibuddha* confers upon *Devadatta* the prophecy of the *Buddha* named *Devarāja*. Besides, there is a daughter of the dragon king *Sāgara*, who is eight years old. She puts the *Lotus* into practice by the strenuous application of vigor, and speedily attains Buddhahood.

vi. **Chapter 13** : The *Buddha* also foretells *bhikṣunīs* about their attainment of Buddhahood — *Mahāprajāpatī* (the Buddha's maternal aunt) and *Yaśodharā* (the *Buddha's* former wife) and six thousand other *bhikṣunīs*.

8) One-Vehicle and *Nirvāṇa*

Nirvāṇa or deliverance, as the *Lotus* understands it, is the single goal or the ultimate, eternally quiescent *Nirvāṇa*, which has two attributes — Omniscience and Emptiness.

"The *Dharma* having a single flavor.

That of deliverance and *Nirvāṇa*."[21]

"Just so is the *Dharma* preached by the Thus Come One of a single mark and a single flavor, namely, the mark of deliverance, the mark of disenchantment, the mark of extinction, arriving completely at knowledge of all modes."[22]

"The Thus Come One knows this *Dharma* of a single mark and a single flavor, namely, the mark of deliverance, the mark of disenchantment, the mark of extinction, the mark of ultimate *Nirvāṇa*, of eternally quiescent *Nirvāṇa*, finally reducing itself to Emptiness."[23] *Nirvāṇa*, in the *Lotus*, cannot be attained and deliverance cannot really take place, for they finally reduce themselves to Emptiness "the mark of deliverance,..., the mark of ultimate *Nirvāṇa*, of eternally quiescent *Nirvāṇa*, finally reducing itself to Emptiness." According to *Nāgārjuna*, *śūnyatā* means nothing acquirable. And emptiness has no properties, no marks, it has nothing by which it could be recognised, and so we can never know whether we have it or not. The Ultimate, eternally quiescent is by definition devoid of any relation to anything else, absolutely isolated and solitary; or being transcendent to all categories of thought. It is therefore impossible for a person to enter into any kind of relation with it, much less to possess or gain it. Hence, *Nirvāṇa*, the single goal of deliverance, is *śūnyatā*. Just as a further explanation, "What is the emptiness of ultimate reality? 'Ultimate reality' means *Nirvāṇa*. And that *Nirvāṇa* is empty of *Nirvāṇa*, on account of its being neither unmoved nor destroyed."[24]

In chapter 7 of the *Lotus*, Parable of the Conjured city, the two *nirvāṇas* of the *śrāvakas* and *pratyekabuddhas* (illustrated with the conjured city in mid-way) are false, they are just devising expedients of the *Buddha* to fit the state of mind of the beings who are of inferior intellect and who can not directly apprehend the difficult and far-reaching teachings of the *Buddha* Vehicle,

> "What you had to do is not yet done. The lands in which you dwell are near to *Buddha*-knowledge. You must observe and consider, weigh and measure. The *Nirvāṇa* you have gained is not the real one."[25]

So, there is a single *nirvāṇa*, which is ultimate, eternally quiescent.

Nirvāṇa, in the *Lotus*, is described as omniscience "the mark of deliverance, the mark of disenchantment, the mark of extinction, arriving completely at knowledge of all modes" or "And the beings, hearing the *Dharma* from the *Buddhas*, shall attain thoroughly the knowledge of all modes."[26] Omniscience or knowledge of all modes in the *Mahāyāna* is unimpeded cognition, knowing correctly all the aspects of existence, in all its details. Phenomena, however, are dependent on conditions. Being so dependent, they are devoid of substantial reality; hence, they are *śūnya*. A finite mind could not understand the workings of an infinite intellect. The *Buddha's* thoughts would really be quite different from ours qualitatively. They would be 'absolute' thoughts which are transcendent, cease to indulge in thought-constructions. According to the *Mahāsaṅghikas*, empirical knowledge could not give us an insight into Reality. Only *śūnyatā* which transcends all wordly things can give us a vision of the Real. All verbal statements give us a wrong view of the Real; they are mere thought-constructions. So omniscience becomes synonymous with *śūnyatā*.

However, one acquires insight into *śūnyatā* not merely by accepting it enthusiastically, nor by logomachy, but by meditation on *śūnyatā*. One has to meditate on *śūnyatā* as the absence of self-hood, on the absence of substantiality in all the *dharmas*, on *śūnyatā* as even the essencelessness of the unconditioned, for according to the *Mahāyāna* such *dharmas* as *saṃsāra* and *nirvāṇa*, the conditioned and unconditioned are not ultimate realities at all, but only mental constructions and are so essenceless (*śūnya*). Finally, one has to abandon *śūnyatā* itself as a mere raft to cross the ocean of ignorance. It is a means to lead the mind up to *prajñā* (transcendental insight), and should not be thought of as an end in itself. *Nāgārjuna* says:

> *"Śūnyatā sarvadrṣṭīnām proktā nihsaraṇam jinaih*
>
> *Yeśām tu śūnyatā drṣṭistan asādhyān babhāṣireh"*
>
> (M.K. 13, 8)
>
> (*Śūnyatā* was declared by the *Buddha* for dispensing with all views or 'isms'. Those who convert *Śūnyatā* itself into another 'ism' are verily beyond hope or help.)

This meditation will, however, be ineffective unless one has cultivated certain moral virtues.

9) One-Vehicle and two truths

According to *Nāgārjuna* there are two kinds of truths: *Paramārtha satya* (Absolute Reality) and *Samvṛti satya* (Empirical Truth or Phenomena).

There are many words used for the Absolute or Reality in the *Mādhyamaka* philosophy, namely, *Tathatā*, *Śūnyatā*, *Nirvāṇa*, *Advayatā* (non-duality or oneness), *Anutpanna* (unproduced), *Nirvikalpa* (the realm of non-discrimination), *Dharmatā* (the essence of being, the true nature of *dharma*), *Anabhilāpya* (the inexpressible), *Tattva* (Reality or Thatness), *niśprapañca* (free of verbalisation and plurality), *Yathābhūta* (that which really is), *Satya* (Truth), *Bhūtatathatā* or *Bhūtatā* (the true reality), *Tathātgatagarbha* (the womb of *Tathāgata*), *Aparapratyaya* (reality which one must realize within oneself). *Dharmakāya*, etc. Each word is used from a particular standpoint.

Through the *Madhyamaka śāstra*, *Nāgārjuna* proves that the Absolute is transcendent to both thought and speech. Neither the concept of *bhāva* (ens) nor *abhāva* (non-ens) is applicable to it. He argues for the inapplicability of these concepts.

> *"Bhāvastāvat na Nirvāṇam jarāmaraṇalakṣaṇam*
> *Prasajyetāsti bhāvo hi na jarāmaraṇam vinā"*
>
> (M.K. 25, 4)

(*Nirvāṇa* or the Absolute Reality cannot be a *bhāva* or positive ens, for in that case it would be subject to origination, decay, and death; there is no empirical existence which is free from decay and death. If it cannot be *bhāva*, far less can it be *abhāva* (non-existence), for *abhāva* (non-exisence) is only a relative concept (absence of *bhāva*) depending upon the concept of *bhāva*).

Or he puts it:

> *"Bhāvasya cedaprasiddhirabhāvo naiva siddhyati*
> *Byāvasya hyanyathābhāvam abhāvam bruvate janāḥ"*
>
> (M.K. 15,5)

(When *bhāva* itself is proved to be inapplicable to Reality, *abhāva* cannot stand scrutiny, for *abhāva* is known only as the disapperance of *bhāva*.)

When the concepts of *bhāva* (empitical existence), and *abhāva* (the negation of *bhāva* cannot be applied to the Absolute, the question of applying any other concept to it does not arise, for all other concepts depend upon the above two. In one word, the Absolute is transcendent to thought, and because it is transcendent to thought, it is inexpressible.

> *"Nivṛttamabhidhātavyam nirvrtte cittagocare*
> *Anutpannāniruddhā hi Nirvāṇamiva dharmatā"*

(What cannot be an object of thought cannot, *a fortiori*, be an object of speech. The Absolute as the essence of all being is neither born, nor does it cease to be)

Candrakīrti says "*Paramārtho hi āryāṇām rūṣṇīmbhāvah*" (P.P. p. 19) (To the saints, the Absolute is just silence i.e. it is inexpressible).

Phenomena have no independent, substantial reality of their own. Relativity or dependence is the main characteristic of phenomena, and that which is relative is not real in the highest sense of the word. The Absolute is the Reality of the appearances.

The Absolute and the world are not two different sets of reality posited against each other. Phenomena viewed as relative, as governed by causes and conditions constitute the world, and viewed as free of all conditions are the Absolute. The Absolute is always of uniform nature. *Nirvāṇa* or the Absolute Reality is not something produced or achieved. *Nirvāṇa* only means the disappearance of the fabrications of discursive thought.

If the Absolute is beyond all thought and speech, how can the Absolute be described ? The answer is — Phenomena do not completely cut us off from Reality. Phenomena are appearances, and appearances point to their Reality. The veil gives a hint of that which is veiled. The philosophy of *Śūnyatā* is meant only to help uncover the veil.

To understand the two truths is very important. *Nāgārjuna* maintains that no one can understand the teaching of the *Buddha* who does not know this distinction.

"Ye'ṅayorna vijñānanti vibhāgam Satyayordvayoḥ

Te tattvam na vijānanti gambhiram Buddhaśāsane"

(M.K. 24, 9)

(Those who do not know the distinction between these two truths cannot understand the deep significance of the teaching of the *Buddha*).

As regards *Samvṛti*, *Candrakīrti* mentions three senses of it.

(a) "*Samantāt sarvapadārthatattvavacchādanāt Samvṛtiḥ*"

(P. P. p. 215)

Samvṛti is that which covers all round the real nature of things. *Candrakīrti* calls it *ajñāna* or *avidyā* (the primal ignorance). *Samvṛti* is due to *ajñāna* or *avidyā* and is identical with it. It is the primal ignorance that throws a veil over Reality.

(b) "*Parasparasambhavanam vā samvrṛtiranyonyasamāśṛayeṇa*"

(P. P. p. 215)

Samvṛti is mutual dependence of things or their relativity. In this sense, it is identical with phenomena.

(c) "*Samvṛtiḥ sayketo lokavyavahāraḥ Sa ca abhidhānābhidheya jnānajneyādilakṣaṇaḥ*"

(P.P. p. 215)

What is conventionally accepted by people at large is *samvṛti*.

Samvṛti or pragmatic reality is the means (*upāya*) for reaching Reality which is the goal (*upeya*). *Nāgārjuna* expressly mentions the importance of *vyavahāra* or empirical reality in attaining *Paramārtha* or Absolute Reality. He says:

"*Vyavahāramanāśritya paramārtho na deśyate*
Paramārthamanāgamya Nirvāṇam nādhigamyle"

(M.K. 24, 10)

(Without a recourse to pragmatic reality, the absolute cannot be taught. Without knowing the absolute truth, *Nirvāṇa* cannot be attained.)

There are two kinds of *Samvṛti* - (i) *Loka-samvṛti* and (ii) *Aloka-samvṛti*. (i) *Loka-samvṛti* refers to the common empirical objects recognized as real by all as, for example, a jar, a cow etc, (ii) *Aloka-samvṛti* refers to objects experienced under abnormal conditions. Illusory objects, distorted perceptions caused by diseased or defective sense-organs, dream objects, etc. are cases of *Aloka-samvṛti,* which are non-empirical, for they are unreal even for the empirical consciousness.

So, *Samvṛti* or pragmatic reality is the means (*upāya*) for reaching *Paramārtha* or the Absolute Reality, which is the goal and truly real alone.

In the chapter 16 of the *Lotus,* the two truths are described through (i) the statement of the *Buddha* and (ii) the parable of 'Physician's ill sons'.

i. the *Buddha* said that since his attainment of Buddhahood it has been a very great interval of time; his life-span was incalculable *asaṃkhyeyakalpas*, ever enduring, never perishing; he was in fact limitless in both time and space, assuring various forms in different ages and under circumstances but all for one and the same purpose, namely, the deliverance of the beings. But, if the *Buddha* lived long in the world, men of thin qualities would not plant wholesome roots; while the lowly and the poor would crave the objects ot the five desires and enter into the net of recollections, notions, and false views. So the *Buddha* by resort to expedient devices manifested himself a historical *Śākyamunibuddha* having birth and death.

ii. Suppose there is a good physician, wise, who intelligently refines medical herbs and skillfully heals many sickness. Returning home from afar the father saw his sons getting unintentional poisoning, some serious and some light. The light sons rook the medicine from their father, but the serious sons did not. Then the father devised an expedient with which to induce them to take the medicine. Straightway he spoke to his sons that he was now aged and infirm, and that his time of death was already at hand; the fine and good medicine he now left there for them to take; no worry about not recovering. When he had given these instructions, he went again to another country and sent a messenger back to declare to his sons that he was dead. The sons thought themselves from now on forsaken and exposed, having nothing further on which to rely, they harbored feelings or sadness. It is only when at length their thoughts were awakened that they understood that the medicine was colorful, fragrant, and tasty. Then straightway they took it, and the poisons and the sickness were all healed.

In the chapter 16, the *Lotus* gives an implication of the two truths: (i) the Empirical truth or phenomena (illustrated with a historical *Śākyamunibuddha* and a dead father), and (ii) Absolute truth or Absolute Reality (illustrated with the countless life-span of the *Tathāgata* and alive father). Since the level of beings was still low, the *Buddha* by resort to expedient devices, spoke to the beings of the Empirical truth, viz., the Three-Vehicles. In fact, there is only OneVehicle or *Buddha* Vehicle, viz., Absolute Reality, which is real and eternal.

10) One-Vehicle and *Madhyamā Pratipad*

In his first sermon, *Dhamma-cakkappavattana Sātta* (Setting the wheel of the *Dharma* into motion), to the five ascetics at *Sārnāth*, the *Buddha* said that Truth did not lie in the extreme alternatives but in the Middle Way (*Madhyamā Pratipad*). We are told in the *Saṃyutta-nikāya*:

"Once the World-Honored One was at *Vārāṇasī* at the deer park called *Isipatana* (presently *Sārnāth*) he addressed the five monks in the following manner: There are two extremes not to be served by a wanderer (seeker of truth). One is the pursuit of desires and the pleasure which springs from desire.... The other is the pursuit of (self-inflicted) pain and hardship.... The Middle Way of the *Tathāgata* (The Thus Come and Gone) avoids both of these two extremes. It is enlightened, it brings clear vision (of the Four Noble Truths) and it leads to peace and *Nirvāṇa*...."[27]

And, *Nāgārjuna* says:

"Kātyāyanāvavāde cāstīti nastīti cobhayam
Prastiṣiddham bhagavatā bhāvābhāvavibhāvina"

(M. K. 15, 7)

(In the *Kātyāyanāvavāda-sūtra,* the Lord who had the right insight into both *bhāva* (ens) and *abhāva* (no-ens) rejected both the extreme alternatives of 'is' and 'is not'.)

In commenting on this, *Candrakīrti* has quoted the relevant passage in the *Kātyāyanāvavāda-sūtra* which is accepted as an authority by all the Buddhists. In this, the *Buddha* says to *Kāśyapa*,

"O *Kāśyapa*, 'is' is one extreme alternative, 'not is' is another extreme alternative. That which is the *madhyama* position is intangible, incomparable, without any position, non-appearing, incomprehensible. That is what is meant by *madhyamā pratipad* (the middle position) O *Kāśyapa*. It is perception of Reality (*bhūta pratyavekṣa*)" (P. P. p, 118).

Thus, the word *madhyama* is not to be taken in its literal sense of 'in between' or a 'mean between the two'. As is clear from the adjectives 'intangible, incomparable, incomprehensible etc.. *madhyamā pratipad* means that Reality is transcendent to the antinomies of Reason, the dichotomies of thought, and cannot be 'grasped, caged and confined' in the alternatives of 'is' and 'is not'. It is on this basis that *Nāgārjuna* called his philosophy *madhyamaka*, i.e., pertaining to the transcendent.

In the Lotus, *Madhyamā Pratipad* (the Middle Way) is illustrated by 'the glow emitted from the white curls between the *Buddha's* eyebrows.' The glow refers to the *Buddhajñāna*, the eyesbrows to the extreme alternatives, and the white curls between the *Buddha's* eyebrows to the Middle Way.

(Chapter 1 of the *Lotus*): Having preached a scripture of the Great Vehicle named the Immeasurable Doctrine (*Anantanirdeśa*), the *Buddha* entered a state of deep contemplation (*samādhi*) called the *Anantanirdeśapratiṣthānasamādhi*, his body and mind motionless, at which the world and the universe itself expressed admiration and joy. While in this state he emits from the white curls between his eyebrows a ray of light that illuminates eighteen thousand worlds in the east. *Bodhisattva Maitreya* asked *Bodhisattva Mañjuśrī* what is the cause of this wonder, and the reply is that the *Buddha* is about to preach the Great *Dharma* (the *Lotus*).

This passage makes use of the wonderful event to reveal the Absolute Truth, which is the *Lotus*, to wit, the *Buddhajñāna* or *Ekayāna*. The reason why the *Buddha* does not express the Absolute by the language but by meditation, it is because the language is verbal expressions belonging to dichotomies of thought or thought constructions. *Candrakīrti* says,

> "*Paramārtho hi āryāṇām tūṣṇīmbhāvaḥ*"
>
> (P. P. p, 19)
>
> (To the saints, the Absolute is just silence, i.e., it is inexpressible).

That is why the *Buddha* enters the meditation, his body and mind motionless, at which the world and the universe itself express admiration and joy. The *Buddha* emits from the white curls between his eyebrows. It gives the implication that with the wisdom transcendent to the antinomies of Reason, the dichotomies of thought the *Buddha* (or we) can see throughout the world and beings (without obstruction), reaching downward as fas as the *Avīci* [the lowest] hell and upward as far as the *Akaniṣṭha* [highest] gods.

So, in a sense, the Great *Dharma* (the *Lotus, Buddhajñāna* or *Ekayāna)* is to express the Absolute, the *Madhyamā Pratipad.*

The analysis of the doctrine of One Vehicle as *Paramārtha* will be continued by further analysing *Upāya-kauśalya,* a means to reach the former, in the next chapter.

References

1. The Diamond sutra.
2. *aprāptvya-sūnyatā.*
3. *pratītyasamutpāda.*
4. *Mūlamadhyamakākrikā* of *Nāgārjuna,* trans. Kenneth K. Inada, Sri Satguru Publications, Delhi, 1993, pp. 38-39.
5. *Saṃyutta Nikāya* II, 17. Cf. Tsa 12.19 (Taishō 2.85C)
6. Leon Hurvitz, *Scripture of the Lotus Blossom of the Fine Dharma,* translated from the Chinese of *Kumārajīva,* Newyork: Columbia University Press, 1976, p. 41.
7. Ibid., pp. 147-148.
8. Ibid., p. 110.
9. Ibid., p. 31.
10. *The Lankavatara Sutra,* translated from the Sanskrit by D.T.Suzuki, Colorado, 1978, p. 116.
11. Ibid., pp. 115-116.
12. Ibid., p. 115.
13. Leon Hurvitz, Op.cit., p. 41.
14. Ibid., p. 180.
15. Ibid., p. 188.
16. Ibid., p. 198.
17. Ibid., pp. 22-23.
18. Ibid., p. 110.
19. *Munimatālāṃkāra* , T. T. fol. 186b-187a.

20. Learners are those who attain the first three grades of saintship, i.e. *Srota-āpanna, Sakradāgāmi-phala, Anāgāmi-phala,* and the last grade of saintship is *Arhat-phala* attained by adepts.
21. Ibid., p. 106.
22. Leon Hurvitz, Op.cit., p. 102.
23. Ibid., p. 103.
24. *The Large Sutra on Perfect Wisdom,* tr. E.Conze, Delhi, 1990, p. 145.
25. Leon Hurvitz. Op.cit., p. 149.
26. Ibid., p. 31.
27. *Saṃyutta-nikāya* V. 421ff.

Chapter IV

Skilful Means (*Upāya Kauśalya*)

Samvṛti also known as *vyavahāra*, pragmatic reality, or provisional truth, is the means (*upāya*) for reaching Reality which is the goal (*upeya*). *Nāgārjuna* expressly mentions the importance of *vyavahāra* or empirical reality in attaining *Paramārtha* or Absolute Reality. He puts it:

"*Vyavahāramanāśritya paramārtho na deśyate*

Paramārthamanāgamya Nirvāṇam nādhigamyle"

(M. K. 24, 10)

(Without a recourse to pragmatic reality, the absolute cannot be taught. Without knowing the absolute truth, *Nirvāṇa* cannot be attained.)

The *Lotus* also emphasizes the important role of *Samvṛti* and uses the term *upāya-kauśalya* for this.

I) Introduction

'Skilful means' is an English translation from the Sanskrit '*upāya-kauśalya*' or from the Pali '*upāya-kosalla*', which means 'skill in means,' 'skill in devices'. Edgerton[1] gives the meaning of this compound as 'skill in expedients'. He also goes on to say that the term 'is extremely common everywhere' (i.e. in Buddhist Hybrid Sanskrit texts, which are almost entirely *Mahāyāna*), 'especially of the *Buddha's* skill in devising means to impress and convert people'. It may be explained as 'skilfulness or wisdom in the choice and adoption of the means or expedients for converting others or helping them.' There are so far two main terms which have been usually translated and linked as follows:

upāya = 'means', 'device', etc.

upāya-kauśalya = 'skill in means', 'skill in devices', etc.

A Buddhist *upāya* is something created on the responsibility of a *Buddha* or a *bodhisattva* who has perfected his 'skill in means' (*upāya-kauśalya*).

The most usual Chinese term for *upāya* is *fang-pien*, which is pronounced in Japanese as *hò-ben*. *Kumārajīva* translated *upāya-kauśalya*, which is the title of the chapter 2 of the *Lotus*, as *fang-pien*.

The concept of 'skilful means' is one of the leading ideas of *Mahāyāna* Buddhism and was first used extensively in the *Lotus* and some other texts. In *Mahāyāna* Buddhism the various forms of Buddhist teachings and practices are declared to be provisional means, all skilfully devised by the *Buddha* for the sake of the unenlightened. A Buddhist who makes progress himself comes to recognise this provisional quality and though using the means provided for him he has to learn not to be wrongly attached to them. They will be left behind, like a raft left lying on the other bank by a man who has crossed a river and needs it no longer, or like a finger pointing to the moon no more needed when a man has seen it. An advanced follower of Buddhism, usually named by *Mahāyāna* Buddhists as *bodhisattva*, continues to use such provisional means in order to lead other living things toward the ultimate goal, *nirvāṇa*.

'Skilful means' is about the way in which the goal of *nirvāṇa* is realised. One cannot go to the goal without taking the proper way or the appropriate means leading to it, or in other words, the way implies the goal. The *Lotus* explains that the *Buddha* himself uses 'countless skilful means' to lead living beings along and to separate them from their attachments. Such skilful means are formulated in terms of the relative ignorance and the passionate attachments of those who need them, but they dissolve into the Buddhist attainment of release. Similarly the great celestial *bodhisattvas* or *buddhas*-to-be are characterised not only by their penetrating insight into the true nature of reality but also by a great compassion for suffering beings. They deploy various kinds of methods for the deliverance of the multitude, skilfully turning them to a variety of needs of beings suffering in ignorance and *saṃsāra* yet consistently intimating the intention of *nirvāṇa* or deliverance. 'Skilful means' can be seen not only from the side of the *Buddhas* and *bodhisattvas* who invent them but also from the side of the sentient beings who need them. However, as the multitude become enlightened the expedients become redundant.

It is therefore of great importance that Mahayanists interpret the Buddhist religion in terms of the *Buddha's* skilful means. For them this leading concept is the appropriate way in which to understand any phase of Buddhism which is supposed to derive from the *Buddha's* initiative, whether it be abstractedly conceptual, concretely narrative, or expressed as meditational practice.

1. Buddha's decision to proclaim *Dharma*

Trully speaking, that the Mahayanists claim that 'skilful means' is the key to the understanding of Buddhism in general is not without some reasons. And, perhaps the most suggestive passages in this connection are those which narrate the *Buddha's* initial decision to teach *Dhamma* after his obtaining enlightenment. Without this decision Buddhism would never have developed any articulate form. The first passage is from the Pali Canon. The simple outline of the story is that the *Buddha*, on attaining enlightenment, is at first not inclined to teach *Dhamma*, "When the Blessed One pondered over this matter, his mind became inclined to remain in quiet, and not preach the doctrine."[2] Afterwards, however, he is inclined towards 'little effort'. The reason is that while the *Dhamma* he attained is deep and subtle,

> "I have penetrated this doctrine which is profound, difficult to perceive and to understand, which brings quietude of heart, which is exalted, which is unattainable by reasoning, abstruse, intelligible (only) to the wise,"[3]

the people who would hear it are too engrossed in sensual pleasure and steeped in ignorance to recognise its value. The *deva Brahmā Sahampati* realises this and regrets what the *Buddha* is thinking. He at once appears miraculously in the world and pleads with the *Buddha* to teach it. He argues that there are those who for not hearing *Dhamma* are decaying, but who on hearing it would grow. The *Buddha* listens to this entreaty and when he looks over the world with his eye of a *Buddha* he perceives the variety of levels, faculties and dispositions of men. These are compared to a pond of lotuses, some of which are born in the water, grow up in the water, grow up through the water and rise above it immaculately. Thereupon he decides after all that he will teach *Dhamma*. Even so, he wonders who might be able to understand the *Dhamma* 'quickly', and this is another evidence of the recognition that there is a problem about relative degrees of understanding among different people. Thereafter is the first teaching to his five former companions, a teaching which includes the teaching of the four Noble Truths, which include the Middle Path and the holy eightfold Path.[4]

The *Lotus* in chapter 2 contains the same story with some different details, and with a greater stress on the reflectiveness of the *Buddha* on what he is doing. Thus he is portrayed as recollecting,

"When I think back on the *Buddhas* of the past,

On the power of the expedient devices put into practice by them."[5]

With this in mind he decides to teach the way in three vehicles, and is encouraged by the *buddhas* of the ten directions,

"I know that in the Way I have now gained

I, too, must preach three vehicles. When I had had these thoughts,

The *Buddhas* of the ten directions all appeared,

Comforting and instructing me with *Brahmā* chant:

Good, *Śākyamuni* !"[6]

It is then stressed that to do this is to follow all the *buddhas* and to use skilful means.

"Follow all the *Buddhas*

In using the power of expedient devices"[7]

Men of little wisdom take delight in petty teachings and lack confidence that they can attain Buddhahood. Hence skilful means are necessary,

"Those of slight wisdom, desiring lesser *Dharmas*,

Would not believe they could achieve Buddhahood.

For this reason, by resort to expedient devices,

We discriminated, preaching various fruits."[8]

The *Buddha* then goes to *Vārāṇasī* and teaches his five former companions. Since the nirvanic character of all existence (of all *dharmas*) cannot be stated in words and so he teaches them by using skilful means. This turning the *Dharma*-wheel', it is said, will lead to the 'Sound' or promise of *nirvāṇa*.

"Straightway I went to *Vārāṇasī*.

Since the quiet and extinct marks of the *Dharmas*

Were not to be proclaimed in words,

By resort to the power of expedient devices

I preach to five *bhikṣus*.

This is called 'turning the *Dharma*-wheel.'

Then there was the sound '*nirvāṇa*,'

As well as '*arhant*,'

'*Dharma*,' and '*saṃgha*' — several and distinct names such as these."[9]

The Pali Canon already contained the idea that there is a problem about communicating *Dhamma* to anybody. However, in spite of the *Buddha's* hesitation, he did go on to convey his teaching to the five ascetics. But the *Lotus* does emphasize the implication of this tradition — the *Buddha's* initial refusal to teach, and then argues that through skilful means it became possible and worthwhile.

2. Skilful means and the inexpressible

As for the *Buddha's* final intention of teaching, 'the supreme way' or 'the undivided *Dharma*', this is in itself inexpressible in words,

"Since the quiet and extinct marks of the *Dharmas*

Were not to be proclaimed in words,"[10]

but is realised when the *Buddha* honestly discards skilful means. When this takes place it is not some new form of teaching, but rather the secret lies in the very discarding of the hitherto cherished concepts such as *nirvāṇa*.

"For their sakes I established an expedient device,

Preaching ways that put an end to woe

And showing them *nirvāṇa*.

Though I preach,

This is no true extinction."[11]

The real meaning of the *Buddha's* teaching can only be recognised in so far as one appreciates that it is at first formulated in a manner appropriate to the entanglement of the hearers in passions and ignorance. The formulations which make possible the escape from passions and ignorance are themselves only necessary in so far as they lead to the disentanglement. As in Pali Canon, the *Dhamma* itself is 'tranquil' and 'beyond dialectic'.[12] This relationship between the conveyed form and inexpressible goal finds many echoes in the passages of Pali Canon, for example in the simile of the raft and in the dialogue of the ten undetermined questions.[13] Meanwhile, what is special to the *Mahāyāna* form of the story is the introduction of the term skilful means when it is a question of communicating the inexpressible. This term emphasizes the difficulty and yet the possibility of the communication of *Dharma*.

3. The role of the skilful means

The role of the term skilful means or expedient devices in the chapter 2 of *Kumārajīva's* translation of the *Lotus* is in its outlines a consistent one. Almost anything in the whole range of Buddhist teachings and practices can be described as skilful means. This applies not only to a *Buddha* image playfully drawn with the finger-nail but also to such a central teaching as that of *nirvāṇa* itself, not only to the *śrāvakas*, *pratyekabuddhas* but also to the *bodhisattvas*. The skilful means used by the *Buddhas* as the provisional teaching which are established only to be dissolved in favour of 'the *Dharma* of only One Vehicle'. And its role still remains until the beings get enlightened ending all defilements of desires, attachments and discriminations.

II. Teaching of Skilful Means in the *Lotus*

1. The new style for understanding the existing teaching of skilful means

In the Sino-Japanese Buddhist tradition the chapter 2 of the *Lotus* has always had a special importance as the key to the understanding of the *sūtra* as a whole. Usually it is coupled with chapter 16 which implies the true character of the *Buddha*.

The narrative framework of the chapter 2 is quite simple. Continuing the preparatory explanation in the chapter 1 the *Buddha* rises from his contemplation and briefly explains to *Sāriputra* and the whole assembly the relation between the insight of the *Buddhas* and their style of teaching. The hearers, including *Sāritputra*[14] who was supposed to be the wisest of his *śrāvakas*, fail to understand his meaning, and so *Sāriputra*, as spokesman, requests a further explanation. At first, the *Buddha* hesitates for it would merely startle and perplex people, but when the request is repeated twice more he agrees to speak. At this time, five thousand hearers of overweening pride withdraw, believing that they have already attained what is to attain, and then the *Buddha* begins again to expound at some length the doctrine of skilful means.

In relation to the theme three questions arise. Firstly, now, why has the *Buddha* made this speech earnestly praising expedient devices?[15] Secondly, why is the *Dharma* which the *Buddha* has gained very hard to understand, whose meaning is hard to know, and which no *śrāvaka* or *pratyekabuddha* can attain?[16] Thirdly, why has the *Buddha* preached the doctrine of unique deliverance, which means that we, too, gaining this *Dharma*, shall reach *nirvāṇa*; yet, now we do not know where this doctrine tends?[17] As for the doubt of the hearers of which *Sāriputra's* request is a representative it seems that what the *Buddha* is about to say is the 'new' teaching. But from the overall standpoint of the *sūtra's* teaching the 'new' teaching is simply the teaching of all *Buddhas* in all times and places.

The very theme of the *Buddha's* discourse in the *Lotus* is supposed to be his 'skilful means'[18], which is intimately connected with his *Dharma* and both are spoken of as the property of all the *Buddhas*. And this skilful means he shares in common with all the *Buddhas*.

> "*Sāriputra*, the *Dharmas* of the *Buddhas* in all ten directions are also of this sort. *Sāriputra*, the *Buddhas* of the past by resort to incalculable and numberless devices and to various means, parables, and phrases proclaimed the *Dharmas* to the beings. These *Dharmas* were all directed toward the One *Buddha* Vehicle. These beings, hearing the *Dharma* from the *Buddhas*, all attain thoroughly to knowledge of all modes (*sarvākāra-jñatā*).
>
> *Sāriputra*, future *Buddhas* shall come into the world, and they, too, by resorting to incalculable and numberless devices and to various means, parables, and phrases, shall proclaim the *Dharmas* to the beings. These *Dharmas* shall all be directed toward the One *Buddha* Vehicle. These beings, hearing the *Dharma* from the *Buddhas*, shall all attain thoroughly the knowledge of all modes.
>
> *Sāriputra*, the *Buddhas*, the World-Honored Ones, in the incalculable hundreds of thousands of myriads of millions of *Buddha*-lands in the ten directions of present time have many beings whom they benefit and put at their ease. These *Buddhas* also, by resort to incalculable and numberless devices and to various means, parables, and phrases, proclaim the *Dharmas* to the beings. These *Dharmas* are all directed toward the One *Buddha* Vehicle. These beings, hearing the *Dharma* from the *Buddhas*, shall all attain thoroughly to knowledge of all modes."[19]

Apart from this theme there is indeed no particular 'content' to the teaching given. It is a *sūtra* therefore not so much about 'new' doctrines, but rather about the inner method of the Buddhist religion. For instance, there is little concern about whether there is an attainable goal, *nirvāṇa*, or not, but there is much concern about the whys and wherefores of such a goal being held out for people to entertain and about what they should do with it.As the perplexity of the hearers refered to above put it: "We, too, gaining this *Dharma*, shall reach *nirvāṇa*; yet, now we do not know where this doctrine tends?"[20] The *sūtra* emphasizes the correct use of existing religious procedures. It does not propose the establisment of new religious procedures, though it perhaps encourages a certain widening of outlook. Since it is about a religious method it is not a speculative writing but an extremely practical, spiritual one.

However, although there is no new 'content', what does emerge is a new style of understanding the existing teaching, and in this sense the *sūtra* is indeed about the same old doctrine. This new style, which touches the very centre of what Buddhism is all about, is inextricably bound up with the elaboration of the notion of skilful means as that which above all characterises the observable activity of a *Buddha* through his exposition. The intention is to bring out the meaning of 'skilful means' as it stands in *Kumārajīva's* Chinese version, and in which various aspects of Buddhist teachings are referred to as skilful means.

2. The brief opening exposition of skilful means of Three Vehicles:

The brief opening exposition contains mainly the same as three points of concern of the hearers as mentioned above, namely: the wisdom or insight of the *Buddhas*, their method or means, and the question relates to the existing *Buddha's* teaching. Great emphasis is placed on the perfection of the

Buddhas, with regard to insight and skilful means, "The Thus Come One's expedient devices, his knowledge and insight, and his *pāramitās* have all been acquired to the fullest measure."[21] The insight of a *Buddha* or a *Tathāgata* is profound and incalculable and not shared by any other beings at all. He achieved profound *Dharmas* that had never been before, and

"Those *Dharmas* profound and subtle,
Hard to see and hard to understand.
...
These *Dharmas* cannot be demonstrated;
Words, which are only signs, are quiescent in them.
Among the remaining kinds of living beings
None can understand them"[22]

This means that the *Buddhajñāna* does realize the true nature of the multiple factors of existence,

"Only a *Buddha* and a *Buddha* can exhaust their reality, namely, the Suchness of the *Dharmas*, the Suchness of their marks, the Suchness of their nature, the Suchness of their substance, the Suchness of their powers, the Suchness of their functions, the Suchness of their causes, the Suchness of their conditions, the Suchness of their effects, the Suchness of their retributions, and the absolute identity of their beginning and end."[23]

Everything is conditioned, and no constituent of thing is real. Hence, though it is said that marks, nature, substance, powers, functions, causes, conditions, effects, retributions, all are falsely-established words. They are falsely-established, that is, their nature is empty.

The double character of the *Buddhajñāna*, its profundity and inaccessibility together with its formulation in teachings appropriate for releasing living beings from their attachment, is found also in the very first paragraph of the chapter 2 of the *Lotus,* which may be quoted now in full.

> "The *Buddha's* wisdom is profound and incalculable. The gateways of their wisdom are hard to understand and hard to enter, so that no voice-hearer or *pratyekabuddha* can know them. Why is it? In former times the *Buddha*, personally approaching hundreds of thousands of myriads of millions of innumerable *Buddhas*, performed exhaustively the *Dharmas* of those *Buddhas'* incalculable paths. His fame for bold and earnest exertion having spread everywhere, he achieved profound *Dharmas* that had never been before. What he preaches accords with what is appropriate, but the end point of its meaning is hard to understaned. *Śāriputra*, since achieving Buddhahood I have, by a variety of means and by resort to a variety of parables, broadly set forth the spoken doctrine, by countless devices leading the living beings and enabling them to abandon their encumbrances. Why is this? The Thus Come One's expedient devices, his knowledge and insight, and his *pāramitās* have all been acquired to the fullest measure."[24]

Consequently, the first two points, means and insight, are inextricable from each other. And the reference to *śrāvaka* and *pratyekabuddha* here raises the third point, the question relates the existing *Buddha's* teaching. The question is the 'newness' sensed by recipients of the skillfully differentiated teaching. The *śrāvaka* and *pratyekabuddha* are presented as not appreciating the full implications of that to which they are attaining. They do not understand it because it is too difficult to understand and because the *Buddha* uses skilful means. In order to benefit from the 'tactful methods' or skilful means of the *Buddha* it is necessary not only to make use of them as they are at first presented but also to discern in them *what they imply or tend to.* And to do so, the hearers must drop all their attachments. In any case the 'newness' causes a crisis point, or the perplexity in the hearers, which leads either to a successful transcending of the means to make further progress or to a haughty refuse in the case of the five thousand proud hearers.[25]

The third point is clearly expressed in the verse form of the brief opening exposition.

"*Śāriputra,* let it be known

That the *Buddhas'* words are without discrepancy,

That toward the *Dharma* preached by the *Buddha*

One should display the strength of great faith.

After the World-Honored One's *dharma* has long been in effect,

He must preach the truth.

I proclaim to the multitude of voice-hearers

Anh to those seeking the vehicle of condition-perceivers[26]

That I am the One who shall cause them to cast off the bonds of suffering

And attain *nirvāṇa*.

The *Buddha*, by the power of expedient devices,

Demonstrates the teaching of the three vehicles.

The living beings, attached to this object and that,

He attracts and thus enables to extricate themselves."[27]

Here the consistency of Buddhism is reasserted, and unless one has the insight of a *Buddha* oneself an act of faith is required to accept that there is a fundamental unity behind the various forms of the *Buddha's* teaching. Most important, the teaching of *nirvāṇa*, which has been the inspiration of the *śrāvakas* and *pratyekabuddhas*, like all the other forms, has to be both used and transcended or superseded. Notably here, there is no further definable point at which the means themselves are either affirmed or rejected. In the Ultimate Truth or emancipation there is no room for the affirmation or the rejection. And only the complete symbiosis leads to deiverence.

The famous 'three' vehicles referred to are: the vehicle of *śrāvakas*, *pratyekabuddhas* and the third, *bodhisattva*, which, like the others, must be understood as being differentiated in accordance with the *Buddha's* skilful means.

3. The skilful means of *Nirvāṇa*

Owing to their ignorance and desires, all beings are subject to suffering forever in the six destinies.

"Because I knew that these beings

Had never cultivated wholesome roots;

That they were firmly attached to the five desires;

That, through delusion and greed, they were subject to agony;

That, by reason of their desires,

They fell into the three evil destinies;

That they spun like wheels in the six destinies[28],

Receiving all manner of woe and harm;

That, receiving the frail form of a foetus,

For generation after generation they would constantly grow;"[29]

Based on the understanding of the conditions of beings, the *Buddha's* teaching of *nirvāṇa* — the extinction of suffering — is given as a skilful means.

"For these reasons, *Śāriputra*,

For their sakes I established an expedient devices,

Preaching ways that put an end to woe

And showing them *nirvāṇa*."[30]

Nirvāṇa which is a central teaching of Early Buddhism is the goal for which the *śrāvakas* and *pratyekabuddhas* seek. The choice of *nirvāṇa* as a goal to be contrasted with ordinary existence is only necessary because sentient beings thought it is a 'thing' attainable and yet do not realize that the basic quality of all existence is nirvanic to start with. Everything is no-self. Everything is a flux.

"Though I preach *nirvāṇa*,

This is no true extinction.

The *Dharmas* from their very origin

Are themselves eternally characterized by the marks of quiet extinction."[31]

The term *nirvāṇa* used here is not true, final because the real nature or marks of all *Dharmas* are extinct, empty, and inexpressible, and it is simply taught by the *Buddha's* power of skilful means. Two different terms seem to distinguish subtly '*nirvāṇa* without residue'[32] as inexpressible, true, final and 'sound *nirvāṇa*'[33] as provisional for the benefit of beings still 'long for and cling to their desires alone.'[34] The two meanings of the term *nirvāṇa*, i.e. provisional and final, are also presented in the reference to the 'entering' *nirvāṇa*[35] instead of 'preaching' it by the *Buddha*. It is by preaching the 'provisional *nirvāṇa*' on the discriminated side he can eventually bring living beings to the pure, indiscriminated Buddhahood or the 'final *nirvāṇa*.'

4. The skilful means of the teaching in nine divisions

The skilful means is also explicitly applied to Early Buddhism in the *Lotus* in terms of the classification of the teaching in nine divisions. The nine referred to are: sermons (*sūtra*), verses (*gāthā*), former matters (*itivṛttaka*), former lives (*jātaka*), things that have never been before (*adbhuta*), cause and condition (*nidāna*), parables (*aupamya*), verses repeating the prose (*geya*), and expositions (*upadeśa*).

"The *Buddha* knows them thoroughly. Knowing them, and

Resorting to various means and parables

And to their powers, and to the powers of phrases and other expedients,

He causes all to rejoice.

Now he preaches *sūtra* [sermons],

Gāthā and former matters (*itivṛttaka*),

Former lives (*jātaka*) and things that have never been before [*adbhuta*]

Again, he preaches cause and condition (*nidāna*),

Parable (*aupamya*) and geya [verses repeating the prose],

And *upadeśa* [dialogue] scriptures."[36]

Those are various kinds of styles of teaching the *Buddha* makes use of, according to the levels of sentient beings, in order to seduce them going from low up to high, finally to the ultimate goal of the Great Vehicle.

"This *Dharma* of mine, in nine divisions,

I preach by matching it to the beings,

Keeping the entry into the Great Vehicle as the basis:

This is why I preach this scripture."[37]

The present scripture is not in itself offering a new teaching, but it points out the real meaning or intention of the existing teaching in nine divisions. This represents an explicit widening out of the way in which various aspects, if not the whole, of Buddhist teachings are referred to as skilful means.

5) The skilful means of the 'six perfections'

The Buddhist teaching as skilful means can be seen when the *Buddhas* are said to use their expedient devices to expound the *Dharma* in terms of the 'six perfections'[38] of the *bodhisattvas* to convert innumerable sentient beings so that they attain the *Buddha*-way or One Vehicle.

"If there are varieties of living beings
Who, having encountered *Buddhas* in the past,
Have heard the *Dharma* of dispensed gifts,
Or else kept the discipline or endured ignominy,
Or advanced with vigor, or cultivated or wisdom
Who, in short, have in various ways cultivated merit and wisdom,
Persons like these
Have all achieved the *Buddha* path."[39]

These activities of the 'six perfections' are not here explicitly identified with skilful means, but the implication is certainly that they also play a similar intermediate role between the condition of the sentient beings and the state of Buddhahood.

6) The skilful means of devotional actions

The *Lotus* teaches that the notion of *nirvāṇa* and the whole nine-fold teaching of the *Buddha* is not to be considered as other than a means or more than a means, while at the same time it teaches that the simple devotional actions such as drawing or painting the images of the *Buddha* are also to be understood in terms of the same implication. The *Lotus* enumerates a great variety of practices, each of which is identical with the attainment of the *Buddha* path. Here are not the central teachings or the central practices of Early Buddhism but a large number of simple devotional actions such as slightly bending the head, merely joining palms, gathering sand and making it into *Buddha stūpas*, using fingernails to draw *Buddha* images, reciting *Namo Buddhāya*, or even making offering a single flower to a painted image with distracted thought, etc. Those who undertake these actions achieve the *Buddha*-path.

"If anyone, even with distracted thought,
And with so much as a single flower,
Makes offering to a painted image,
He shall at length see numberless *Buddhas*.
There will be some who prostrate themselves ceremoniously;

Others, again, who merely join palms;
Others yet who do no more than raise one hand,
Others yet again who incline their heads but slightly-
All, in these several ways, honoring the images.
They shall at length see incalculable *Buddhas*,
Themselves achieve the Unexcelled Path,"[40]

"If any, even with distracted thought,
Shall enter a *Stūpa* or mausoleum
And recite [Homage to the *Buddha*] but once,
They have all achieved the *Buddha* Path,"[41]

"Or with their fingernails,
Draw *Buddha* images,
Persons like these,
Gradually accumulating merit
And perfecting thoughts of great compassion,
Have all achieved the *Buddha* Path."[42]

"There are even children who in play

Gather sand and make it into *Buddha*.

Persons like these

Have all achieved the *Buddha* Path."[43]

The sentence 'Have all achieved the *Buddha* Path' gives a special emphasis to a meaning: All living beings have already their own *Buddhajñāna*, *Buddhatā* immanent in them, but due to ignorance and fogetting it they have spun cobwebs like wheels in the six destinies. However, once they awake they will attain the Buddhahood soon. Because the available seedlings when properly cultivated will sooner or later give their fruits. Those who put their faith in the *Buddha* 'have all achieved the *Buddha* Path.'

III. Time to Discard the Skilful Means

After teaching in terms of various distinctions the *Buddha* finally declared his intention,

"Frankly casting aside my expedient devices

Merely preach the Unexcelled Path."[44]

Just as a law is true all the time, just so the *Buddha* now follows the *same manner* done by innumerable former *Buddhas*,

"As has been, for the *Buddhas* of the three ages,

The manner in which they preach the *Dharma*,

So I, too, now

Preach a *Dharma* without distinctions."[45]

All *Buddhas* have the same activity: first, based on skilful means, setting up a teaching based on discrimination and then resolving it in favour of the teaching without distinctions or of the undivided *Dharma*. This idea of two stages, provisional and final, was later developed in China under the name of *five periods and eight kinds of doctrine*. This is a *T'ien-t'ai* classification of the *Buddha's* teaching into five periods and eight kinds of doctrine, which are subdivided into two groups:

1. **Five periods:** According to the *T'ien-t'ai* they are (1) the *Avataṃsaka* or first period in three divisions each of seven days, after his enlightenment, when he preached the contents of this *sūtra*; (2) the twelve years of his preaching the *āgamas*, in the deer park; (3) the eight years of preaching *mahāyāna*-cum-*hīnayāna* doctrines, the vaipulya *sūtras*; (4) the twenty-two years of his preaching the *prajñā* or wisdom *sūtras*; (5) the eight years of his preaching the *Lotus* and, in a day and a night, the *Nirvāṇa sūtra*.
2. **Eight kinds of doctrine:** The eight *T'ien-t'ai* classifications of *Śākyamuni's* teaching, from the *Avataṃsaka* to the *sūtras* of *Lotus* and *Nirvāṇa*, divided into the two sections **(1)** his four kinds of teaching of the content of the Truth accommodating to the capacity of his disciples: (a) The *Tripiṭaka* or *Hīnayāna* teaching, for *śrāvakas* and *pratyekabuddhas*, the *bodhisattva* doctrine being subordinate; it also included the primitive *śūnya* doctrine as developed in the *Satyasiddhi śāstra*. (b) His later "intermediate" teaching which contained *Hīnayāna* and *Mahāyāna* doctrine for *śrāvaka*, *pratyekabuddha*, and *bodhisattva*, to which are attributed the doctrines of the *Dharmalakṣaṅa* (or *Yogācāra*) and *Mādhyamika* schools. (c) His differentiated, or separated, *bodhisattva* teaching, definitely *Mahāyāna*. (d) His final, perfect, *bodhisattva*, universal teaching as preached, e.g. in the *sūtras* of *Lotus* and *Nirvāṇa*. **(2)** The four methods of instruction are: (a) Direct teaching without reserve of the whole truth, e.g. the *Avataṃsaka-sūtra*. (b) Gradual or graded, e.g. the *Āgama*, *Vaipulya*, *Prajñā sūtras*. (c) Esoteric teaching, only understood by special members of the assembly. (d) General or indeterminate teaching, from which each hearer would derive benefit according to his interpretation.

Thus, according to the *T'ien-t'ai's* classification, the final and perfect teaching of the *Buddha* is in the *sūtras* of *Lotus* and *Nirvāṇa*. And, what is the final and perfect teaching of the *Buddha* in the *Lotus*? In this *sūtra*, various terms for *the unified meaning* of diverse teachings are 'the One Vehicle',[46] 'the *Buddha* Vehicle',[47] 'the *Dharma* of only One Vehicle',[48] 'this unsurpassed *Dharma*',[49] 'this most subtle prime *Dharma*',[50] '*Dharma* without distinctions',[51] 'the Path of the One Vehicle',[52] 'the Unexcelled Path',[53] 'the *Buddha* Path',[54] '*Nirvāṇa* without residue',[55] 'the Prime Meaning',[56] 'the Seal of reality-marks',[57] 'the *Buddha's* knowledge and insight'.[58]

The unified meaning mentioned above can only be exhausted by the *Buddhas*, and others, even the *śrāvakas*, *pratyekabuddhas*, and *bodhisattvas* can not understand it.

"If all were like *Śāriputra*,

And if, exhausting their thoughts, all calculated together,
Could not fathom the *Buddha's* knowledge.

....

If *Pratyekabuddhas* of keen intelligence (*tīkṣṇendriya*),

....

None could know a slight portion thereof.

If *bodhisattvas* who have recently launched their thoughts

....

Still they could not undestand the *Buddha's* knowledge.

If *bodhisattvas* who do not backslide

....

They still could not know it."[59]

The reason why the others except the *Buddhas* cannot know the unified meaning is because of their desires, attachments or their mind of discrimination,

"Because I knew that these beings
Had never cutivated wholesome roots;
That they were firmly attached to the five desires;
.....
That men of slight virtue and little merit
Were attacked by multitudinous woes;
That, entering into the luxuriant forest of wrong views,
Whether of existence, or of nonexistence, or the like,
And relying on these views,
They fulfill sixty-two of them;
That, profoundly attached to vain and arbitrary *Dharmas*,
.....
That men the likes of these are hard to save;"[60]

"This *Dharma* is not a thing that discursive or discriminatory reasoning can understand. Only *Buddhas* can know it."[61]

It is these defilements which are the obstructions for the 'beings' progress on the way to the final goal. Consequently, they should be dismantled. The *bodhisattva* vehicle itself is still on the side of the three, that is, it still belongs to discriminatory exposition. Therefore the *bodhisattva* vehicle is also required to be transformed and superseded by the one *Buddha* vehicle which gives an equal validity to the other two.

"*Śāriputra,* since achieving Buddhahood I have, by a variety of means and by resort to a variety of parables, broadly set forth the spoken doctrine, by countless devices leading the living beings and enabling them to abandon their encumbrances."[62]

"The *Buddha,* by the power of expedient devices,

Demonstrates the teaching of the three vehicles.

The living beings, attached to this object and that,

He attracts and thus enables to extricate themselves."[63]

And, the great cause of the appearance of the *Buddhas* on the world is simply because of a purpose, e.g. showing the *Buddhajñāna* for the beings to enter into it and that *Dharma* is the One *Buddha* Vehicle.

"The *Buddhas,* the Thus Come Ones, teach the *bodhisattvas* merely that whatever they do is for one purpose, namely, to demonstrate and make intelligible the *Buddha's* knowledge and insight to the beings. *Śāriputra*, the Thus Come One by resort to the One *Buddha* Vehicle alone preaches the *Dharma* to the beings. There are no other vehicles, whether two or three."

IV. Parables about Skilful Means in The Lotus and their Philosophical Implications

There are several parables in the *Lotus* which illustrate in various ways the concept of skilful means. Skilful means is provisional because of the conditions of beings and should be superseded to attain the final goal, which is the *Buddhas*' intention. In the *Lotus*, the parables are not very systematically arranged and they may have been composed at various stages in the compilation of this *sūtra*. The parables have been widely known in East Asia, partly because they are easier to remember than philosophical dialogues, but partly also because they have often formed the subject of paintings. All nine parables are arranged in the chapters 3, 4, 5, 7, 8 and 16. Among these the 16 is the most important in the latter half of the *Lotus*. These parables indeed represent a dramatic extension of the implication of the concept of skilful means in chapter 2.

Nine parables, which we have earlier stated also, are: the 'burning house' (chapter 3); the 'poor son' (chapter 4); the 'rain,' the 'sun and moon light,' the 'pots' (chapter 5'); the 'conjured city' (chapter 7); the 'priceless jewel in the interior of the garment' (chapter 8); the '*Buddha's* life span,' and the "physician' ill sons" (chapter 16).

Since the parables are rather verbose and mentioned earlier, their brief summaries will not be repeated here.

The burning house : At the *Śāriputra's* request, the *Buddha* expounded the *Dharma*, Unexcelled Path, *Anuttarasamyaksaṃbodhi*, with the parable of burning house. After that, the question is raised whether the old man was guilty of a falsehood. *Śāriputra's* answer to this is that he was not because of the old man's first thought to bring them out from the flames. "By resort to an expedient device I will enable the children to get out."[64]

After *Śāriputra's* first answer that the old man is not guilty of falsehood there follows a longer explanation of the story. According to this the old man is the *Tathāgata*, the house is the world, and the children are the beings of the world. These beings are too blinded by their desires and attachments to be able to be saved from the round of birth and death by a direct ultimate teaching of the *Tathāgata*. Hence he makes use of the three vehicles, namely the *śrāvaka-yāna*, the *pratyekabuddha-yāna* and the *Buddha-yāna*,[65] as a skilful means. These three vehicles are identified with the goat-cart, the deer-cart and the oxen-cart respectively and the basic implication is that various paths within Buddhism are distinguished because of varying needs while all of them have the same fundamental intention and meaning.

There is a complication here because the third vehicle is referred to again as 'the great vehicle' (i.e. the *Mahāyāna*)[66] and one who follows it is a *bodhisattva* or a *Mahāsattva*, that is an 'enlightened being' or a 'great being'. At the same time the vehicle which all receive equally at the end is also called the great vehicle.[67] This may seem, at first sight, that the vehicle of *bodhisattvas* or *Mahāsattvas* are as opposed to those of the *śrāvakas* and *pratyekabuddhas*. However, such an interpretation would fail to take into account that the third vehicle, as a differentiated vehicle, is itself superseded in so far as all three are replaced by the single consistent vehicle. And this is supported by the concluding comments in the text, "just so in the same way is the Thus Come One free of falsehood, though he first preached the three vehicles in order to entice the beings, then conveyed them to deliverance by resort to only the One Great Vehicle."[68] And, it is because of the inablility of the beings to receive the great vehicle teaching[69] directly that "the *Buddhas,* by resort to the power of expedient devices, divide the One *Buddha* and speak of three."[70]

The term '*Buddha-yāna*' is used equivocally just as is *Mahāyāna*. Sometimes it refers to the third of the three, as earlier,[71] but sometimes, as in the case quoted immediately above, it is not a further differentiated vehicle, neither a third nor a fourth. Rather it refers, in this special sense, to that single vehicle which takes over when the differentiated vehicles are seen in their true character as skilful means. This One *Buddha* Vehicle brings *bodhisattvas* and *śrāvakas* alike directly to the 'Platform of the Way'.[72] Thus the *Buddha*-vehicle which transcends the differentiated vehicles is also radically identified with them. As the verse continues to say: 'There is no other vehicle, apart from the expedient devices of the *Buddhas*.'[73]

This parable of 'burning house' confirms the pattern of thinking already observed in chapter 2 of the *Lotus*,

> "by resort to the expedient power of various means, parables, and phrases, I preach the *Dharma* to them. *Śāriputra*, I do this only in order that they may gain the One *Buddha* Vehicle and knowledge of all modes."[74]

The similar forms of teaching occurs half a dozen times in chapter 2, as well as again here, and symbolizes articulated Buddhist tradition in general. The meditation or spiritual aspects of Buddhist religion, if these may be referred to separately from the conceptual formulations, are also treated as part of the whole matter to be understood in terms of skilful means. In the interpretation of the parable the *Lotus* puts it:

> "By such devices as this the Thus Come One attracts and urges the beings. He also says : 'You all are to know that the *Dharmas* of these three vehicles are praised by the saints, [and they who mount them] are their own masters, unbound, depending on nothing and seeking nothing. Mounted on these three vehicles, one gains for oneself the pleasure of faculties, strengths, intuitive perceptions, paths, *dhyāna*-concentrations, deliverances, *samādhis*, and the like, all without outflows, then gets incalculable tranquil joys'."[75]

Therefore, in general, it is the Buddhist religion as a whole which is to be understood as arising from the *Buddha's* use of skilful means.

The doctrine of *Hīnayāna*, the four Noble Truths, are also brought into this context. It is in fact a skilful means of the *Buddha*.

> "If there are persons of slight understanding
>
> Profoundly addicted to lust and desire,
>
> For their sakes
>
> I preach the Truth of Suffering
>
> .....
>
> If there are beings
>
> Who, not knowing the origin of woe,
>
> .....

The extinction of woes
Is called the Third Truth.
For the sake of the Truth of Extinction
One cultivates the Path.
Separation from the bonds of woe
Is called the attainment of deliverance.
.....
That is called 'deliverance.'
In fact, however, they have not yet attained
Total deliverance
The *Buddha* says that these men
Are not truly extinguished,
For these men have not yet attained
The Unexcelled Path."[76]

This verse is also a teaching about *nirvāṇa* or extinction, deliverance. And the emphasis here is that the initial teaching of extinction is given because the unenlightened 'beings' submersion in the suffering of birth-and-death (Skt. *saṃsāra*). This contrasted differentiation between *saṃsāra* and *nirvāṇa* was uttered distinctly as a skilful means, but in itself it is not '*Buddhajñāna*', nor 'total deliverance' nor 'the Unexcelled Path.'

The Poor son : Another well known parable is Poor son found in chapter 4 of the *Lotus*. It is not told by the *Buddha* but by four great *śrāvakas*, namely, *Subhūti*, *Mahā-kātyāyana*, *Mahā-Kāśyapa* and *Mahāmaudgalyāyana*, to clarify what they believed and understood as in the *Kumārajīva's* title for the chapter: 'Belief and understanding.'

In this parable the father has three actions which are explicitly referred to as skilful means. Firstly, when he realizes that he himself, being rich and powerful, would be a source of fear to his son's abject disposition he "...for reasons of expediency would not tell others, 'This is my son'."[77] Secondly, in order to entice his son the father "devised an expedient"[78] which is a low job — sweeping the dung. Thirdly, the father himself puts on working clothes and goes to urge on the workmen. 'By this means contriving to approach his son' the father offers him more wages and security, praise his diligence and intimates that he is willing to adopt him. Each of these three actions is necessary because of the low disposition of the son, each involves a provisional disguising of the true situation, and when the purpose is attained all skilful means are superseded as redundant. As for the sons disposition, it progresses from fear to perplexity and a degree of confidence, until finally satisfaction with joy over the quite unexpected treasure.

After the parable, according to the interpretation, the rich father is identical with the *Buddha* while the son is taken to represent his disciples. The disciples declare themselves to be all, as it were, sons of the *Buddha*; and, the *Tathāgata* has constantly declared them to be his sons.[79] Knowing the disciples taking delight in lesser teachings, which is treated as equivalent to the one day's wages of sweeping the dung, the *Buddha* taught them according to their capacity by his power of skilful means. However, the *Buddha* did not stop here, for "The World-Honored One by resort to the power of expedient devices preaches the wisdom of the Thus Come One,"[80] and "Yet the *Buddha* teaches and converts by recourse to the Great Vehicle."[81] According to this viewpoint, the *Mahāyāna* does not seek a specified one of vehicles, some to be confirmed and some to be rejected, but rather it implies an inclusive universalism. The final words of this chapter 4 present the *buddhas'* activity as follows:

"In accord with the beings'
Wholesome roots from former ages,
Also knowing who is ripe
And who unripe,
When, as a result of varied weighing and measurings,
He knows [these things] with discrimination,
Then, for the Path of the One Vehicle,
In accord with what is peculiarly appropriate, he preaches three."[82]

The rain and other parables : The main parable of chapter 5 is about 'rain' which water various kinds of plants, and it is the plants or herbs which have provided the chapter with its title: 'Medicinal Herbs.' Although the variety of the plants and the amount of moisture they need referring to the *śrāvakas*, *pratyekabuddhas* and *bodhisattvas* or Three-Vehicles is part of the point of the parable, the consistency of the rains or *Dharma*, One Vehicle is if anything more important, and it may be that the parable was expanded from the widely used simile found in chapter 1 of the *Lotus* itself.

"Thus do I know that the present *Buddha*
Wishes to preach the Scripture of the *Dharma* Blossom.
The present signs are like the former portents;
They are the *Buddha's* devices.
The present *Buddha* emits a glow
Which helps to set forth the doctrine of the reality-marks.
Men, the time has now come to know [the answers to all questions].
Join palms and single-mindedly wait,
For the *Buddha* shall now precipitate a *Dharma*-rain

That shall satisfy the seekers of the Path.

As for those who seek the rank of the three vehicles,

If they have doubts or regrets,

For their sakes the *Buddha* shall remove them,

Causing them to vanish without a trace."[83]

The parable is not really a story so much as an extended simile. A single great cloud waters all over the world, giving moisture equally to plants, trees, thickets and forests of all sizes. Each of them develops in its own way, blossoms and bears its fruit, "Though produced by the same earth, and moistened by the same rain, yet the grasses and trees all have their differences."[84] The explanation is given in the text itself as follows. The *Tathāgata* is like the cloud pervades and the great sound of his voice covers all the worlds. He knows the disposition and abilities of all the beings in the world, and proclaims the same *Dharma* to them all in various ways so that they can benefit from it. Only the *Tathāgata* can clearly perceive the stages in which living beings find themselves. They themselves do not understand this clearly, just as the plants and trees have no knowledge of their sizes. Nor can living beings immediately or directly accept the undivided *Dharma*, because they are hindered by the great variety of thoughts which they entertain. Hence the teaching is related to these thoughts and to the practices which seem so indispensable to them. In reality however the *Dharma* is unified as the rain-cloud.

This chapter emphasizes again the nature of the *Buddha's* teachings which are skilful means and not false, and the nature of the *Dharma*[85] which are unified, single, equal and indiscriminated.

"The *Buddha's* use of these parables

And expedient devices to demonstrate"[86]

"The Thus Come One is King of the *Dharmas*. If he has anything to say, it is never vain. He sets forth all *Dharmas* by resort to wisdom and practical expedients. Without exception, the *Dharmas* he preaches all reach to the ground of All-Knowledge. The Thus Come One sees and knows that to which all *Dharmas* tend, that to which they are reduced. He also knows what the profound thoughts of all living beings can do, penetrating them without obstruction. Furthermore, with respect to the *Dharmas* he is perfectly clear, demonstrating all manner of wisdom to the beings."[87]

"Just so is the *Dharma* preached by the Thus Come One of a single mark and a single flavor, namely, the mark of deliverance, the mark of disenchantment, the mark of extinction, arriving completely at knowledge of all modes."[88]

Extinction here does not mean annihilation but rather that *nirvāṇa* of a *Tathāgata* with respect to which the dichotomy of annihilation or existence or the like is no longer applicable as seen in the following expression.

"The Thus Come One knows this *Dharma* of a single mark and a single flavor, namely, the mark of deliverance, the mark of disenchantment, the mark of extinction, the mark of ultimate *nirvāṇa,* of eternally quiescent *nirvāṇa*, finally reducing itself to Emptiness."[89]

"I, in viewing all,
Regard all without exception as equal,
Since I have neither 'that' nor this,'"[90]

The verse form of the parable also allegorises the different types of plants, making various kinds of *śrāvakas* and *pratyekabuddhas* the smaller and larger herbs respectively, *bodhisattvas* the shrubs and especially advanced and effective *bodhisattvas* the trees. In the closing lines of *Kumārajīva's* verse say that the *śrāvakas* do not attain extinction, while those directly addressed are told that they will pursue the *bodhisattva* way until they become *Buddhas*. On the other hand the unity and equality of the *Buddha's* teachings has already been thoroughly avowed by the whole chapter, and it seems consistent to say that the *śrāvakas* will not attain the final goal in their capacity as *śrāvakas*. Even the *bodhisattvas* are only predicted to buddhahood in this context after gradual discipline,[91] and they are not equated with the *Buddhas* over against the *śrāvakas*.

Extensions of this chapter 5 in the Sanskrit version contain *three further parables* which are not found in *Kumārajīva's* version. The first is the light of the sun and the moon which falls everywhere in the whole world equally. The second speaks of a number of pots made out of the same clay by the same potter, but used for containing different things such as sugar, butter, curds or milk. The meaning of these two is the same as that of the rains and the plants. The third is a longer story about a blind man who recovers his sight as a result of healing, and who thereupon thinks of his power to see as an unsurpassed achievement, only to be told that there is much else which he could still attain such as supernormal powers. It is noteworthy that the four herbs used to cure his blindness are allegorised as 'the gate to *nirvāṇa*, the empty, the signless, and the wishless,'[92] so that in effect all of these must be supposed to be on the level of skilful means. The three vehicles are in this passage too said to shown by the skilful means of the *Tathagata*,[93] and "For there is no triad of vehicles, but only One Vehicle."[94] In general these extra parables do not seem to add anything of fundamental importance to the parable of the rains.

The priceless in the interior of the garment : Like the parable of the 'poor son' this parable is told not by the *Buddha* but by his five hundred *śrāvakas*. After the *Buddha* has predicted future Buddhahood for all of them, this parable is told to express their feelings of surprise and joy. They are compared to a man who went to visit a friend, drank too much and fell asleep. On waking he travels to another country where he gets into such severe difficulties over feeding and clothing himself that he is content to labour very hard for little reward. He does not realize that the friend in whose house he had got drunk had sewn a precious jewel into his garment before going away on business. When the friend encounters him again, and points the jewel out to him, his worries are over.

This parable and its explanation given are relatively short. The *bhikṣus* had laboured hard for a mere trifle, namely that which they supposed to be *nirvāṇa*, forgetting in the meanwhile the goal of the *Tathāgatajñāna*, or *Sarvajña* (Omniscence). The *Buddha* has then declared the provisional nature of their achievement,

> "*Bhikṣus* ! What you have gained is not ultimate extinction. I have long caused you to plant the roots favorable to Buddhahood, and [recently] by resort to an expedient device I made a display of the signs of *nirvāṇa*. You have been imagining, however, that you had in fact achieved the passage into extinction."[95]

The main goal of Buddhism is again put into question, in the verse 'a trifling portion of *nirvāṇa*' is contrasted with 'no real passage into extinction.' And it is gaining the *Buddha's* unexcelled wisdom which is true extinction.[96] As a result, the teaching of *nirvāṇa* is here described explicitly as the *Buddha's* skilful means.

The conjured city : This parable also speaks of the skilful means of the *Buddha* and it is in the One Vehicle the *Buddha* by resort to his expedients speaks of Three Vehicles. However, before the parable of the conjured city in chapter 7 is an account of a long distant previous *Buddha's* decision to preach *Dharma*. This decision is presented on the same model in two phases: firstly, the doctrine of the four noble truths and the twelve links of dependent origination, of which the goals are *nirvāṇas* of the *śrāvakas* and *pratyekabuddhas*, and secondly, the teaching of the *Lotus*, of which the real goal is the ultimate *nirvāṇa*, or the *Buddhajñāna*.

The guide of the band of travellers is described as having many skillful devices and his creation of the conjured city for his exhausted members to take a rest before proceeding to the real goal is one such.[97] In the interpretation of the parable, the *Buddha*, who is of course the guide, having known the low temperament of beings, proclaims two *nirvāṇas* midway by his power of skilful means for the living beings may stop for rest.[98] If the beings take up residence in either of these 'two places' they are told that the place where they are staying are near to *Buddhajñāna* and that the *nirvāṇa* which they have gained is not the real one. And next is the familiar formula "This is simply the Thus Come One's power to device expedients: within the one *Buddha* Vehicle he speaks of a threefold distinction."[99]

The point of the parable is that the teaching of *nirvāṇa* as given in the four noble truths and in the teaching of dependent origination is only a restful preliminary to the real attainment required. According to this parable it is only by recognising the 'magic' or provisional character of that which is at first manifested, that the travellers are able to proceed to real extinction and *Buddhajñāna*. At the same time there is no other picture of 'real extinction' than the original teaching of *nirvāṇa*. However, the conjured city is intended to be mistaken for the place of precious jewels. Here, the conjured city is compared to the finger pointing to the moon and the *Lotus* tells us now it is time to drop the finger so that we can see the moon.

The *Buddha's* life-span and the parable of the physician's ill sons : These two parables lie in the chapter 16 of *Kumāravijīva's Lotus*. This chapter is considered as the most important one of all and it is still used liturgically today, along with chapter 2, in a manner representative of the *sūtra* as a whole. It raises questions about the nature of the *Buddha* which is relevant to many discussions of *Mahāyāna* Buddhism.

Before coming to the parable itself some attention must be paid to the opening portion of the chapter which the parable of the physician's ill sons then illustrates, and first of all to the title of the chapter. The title is 'The Life-span of the *Tathāgata*.' It is very important to notice this precise formulation as well as some others in the body of the *Lotus* because it is largely on the basis of this chapter that the *Lotus* is sometimes represented as replacing the human *Buddha* with an eternal, transcendent *Buddha* who may be mistaken as equivalent to the God of the main theistic religions. However, such an interpretation is not accurate. The whole purport of this chapter is to argue that the manifestation of the attainment of enlightenment and of *nirvāṇa* to be seen in the life of the *Śākyamunibuddha* (i.e. the historical *Buddha*) are as much to be understood in terms of the concept of skilful means as his teachings about the four noble truths and *nirvāṇa*. By contrast to the idea that the *Buddha* attained enlightenment after a certain number of years in a historical life, it is said that he had already attained true Buddhahood an incredibly long time previously. The purpose of saying this is to disperse the fixed idea that it took a small number of years. In other words the argument is conceived on an entirely dialectical basis. And, to think that the *Lotus* is gratuitously advancing the conception of an eternal *Buddha* as a God or alike, in a manner which would run contrary to the whole trend of Buddhism in general, both before and after the appearance of this *sūtra*, would be to misconstrue it completely.

The difference of the terms 'eternal' and 'immeasurable' may be worth noticing. 'Eternal' is considered as an attribute of an independent thing which is not subject to the cycle of birth-and-death, and which is identical with the so-called 'God.' Whilst, 'Immeasurable' means exactly that one with the limited knowledge would not in practice be able to measure it; for *Bodhisattva Maitreya* and the assembly are asked whether supposing vast quantities of worlds were crushed into atoms, and then each atom were eastward deposited every distance of vast quantities of realms one by one till the last one, they would be able to calculate the numbers of world-spheres so treated.[100] Of course, they would not be able to, and likewise the length of time which has passed since the *Buddha* attained the supreme perfect enlightenment is so long that it cannot be calculated.

The argument of the chapter 16 as a whole arises out of a fantastic event described in the preceding one, chapter 15. While numerous *bodhisattvas* are promising that they will protect, read, recite and copy the *Lotus* after the passing away of the *Buddha*, the latter to their great astonishment says that there really is no need for them to be concerned. Because there already are innumerable *bodhisattvas* ready to do it. These countless *bodhisattvas* then appear from out of the earth and establish themselves in a marvelous tableau. This gives rise to considerable perplexity, and the *Buddha* assures *Maitreya* and the original assembly that all of these new arrivals were converted to Buddhism after the *Buddha's* own enlightenment. Even so, it does not seem possible that so many were converted in the mere forty years which have elapsed since the *Buddha* was enlightened. *Maitreya* and other *bodhisattvas* say that it is as if a young man of twenty-five were to claim numerous old men as his sons, while the latter recognised him as their father. Since such a thing seems inconceivable they beg the *Buddha* to explain, and it is this explanation which is given in chapter 16 on 'the life-span of the *Tathāgata*.'

The preparation for what is about to be said is very similar to that in chapter 2. The *śrāvakas* are in a state of perplexity, and they must be prepared to receive what will be said with belief and understanding.[101] Three times the *Buddha* enjoins the *śrāvakas* to receive his sincerely true word. Three times they promise to listen with faith and understanding. And the *Buddha* must repeat three times for the *śrāvakas* to pay attention to listen.

The *Buddha* then explains that although he is usually thought of as leaving the palace of the *Śākya* clan, taking up a place of meditation not far from the city of *Gayā* and there attaining *anuttarasamyaksaṃbodhi*, the reality is that innumerable world-systems have come to be and passed away since he originally became a *Buddha*. Ever since an inconceivably long time ago he has been constantly teaching both in this world and in innumerable others. This marvellously different reality is termed 'the power of *Buddha's* supernatural penetrations'[102] and we may ask whether it be linked with skilful means for the whole matter of deflating the historical view of the *Buddha's* life is explained further in terms of 'the power of an expedient device.'[103]

It is as skilful means that various other *Buddhas* such as the *Dīpaṃkarabuddha* are discriminated and described as entering *nirvāṇa*. The various details are framed in accordance with the capacities of those who are to be saved, and "Further, by resort to sundry expedient devices I preach a subtle *Dharma*, being thus able to cause the beings to open their thoughts to joy."[104] The matter is then related to the historical life-span of the *Buddha*,

> "The Thus Come One, seeing the beings' desire for a lesser *Dharma*, their qualities thin and their defilements grave, preaches to such persons, saying, 'In my youth I left my household and attained *anuttarasamyaksaṃbodhi*.'

> However, since in fact I achieved Buddhahood it has been as long a stretch of time as this. It is merely by resort to an expedient device, in order to teach and convert living beings, to enable them to enter upon the *Buddha* Path."[105]

The skilful means is applied to the opening of the *Buddha's* life as well as to its end, "Though in reality I am not to pass into extinction, yet I proclaim that I am about to accept extinction. By resort to these expedient devices the Thus Come One teaches and converts the beings."[106] Since the *Buddha* is a great psychologist who knows the psychological trends of living beings, he, by resort to expedient devices, demonstrates his extinction and "his emergence into the world is a thing difficult to encounter."[107] This is necessary to prevent people from becoming complacent as a result of the *Buddha's* presence. In this way the understanding of Buddhist teaching in terms of skilful means which has already been more or less systematically advanced throughout the *sūtra* is here applied to the *Buddha's* own life story.

In this chapter 16 the *Lotus* expresses its viewpoint on the world like *Nāgārjuna's* eightfold negations or the *Prajñāpāramitā-sūtras*, when it reads,

> "The Thus Come One in full accord with Reality knows and sees the marks of the triple sphere. There is no birth and death, whether withdrawal from or emergence into the world, nor is there any being in the world nor anyone who passes into extinction. [The triple sphere] is neither Reality nor vanity, neither likeness nor difference. Not in the manner of the triple sphere does he view the triple sphere. Such matters as these the Thus Come One sees clearly, without confusion or error."[108]

It is this understanding of the nature of the world which subverts the historical view of the activity of a *Buddha*. The historical view is provisionally accepted and encouraged through skilful means, but there comes a time when it is also necessary to indicate the redundancy of the terms in which the real meaning is lurked.

The opening exposition of chapter 16 mentioned above is followed by a parable of **the physician's ill sons** to illustrate the argument. Contiguously following the parable the question is raised as to whether the physician in this case was guilty of a falsehood, and the reply is that he was not. A skilful means to save living beings cannot be said to be a sin. Then the *Buddha* declares:

> "So, too, am I. Since my achievement of Buddhahood it has been incalculable, limitless hundred thousands of myriads of millions of *nayutas* of *asaṃkhyeyakalpas*. For the beings' sake, by resort to my power of expedient devices I say that I shall pass into extinction. Still there is no one who can, in keeping with the *Dharma*, say that I am guilty of the sin of willfully false speech."[109]

The invented death of the physician puts the *nirvāṇa* of the *Buddha* at the level of provisional truth devised to meet the psychological needs of the *Buddha's* followers.

This chapter and this parable really represent a radicalisation of such an understanding of the Buddhist religion, because the *Buddha's* own entry into *nirvāṇa* (i.e. his death at the end of a life-span of eighty years) is now treated as being a supreme skilful means to bring about regret and self-examination on the part of the living being.

The concluding verses confirm that the *Buddha's nirvāṇa* is given out as a skilful means to bring about right attitudes among the living beings, thus:

> "And as an expedient device, I make a show of *nirvāṇa*;
>
> Yet in fact I do not pass into extinction,
>
> ......
>
> The multitude, seeing me passed into extinction,

Broadly make offerings to my *śarīra*,

All harboring feelings of longing

And conceiving the thought of looking up in thirst."[110]

This is important as bringing in the main focal point of Buddhist devotions from earliest times to the context of the thought of skilful means. It is not only doctrinal concepts which are to be understood as skilful means but also ritual practice.

The pragmatic, soteriological criterion for every form of Buddhist teaching is clearly expressed in the closing verses of the chapter:

"I, ever knowing the living beings

Who tread the Path and those who do not,

In response to those who may be saved

Preach to them a variety of *Dharmas*,

Each time having this thought:

'How may I cause the beings

To contrive to enter the Unexcelled Path

And quickly to perfect the *Buddha*-body?'"[111]

From all mentioned above, it may be concluded that *Mahāyāna* Buddhism as a working religion is altogether controlled by the concept of skilful means.

V. Mythology and Skilful Means in the *Lotus*

So far the concept of skilful means discussed is in chapter 2 and in a series of parables following it. However, in the *Lotus*, mythological perspectives as symbols are also used as skilful means and their role of taking part in understanding the meaning of true reality is not less important. The *Mahāvastu*, a *Mahāyāna* work contemporary with the *Lotus*, though is fully developed mythologically but without any central emphasis on insight and skilful means, and hence the famous account of the *lokottara* character of the *Buddha* in it remains mere supernaturalism, unlike the understanding of the *Buddha* in the *Lotus*. And in this *sūtra*, chapters 1, 11 and *25*, make use of the term skilful means in a manner which throws light on this subject, mythology.

1. Illumination of all worlds :

Those impatient with the symbols of *Mahāyāna sūtras* might dismiss chapter 1 of the *Lotus* as a mythological opening of little doctrinal interest. The *Buddha* does not speak, only keeping silent and yet emitting a light illuminating all worlds, until chapter 2. However, what the *Buddha* is said to have done in chapter 1 is as important for the understanding of true reality as what he intends to have taught in words and although in this case the action of the *Buddha* is mythic, the meaning of the myth is partially explained within the narrative itself by the *bodhisattva Mañjuśrī*. He is famous for his insight, and his recollection of past *Buddha*-events enables him to interpret those of the present. And his explanation provides the link between the opening mythology of the chapter 1 and the doctrinal exposition of chapter 2.

Chapter 1, first describes the *Buddha* enthroned in state surrounded by a multitude of devotees including *arhants*, *bodhisattvas*, gods, dragons, humans and many others. First, he preached "a scripture of the Great Vehicle named the Immeasurable Doctrine (*Anantanirdeśa*)"[112] and entered into "a *samādhi* called the Palace of the Immeasurable Doctrine (*Anatanirdeśapratiṣṭhāna*)."[113] He then "emitted a glow from the tuft of white hair between his brows that illuminated eighteen thousand *Buddha*-lands to the east, omitting none of them."[114] These extraordinary signs causes a question among the multitude. *Bodhisattva Maitreya* asked *Mañjuśrī* if he was able to explain it. The latter — ever living under countless past *Buddhas* who have the same name, Sun-and-

Moon-Glow, and have the same framework; and thus, being able to understand the intention of the present *Buddha* when he does likewise — said it indicated that the *Buddha* "wished to preach the great *Dharma*"[115] and "will this day preach a scripture of the Great Vehicle named the *Lotus* Blossom of the Fine *Dharma*."[116] Or again "The present *Buddha* emits a glow, which helps to set forth the doctrine of the reality-marks."[117]

•The term "skilful means" itself occurs but once only in the whole of chapter 1, and that right at the end of the verses as quoted earlier.[118] However, the term is here closely and importantly linked with the central symbol, namely the glow from the tuft of white hair between the eyebrows of the *Buddha*. On account this link the whole mythological preface emerges as an indirect prediction of the teaching of the whole *sūtra*.

Thus although this chapter 1 may seem at first sight like an irrelevant mythological scenario, its patterns reflect the same understanding of Buddhism which appears more explicitly in the main body of the *sūtra*.

2. The tableau in mid-air :

One more mythological pattern linked with the concept of skilful means is described in the chapter 11 of the *Lotus*, 'Apparition of the Jeweled *stūpa*.'

First, a seven-jeweled *stūpa* seated by the whole body of a *Prabhūtaratnabuddha* wells up out of the earth and rests in mid-air. From within it is heard a loud voice which praises the proclamation of the *Lotus* by *Śākyamunibuddha*. *Prabhūtaratnabuddha*, when he was still a *bodhisattva*, had made a vow that on becoming a *buddha* and attaining extinction he would cause the *stūpa* containing his whole body to come to any place where the *Lotus* is preached, thus bearing witness to it by praising its excellence.

The fourfold assembly on the earth then wish to see the whole body of the *Prabhūtaratnabuddha* within the *stūpa*, and they are told that for this to be possible it will he necessary for the present *Śākyamunibuddha* himself to draw back all his emanated *Buddhas* now preaching in all different worlds. To do this he emits a single glow from his white hair-tuft, just as in the chapter 1, by which immediately were seen the *Buddhas* of all these worlds. Then all of them converge to this very world of *Śākyamunibuddha*, which is straigthtway purified and bedecked with jewels for their reception. Each one takes his place on a lion-throne beneath a jewel-tree, then *Śākyamunibuddha* himself rises up into the air where the *stūpa* is suspended and opens the door with his right finger causing a great sound. *Prabhūtaratnabuddha* is then visible to all, seated on the lion-throne in a posture of meditation. Once again he certifies the *Lotus*, receives homage, and gives half seat to *Śākyamunibuddha*. The fourfold assembly, due to their wish, are also raised up to the air by the *Śākyamunibuddha's* supernatural powers. In mid-air they too are urged to preserve and transmit the *Lotus*, for *Śākyamunibuddha* is about to enter *nirvāṇa*.

The verse account which follows is a very briefly summarised repetition of the prose, followed by extended verses of exhortations to preserve and to transmit the *Lotus*. And just between the description of the tableau itself and the beginning of the consequent exhortations there is a line of great importance:

"For by this expedient device

They enable *Dharma* long to endure."[119]

That the arrangement of the term 'expedient device' here refers not to some miscellaneous aspect of the scene but indeed to the whole story of the appearance of the *stūpa*, the *Prabhātaratnabuddha*, and the emanated *Buddhas* of *Śākyamunibuddha*. The gathering of *Prabhūtaratnabuddha*,

Śākyamunibuddha, and the emanated *Buddhas* of *Śākyamunibuddha* in mid-air is an implication of the *Lotus*. Those who preserve and transmit the *Lotus* see the *Trikāya* as under:

"The Thus Come One Many Jewels,
As well as I myself
And the magically conjured *Buddhas* here assembled,
Will know this meaning.
.....
If there is one who can keep
This Scripture-*Dharma,*
Then thereby he shall have made offerings
To me and to Many Jewels.
.....
If they only preach this scripture,
They shall then, on that account, see me,
The *Buddha* Many Jewels,
And the magically conjured *Buddhas*."[120]

Three kinds of *Buddhas* here imply the Three Bodies of the *Buddha* in the *Mahāyāna*, i.e., *Prabhūtaratnabuddha* (*Dharmakāya*), *Śākyamunibuddha* (*Nirmāṇakāya*), and the emanated *Buddhas* of *Śākyamunibuddha* (*Sambhogkāya*). The mid-air implies voidness (*śūnyatā*). The *Lotus* is the *sūtra* of the *Buddhajñāna*, avoiding the extremes, which is illustrated with 'a single glow emitted from the *Buddha's* white hair turf between eyebrows.' It is this non-dual knowledge which is able to see the voidness or the same nature of differentiated things, which is illustrated with the gathering of three kinds of *Buddhas* in mid-air.

Thus, the purpose of the complete operation as a skilful means is to establish the meaning of Buddhism.

3. Transformations by a *bodhisattva*

One more mythological pattern related to the term 'skilful means' is to be found in chapter 25 of the *Lotus*, which is about *Bodhisattva Avalokiteśvara*. This *bodhisattva* is very commonly known in China, Korea, Japan, Taiwan and Vietnam. He is a good example of celestial *bodhisattvas* who play an important role in the devotional side of *Mahāyāna* Buddhism.

The figure of *Avalokiteśvara* is found in various *Mahāyāna* texts, but most later developments of this saviour *bodhisattva* seem to carry the characterisation of *Avalokiteśvara* which is already found in the *Lotus*. Indeed this chapter 25, which was certainly an addition to the main body of the *Lotus*, is so important that it can exist independently.

The characterisation of *Avaiokiteśvara* in this chapter has three phases, and the first of them portrays him as a miracle worker. In response to the question put to the *Buddha* about why *Avalokiteśvara* has this name. The answer is that he uses supernatural powers to deliver living beings who suffer pain and distress. Such super-natural powers are supposed to be available to *Buddhas* and *bodhisattvas* generally in any case, but the stress here is on the compassion shown by this *bodhisattva* and the practical forms which it takes. Those in need should call upon his name and they will be delivered from such things as fire, flood, shipwreck in a land of demons, violent attack, and the bondage of stocks, pillory, or chains, whether one is guilty or guiltless,[121] or from such spiritual things as lust, anger, folly.[122] Next comes a passage, which says that a woman devoted to *Avalokiteśvara* will give birth to a son if she desires a son and to a daughter if she desires a daughter. Finally it is argued that anyone who reveres this *bodhisattva* though only for a moment will obtain innumerable blessings, equal to those obtained by a person who reveres innumerable other *bodhisattvas*.[123]

The second phase of the characterisation of *Avalokiteśvara* is his transformations. *Bodhisattva Akṣayamati* (Inexhautible Mind) who puts the questions in this chapter, now asks how *Avalokiteśvara* travels in this world, how he preaches *Dharma* to living beings and how his power of skilful means may be described.[124] The *Buddha* answers with a long catalogue of the forms taken by *Avalokiteśvara*: *Buddha*, *Pratyekabuddha*, *Śrāvaka*, *Brahma*, *Śakra*, *Iśvara*, *Maheśvara* and many others including elders and citizens, monks and nuns, wives of elders and citizens, boys and girls, gods, dragons and demons. All of these have in common that *Avalokiteśvara* may appear as one such for the benefit of those who are to be saved by him in just that particular form. This is how he wanders in the world, this is how he proclaims the *Dharma*, and this is the power of his skilful means.

The first two phases of characterisation are intermingled in the concluding passages, "This *bodhisattvva-mahāsattva* He Who Observes the Sounds of the World in the midst of terror, emergency, and trouble can confer the gift of ferarlessness. For this reason the whole *Sahā* world-sphere calls him the One Who Confers the Gift of Fearlessness."[125]

The third phase of charactensation of *Avalokiteśvara* links with the Buddhahood. *Akṣayamati* speaks first to *Śākyamunibuddha* and asks permission to make an offering to *Avalokiteśvara*. He then offers a necklace of precious jewels, which *Avalokiteśvara* however declines to accept. *Akṣayamati* presses him to accept it out of compassion. *Śākyamunibuddha* adds his voice and says that *Avalokiteśvara* should accept it out of compassion for *Akṣayamati*, for the fourfold assembly and for gods, dragons and many types of beings. So *Avalokiteśvara* does accept it, out of compassion. He then divides it into two parts and offers one part to the *Śākyamunibuddha* and another to the *stūpa* of the *Prabhūtaratnabuddha.*[126] The necklace is redistributed to the *buddhas*. This means that, in principle, any offering to *Avalokiteśvara* is an offering to the *Buddhas*.

This mythological pattern as a skilful means also conveys a meaning of Buddhism. The whole passage on the transformations of *Avalokiteśvara* is an exposition of the power of his skilful means, and it belongs to the total dialectic of his activity that the merits which accrue to him, symbolised by the costly pearl necklace, is redirected to the *Buddhas*. The conveyance to the *Buddhas* contains an implication: Innumerable differentiated thoughts of living beings, symbolised by *Akṣayamati* (Inexhaustible Mind), lead to fear and distress. But when being mindful of *Avalokiteśvara*, all of them will stop, hence, no more suffering. Why ? Because being mindful of *Avalokiteśvara* is to return back to the inner hearing nature, which is pure and calm. The role of this *bodhisattva* will be analysed further in the chapter 5 of the thesis.

The *Lotus* belongs to Buddhism. So its philosophy is a kind of religious philosophy, which requires not only the aspect of philosophy but also the aspect of religion, i.e., deliverance. This will be discussed in the next chapter.

References

1. The author of the text, *Buddhist Hybrid Sanskrit Language and Literature*, Banaras Hindu University, Banaras, 1954.
2. *Vinaya Texts*, part I, trans. by T. W. Rhys Davids & Hermann Oldenberg, Motilal Banarsidass, Delhi, 1996, p. 85.
3. Ibid., p. 84.
4. Ibid., pp. 84-97.
5. Leon Hurvitz (trans.), *Scripture of the Lotus Blossom of the Fine Dharma*, NY, 1976, p. 43.
6. Ibid., p. 43.
7. Ibid., pp. 43-44.
8. Ibid., p. 44.
9. Ibid., p. 44.

10. Ibid., p. 44.
11. Ibid., pp. 36-37.
12. I. B. Homer (trans.), *The Middle Length Sayings I*, Luzac & Co. 1967, p. 211.
13. See I. B. Homer (trans.), *The Middle Length Sayings II*, 1957.
14. *Sāriputra* is traditionally supposed to have been converted along with five hundred followers after an encounter with one of the original five hermits converted by the Buddha. He frequently appears in dialogues with the Buddha to represent the Hinayana viewpoint in Mahayana writings. In the text *Teachings of Vimalakīrti* he is made to seem rather foolish, worrying over where the assembly will sit down in *Vimalakīrti's* magically emptied room (Chapter VI).
15. Leon Hurvitz. Op.cit., p. 25.
16. Ibid., pp. 25-26.
17. Ibid., p. 26.
18. Chapter II "Skilful Means" of the *Lotus* is considered as the most impotant of the *sūtra*.
19. Leon Hurvitz, Op.cit., pp. 30-31.
20. Ibid., p. 26.
21. Ibid., p. 22.
22. Ibid., p. 23.
23. Ibid., pp. 22-23.
24. Ibid., p. 22.
25. See Leon Hurvitz. p. 29.
26. *pratyekbuddhas*.
27. Ibid., p. 25.
28. The six directions of reincarnation, (1) *naraka-gati*, or that of the hells; (2) *preta-gati*, of hungry ghosts; (3) *tiyagyoni-gati*, of animals; (4) *asura-gati*, of malevolent nature spirits; (5) *manusya-gati*, of human existence; (6) *deva-gati*, of deva existence.

29. Leon Hurvitz, Op.cit., p. 35.
30. Ibid., pp. 36-37.
31. Ibid., p. 37.
32. Ibid., p. 40.
33. Ibid., p. 44.
34. Ibid., p. 46.
35. Ibid., p. 43. "I had rather not preach the *Dharma* / But enter speedily into *nirvāṇa.*"
36. Ibid., pp. 32-33.
37. Ibid., p. 33.
38. The six things that ferry one beyond the sea of mortality to *nirvāṇa*, i.e. the six *pārāmitās*: (1) *dāna*, charity, or giving, including the bestowing of the truth on others; (2) *sīla*, keeping the commandments; (3) *kṣānti*, patience under insult; (4) *vīrya*, zeal and progress; (5) *dhyāna*, meditation or contemplation; (6) *prajñā*, wisdom, the power to discern reality or truth. It is the last which carries across the (sea of incarnate life) to the shores of *nirvāṇa*.
39. Ibid., pp. 37-38.
40. Ibid., p. 40.
41. Ibid., p. 40.
42. Ibid., p. 39.
43. Ibid., pp. 38-39.
44. Ibid., p. 45.
45. Ibid., p. 45.
46. Ibid., p. 46.
47. Ibid., p. 43.
48. Ibid., p. 34.
49. Ibid., p. 43.
50. Ibid., p. 44.

51. Ibid., p. 45.
52. Ibid., p. 46.
53. Ibid., p. 40.
54. Ibid., p. 40.
55. Ibid., p. 40.
56. Ibid., p. 37.
57. Ibid., p. 35.
58. Ibid., p. 30.
59. Ibid., pp. 24-25.
60. Ibid., pp. 35-36.
61. Ibid., p. 29.
62. Ibid., p. 22.
63. Ibid., p. 25.
64. Ibid., p. 60.
65. Ibid., p. 62.
66. Ibid., p. 63.
67. Ibid., p. 64.
68. Ibid., p. 64.
69. Ibid., p. 64.
70. Ibid., p. 64.
71. Endnote 64.
72. Leon Hurvitz, Op.cit., p. 74. This phrase is also translated 'throne of enlightenment'.
73. Ibid., p. 74.
74. Ibid., p. 31.
75. Ibid., p. 62.
76. Ibid., pp. 74-75.
77. Ibid., pp. 86-87.

78. Ibid., p. 87.

79. Ibid., p. 89.

80. Ibid., p. 89.

81. Ibid., p. 89.

82. Ibid., pp. 99-100.

83. Ibid., p. 21.

84. Ibid., pp. 101-102.

85. The Sanskrit term '*Dharma*', or '*dharmas*' can be used both for the normative teaching of the Buddha, his 'Law' or *Dharma*, and in the plural for the factors of existence into which world of our experience is analysed in Buddhist thought. Though we might expect 'King of *Dharma*' (cf. Skt. *dharmarāja*) we definitely find in *Kumārjīva's* version 'king of *dharmas*', *dharmas* here should be taken as 'teachings' in plural.

86. Leon Hurvitz, Op.cit., p. 108.

87. Ibid., p. 101.

88. Ibid., p. 102.

89. Ibid., p. 103.

90. Ibid., p. 106.

91. Ibid., p. 109.

92. Ibid., p. 114.

93. Ibid., p. 113.

94. Ibid., p. 119.

95. Ibid., p. 165.

96. Ibid., p. 167.

97. Ibid., p. 148.

98. Ibid., p. 149.

99. Ibid., p. 149.

100. Ibid., pp. 237-238.

101. This phrase appeared as the title of Chapter IV.
102. Leon Hurvitz, Op.cit., p. 242.
103. Ibid.
104. Ibid., p. 238.
105. Ibid., pp. 238-239.
106. Ibid., p. 239.
107. Ibid., p. 240.
108. Ibid., p. 239.
109. Ibid., p. 241.
110. Ibid., p. 242.
111. Ibid., p. 244.
112. Ibid., pp. 13-14.
113. Ibid., p. 14.
114. Ibid.
115. Ibid., p. 12.
116. Ibid., pp. 15-16.
117. Ibid., p. 21.
118. Chapter IV, part IV, 'the rain and other' of this thesis.
119. Ibid., p. 190.
120. Ibid., pp. 190-191.
121. Ibid., pp. 311-312.
122. Ibid., pp. 312-313.
123. Ibid., p. 313.
124. Ibid., p. 314.
125. Ibid., p. 315.
126. Ibid., p. 315-316.

Chapter V

Bodhisattva, Buddhahood and Dhāraṇī

Broadly speaking, the previous chapter mentions the doctrine of *upāya-kauśalya* as a means to reach Reality, which the *Lotus* terms as *Ekayāna*. The *Lotus*, however, contains a kind of religious philosophy, which aims at the goal of life, i.e., deliverance. To exercise this noble duty the *Lotus*, as other *Mahāyāna sūtras*, advocates the doctrine of *bodhisattva*.

But, what is the *bodhisattva* doctrine ? And, how is this *bodhisattva* doctrine used in the *Lotus* ?

I. The *Bodhisattva* Doctrine

1. The need of a new doctrine

Early Buddhism lays stress on the double ideal of *arhatva* (*Pāli*: *arahatta*) and *nirvāṇa* (*Pāli*: *nibbāna*). *Gautama Buddha* preached his first disciples the four Noble Truths and the Eightfold Way and emphasized the transitoriness, suffering and non-substantiality of all the constituents of human personality. He had no craving or attachment to the *pañcaskandha* that constitute human personality, viz. *rūpa* (form), *vedanā* (feeling), *sañjñā* (perception), *saṃskāra* (volitions), and *vijñāna* (consciousness)[1]. The *śrāvakas* were called *arhats* (*Pāli*: *arahā*, *arahant*)[2], and *Buddha* himself was described as an *arhat*[3]. *Pāli* texts describes a variety of specific features of an *arhat*, of which some are listed. He freed himself from the three 'Roots of Evils': sense-desire, hatred and delusion. He fulfilled the triple discipline of Virtuous conduct (*sīla*) Concentration (*samādhi*) and Wisdom (*prajñā*).[4] He practised the four Meditations, the four ecstatic Attainments and the supreme condition of Trance. He avoids the extremes of severe austerities and sensual self-indulgence[5]. He was absolutely free from the three or four *āsravas*, and this freedom made him an *arhat*.[6]

An *arhat*, who was thus liberated, knew that he would not be reborn; he had accomplished what was to be done; he had laid down his burden; he had lived the holy life; he attained undefiled and final emancipation of mind and heart; he was alone, secluded, zealous, earnest, master of himself.[7]

An *arhat* also went forth as a preacher and taught the doctrine of the *Buddha* to the people. Because the *Buddha* had exhorted his disciples to wander every directions and preach the truth for the welfare and liberation of the multitude, as he loved his fellow-creatures and had pity on them.[8]

Such was the ideal of the *arhat*, as it was understood during the three centuries after *Gautama Buddha's* passing away. But it seems that the Buddhist monks began to neglect certain important aspects of it. They became too self-centered and contemplative, and did not evince the old zeal for missionary activity among the people.[9] They seemed to have cared only for their own liberation from sin and suffering.[10] The *arhats* also believed that a monk, who attained *nirvāṇa* in his life, could not remain in touch with this world of conditioned phenomena after his death.[11] Besides, the ideal of a *pratyekabuddha* was also evolved during this period (*Pāli:paccekabuddha*). Such a *Buddha* is "one enlightened by himself, i.e. one who has attained to the supreme and perfect insight, but dies without proclaiming the truth to the world."[12] Some Buddhists thought that one could not be very wise and holy through personal self-culture without fulfilling the equally important duty of teaching and helping suffering humanity. As a result, the *bodhisattva* doctrine was taught and promulgated by some Buddhist leaders as a protest against this lack of true spiritual fervour and altruism among the monks of that period. The coldness and aloofness of the *arhats* and *pratyekabuddhas* led to a new movement in favour of the old gospel of 'saving all creatures.' The *bodhisattva* ideal can be understood only against this background of a saintly and serene, but inactive and indolent monastic Order. And *Mahāyāna* doctrine is developed, religiously and philosophically, with the *bodhisattva* ideal as its center.

The exponents of the new ideal also protested against the *arhat's summum bonum* of *nirvāṇa*. They declared that mere cessation of *duḥkha* (pain, evil) or the conquest of the *āsravas* was not enough and the *arhat's* ideal of *nirvāṇa* did not include intellectual Perfection and supreme Wisdom. According to them *nirvāṇa* is the realm of self-realisation attained by noble wisdom, which is free from the discrimination of eternality and annihilation, existence and non-existence, not the one consists in recognising individuality and generality, in escaping social intercourse, in not having a perverted view of the world, and not having discrimination, as conceived by the *śrāvakas* and *pratyekabuddhas*.[13] The *nirvāṇas* of the *śrāvakas* and *pratyekabuddhas* were even compared to the dung or lesser things,

> "World-Honored One ! By reason of the three kinds of woe, in the midst of birth and death we suffer various annoyances. Erring ignorant, we cling in desire to lesser *dharmas*. This day the World-Honored One commands us to take thought and to clear away the dung of frivolous assertions concerning the *dharmas*. In the course of this we, striving all the more earnestly, contrive to arrive at *nirvana*. Having earned one day's wages, we rejoice greatly at heart, imagining this to be enough."[14]

The *bodhisattva* doctrine was thus spread as a protest against the theory of arhatship, which was regarded as doubly defective. It disregarded the higher duty of acquiring the perfect wisdom of a *Buddha*; and it deprived the world of the services of the holy men and women who had attained *nirvāṇa* and passed away. A *bodhisattva* was defined as one who strove to gain *Bodhi*, *Buddhahood* and delayed such *nirvāṇa*, as he wished to help and save all his fellow-creatures in the world of suffering. For indeed all beings, according to the *Mahāyāna*, participate in the *Buddhatā* and can attain the total enlightenment. And the *bodhisattva* ideal receive its significance from the basic Mahayanist doctrine.

2. The meaning of the word '*bodhisattva*'

The Sanskrit word *bodhisattva* is a compound noun including two words, i.e. *bodhi* and *sattva*, and has been explained in different ways. *Bodhi* means 'enlightenment.' But *sattva* has a variety of interpretations.

- *Sattva* means essence, nature, true essence' (Skt. Dicy. Pbg. & Skt. Dicy. M. W.). The Pali word *satta* means 'substance' (Pali Dicy.s.v.).
- *Sattva* means 'any living or sentient being' (Skt. Dicy. M.W.). The Pali word *satta* means 'a living being, creature, a sentient and rational being, person' (Pali Dicy.s.v.). Most modem scholars adopt this interpretation. So, a *bodhisattva* may mean 'A being possessing or seeking for *bodhi*.'
- *Sattva* means 'spirit, mind, sense, consciousness' (Skt. Dicy. M.W. and Pbg.). The Pali word *satta* means 'soul' (Pali Dicy. s.v.). Thus, in this case, the word would mean 'one whose mind, intentions, thoughts or wishes are fixed on *bodhi*.'
- *Sattva* means 'embryo' (Skt. Dicy. M.W.). And the word may mean 'In whom enligtenment is latent and undeveloped.'

- *Sattva* may be a wrongly Sanskritized form of the Pali word *satta*, which may correspond to Skt. *Sakta*. *Sakta* (from the root *sañj*) means 'clung, stuck or attached to, joined or connected with, addicted or devoted to, fond of, intent on' (Skt. Dicy. M.W.). Thus, from the Pali *bodhisatta*, the corresponding Sanskrit word would mean *bodhi-sakta*, 'one who is devoted or attached to *bodhi*.'
- *Sattva* means 'strength, energy, vigour, power, courage' (Skt. Dicy. M.W. p. 1052). Then, the word *bodhisattva* would mean, 'one whose energy and power is directed towards *bodhi*.'

Noteworthy, the word *bodhisattva* is often coupled with *mahā-sattva* (great Being).

3. The *bodhisattva* as distinct from the *arhats* (*śrāvakas*) and the *pratyekabuddhas*

According to the exponents of the new ideal, *a bodhisattva* is regarded as superior to a *śrāvaka* and a *pratyekabuddha*, and the new ideal is established as the *summum bonum* of the religious life. It seems that the reformers objected to the old adherents on two main aspects:

1. A *bodhisattva* aims at the acquisition of *Bodhi* and *Buddhajñāna*, while a *śrāvaka* and a *pratyekabuddha* are content with the *nirvāṇa* that is attained by the destruction of the *āsravas*. Three types of *bodhi* are recognised: *śrāvaka-bodhi*, *pratyekabodhi* and *anuttarāsamyak-sambodhi* (the supreme and perfect *bodhi*), in which the last is declared to be the highest as mentioned in the texts.[15] *Arhatva*, *pratyeka-bodhi* and *sarvākāra-jñāna* (omniscence) are mentioned as successive stages.[16] *Śrāvaka-bhūmi* and *pratyeka-bhūmi* are contrasted with *sarvākāra-jñāna*.[17] Corresponding to the three kinds of *bodhi*, there are three *yānas* or 'ways.' The third *yāna* was at first called the *boddhisattva-yāna,* but it was then renamed *mahā-yāna*. The other two *yānas* were called

the *hīna-yāna*.[18] In the later texts, the term *bodhisattva-yāna* is very rare, as *mahā-yāna* has taken its place. This is sometimes called the *Tathāgata-yāna*.

The *Mahāyāna* texts frequently explain, compare and contrast the two ideals of *nirvāṇa* and *anuttarā-samyak-sambodhi* (supreme and perfect enlightenment), and through which the achievements of the *śrāvakas* and *pratyekabuddhas* are recognized by some Mahayanist authors as the preliminary stages of a *bodhisattva*' career:

> "To the disciples he preached the law containing the four Noble Truths, and starting from the chain of causes and effects, tending to overcome birth, decrepitude, sickness, death, sorrow, lamentation, woe, grief, despondency, and finally leading to *Nirvāṇa*; and to the *Bodhisattvas* he preached the law connected with the six Perfections, and terminating in the knowledge of the Omniscient, after the attainment of supreme, perfect enlightenment."[19]

> "Having gained a trifling portion of *nirvāṇa*
>
> We were satisfied, and sought no further.
>
> Now the *Buddha* has made us aware,
>
> Saying that his is no real passage into extinction.
>
> We have gained the *Buddha's* unexcelled wisdom,
>
> Which now for the first time we take to be true extinction."[20]

> "Those *Bodhisattva-Mahāsattvas* who have reached the sixth stage as well as all the *Śrāvakas* and *Pratyekabuddhas* attain perfect tranquillisation (*nirodha*). At the seventh stage, the *bodhisattva-mahāsattvas*, giving up the view of self-nature as subsisting in all things, attain perfect tranquillisation in every minute of their mental lives, which is not however the case with the *śrāvakas* and *pratyekabuddhas*; for with them there is something effect-

producing, and in their attainment of perfect tranquillisation there is a trace [of dualism], of grasped and grasping. Therefore, they do not attain perfect tranquillisation in every minute of their mental lives which is possible at the seventh stage. They cannot attain to [the clear conviction of] an undifferentiated state of all things and the cessation of [all] multiplicities. Their attainment is due to understanding the aspect of all things in which their self-nature is discriminated as good and as not-good. Therefore, until the seventh stage there is not a well-established attainment of tranquillisation in every minute of their mental lives."[21]

2. A *bodhisattva*, who follows the ideal of the *Mahāyāna*, is of altruism and aims at the highest Good for himself and also for others. Meanwhile, an *arhat* is represented by the Mahayanists as self-regarding and unsocial, solving his own problem and nor thinking of others.

"Here, a *bodhisattva*, a great being, produces a thought thus : 'After I have in the measureless stream of *Saṃsāra* put on the armour, I should become one who never abandons all beings. Towards all beings should I adopt the same attitude of mind. All beings should I lead to *Nirvāṇa*, by means of the three vehicles. And even when I have led all beings to *Nirvāṇa*, no being at all has been led to *Nirvāṇa*. And why ? I should look through to the nonproduction and nonstopping of all *dharmas*."[22]

"Further again, *Mahāmati*, in the life of the *śrāvaka*-vehicle, there are two aspects to be distinguished, namely, the excellent and exalted state of self-realisation, and the attachment to the notion of self-nature arising from discrimination. What is the excellent, exalted state of self-realisation belonging to the *śrāvakas* ? This is a state of mental concentration which is attained when one realises states of emptiness, egolessness, suffering, and impermanence, and the truth that is free from passions and is ever serene; when one annihilates notions belonging to the externality of things, such as the *Skandhas*, *Dhātus*, *Āyatanas*, individuality and generality; and when one has an insight into reality as it is. Entering upon this state of mental concentration the *śrāvakas* will attain the blissful abode of exalted self-realisation in which there is the emancipation belonging to a *Dhyāna*, the path and fruit of a *Samādhi*, and the deliverance of a *Samāpatti*, but in which there is as yet no discarding of habit-energy and no escape from the imperceivable transformation of death. This, *Mahāmati*, is the *śrāvakas'* exalted state of self-realisation. Having attained this exalted and blissful condition of self-realisation as realised by the *śrāvakas*, *Mahāmati*, the *Bodhisattva-Mahāsattva* may not enjoy by himself the bliss of cessation, the bliss of *Samāpatti*, but should think compassionately of other beings and keep ever fresh his original vows."[23]

4. The characteristics of a *bodhisattva*

Througout what are mentioned above about *bodhisattva* one may put a question, "So, what may be the characteristics of a new hero, viz. *bodhisattva* ?" The reply is that there may be three characteristics of a *bodhisattva*, i.e., (a) firstly, seeking for *bodhi* or *Buddhajñāna*, (b) secondly, aiming at *Buddhahood*, and (c) thirdly, helping and leading others to the same goal as his.

These three characteristics frequent in *Mahāyāna* texts:

"The Lord : Much great merit will that son or daughter of good family beget who will take up this deep perfection of wisdom, bear it in mind, preach and study it, will wisely attend to it, and who will progress to its Thusness. And why ? So greatly profitable is the perfection of wisdom of the *bodhisattvas*, the great beings, as productive of the supreme enlightenment ! A *bodhisattva* should therefore train in just this perfection of wisdom if he wants to arrive at the supreme position among all beings, to become a saviour of all those who are helpless, a refuge and final relief to those who so far have found no refuge or final relief; an eye to the blind, a lamp to those plunged into the darkness of igorance; if he wants to reach *Buddhahood*, to arrive at the domain of the *Buddhas*, to sport with a *Buddha's* sport, to roar a *Buddha's* lion's roar, to beat the drum and to blow the conch-shell of a *Buddha*, and to explain the *Dharma* as only a *Buddha* can do. And why ? When the *bodhisattva* trains in perfect wisdom, he acquires all the accomplishments which he should acquire."[24]

"At that time, there was a *Buddha* named Sun-and-Moon-Glow, a Thus Come One... For the sake of the *bodhisattvas*, his preachings corresponded to the six *pāramitās* [perfections], with which he caused them to gain *anuttarasamyaksaṃbodhi* and to perfect the knowledge of all modes."[25]

"I dare not hold you all in contempt, since you are all to become *Buddhas* !"[26]

"If there are beings who, having heard the Dharma from the World-Honored One, believe and accept it; who, vigorously practicing and striving, seek All-Knowledge, *Buddha*-Knowledge, the knowledge which is so of itself, knowledge without a teacher, the knowledge and insight of the Thus Come One, his strengths, and his fearlessness: who, mercifully recalling and comforting incalculabe living beings and benefiting gods and men, convey all to deliverance: these are named [Those Who Mount] the Great Vehicle. It is because the *bodhisattva* seek this Vehicle that they are named *mahāsattva* [great beings]."[27]

a. ***Bodhi*** : The word *bodhi* is derived from the root *budh* which has many meanings.

> "The original sense may have been 'to fathom a depth, penetrate to the bottom'; to observe, mark, heed, regard, attend to; to perceive, notice, become acquainted with, recognise; to know, understand, comprehend; to think, reflect; to deem, consider, regard as, esteem as; to recover consciousness (after a swoon or after sleep, etc.), come to one's senses; to wake up, awake; to admonish."[28]

In Buddhist philosophy, it signifies 'supreme Knowledge,' 'Enlightenment,' 'perfect Wisdom.'[29] Three qualifying adjectives are commonly accompanied with it: *sam* (excellent, complete), *samyak* (right, perfect) and *anuttara* (nothing higher, supreme). Hence the usual appellation *anuttara-samyak-saṃ-bodhi*.

According to the *Yogācāra* or *Vijñaptimātratā* school, there are three forms of knowledge: (1) Illusion (*parikalpita*), (2) Relative Knowledge (*paratantra*), and (3) Absolute Knowledge (*painiṣpanna*). *Painiṣpanna-lakṣana* literally means the world-view founded on the most perfect knowledge. According to this view, the universe is a monistic or pantheistic system. Whilst phenomenal existences are regulated by natural laws characterised by conditionality and individuation, they by no means exhaust all our experiences which are stored in our inmost consciousness. They must be something, - be it Will, or Intelligence, which, underlying and animating all existences, forms the basis of cosmic, ethical, and religious life. This highest Will, or Intelligence, or both may be termed God, but the Mahayanists call it religiously *Dharmakāya*, ontologically *Bhūta-tathatā*, and psychologically *Bodhi* or *Sambodhi*. And they think it must be immanent in the universe manifesting itself in all places and times; it must be the cause of perpetual creation; it must be the principle of morality. This being so, then, how do we come to the recognition of its presence ? This happens when our minds are clear of illusions, prejudices, and egotistic assumptions, they become transparent and reflect the truth like a dust-free mirror. The illumination thus obtained in our consciousness constitutes the so-called *painiṣpanna*, the most perfect knowledge, that leads to *nirvāṇa*, final deliverance, and eternal bliss.

Meanwhile, the other philosophical school of Mahayanism, the *Mādhyamika* of *Nāgārjuna*, distinguishes two, instead of three, kinds of knowledge, but practically the *Yogācāra* and *Mādhyamika* come to the same conclusion. The two kinds of knowledge or truth distinguished by the *Mādhyamika* philosophy are *Saṁvṛti-satya* and *Paramārtha-satya*, that is, conditional truth and transcendental truth.

"On two truths is founded
The holy doctrine of *Buddhas*:
Truth conditional,
And truth transcendental.

Those who verily know not
The distinction of the two truths
Know not the essence
Of Buddhism which is meaningful."[30]

The conditional truth includes illusion and relative knowledge of the *Yogācāra* school, while the transcendental truth corresponds to the absolute knowledge, which unifies all contrasts and antitheses in its absolute oneness.

The final goal of a *bodhisattva's* career is always indicated by such words as *Anuttarasamyaksaṃbodhi* (superior enlightenment),[31] *Sarvākārajñatā* (knowledge of all modes, omniscience),[32] *Buddhajñāna* (*Buddha's* knowledge and insight).[33] *Bodhi* has been described as "beyond reckoning and discussion,"[34] "broad and great, profound and recondite, without measure and without obstruction,"[35] "viewing the nature of the *dharmas* ['things,' phenomena] as unmarked by duality, just like space."[36] It is not limited by time "Thanks to the Thus Come One's power of knowledge and insight, I see that time in the remote and distant past as if it were this very day."[37] It is not limited by space,

> "When the *Buddha* Victorious through Great Penetrating Knowledge attained *anuttarasamyaksaṃ-bodhi*, in each of the ten directions five hundred myriads of millions of *Buddha*-worlds trembled in six different ways, and in the intervals between those lands, dark and obscure places that the glorious light of the sun and moon could not illuminate were all very bright. The living beings within them were all enabled to see one another."[38]

It is identical with *nirvāṇa* "We have gained the *Buddha's* unexcelled wisdom, which now for the first time we take to be true extinction."[39]

The *bodhisattva* state is characterized by the *Prajñā-pāramitā.* Without wisdom, the other five virtues, as well as skill in expedients, are worthless. The *Prajñāparamita-sūtra* says:

> "Though a *bodhisattva* should bestow gifts through aeons as numerous as the sands of the Ganges, and should observe morality, practice patience, apply energy, and persist in meditation....If he were not embraced by the Perfection of Wisdom and emptied by skill in expedients, he would fall to the level of a hearer (*śrāvaka*) or a *pratyekabuddha...*"[40]

The *bodhisattva* does not grasp at any concept; he clings to nothing. His Perfect Wisdom is void. This is the essence of highest wisdom: "A *bodhisattva-mahāsattva* should abide himself in the Perfection of *Prajña* by abiding in emptiness."[41]

Besides, as a *bodhisattva* it is only possible to fulfil his or her aspirations and duty to all sentient beings by becoming a fully enlightened *Buddha*, with all the abilities and powers of a *Buddha* to help others. Thus the *bodhisattva* generates the *bodhicitta*, the altruistic aspiration to perfect enlightenment for the benefit of all sentient beings.

b. *Buddhahood* : A *Buddha*, according to the Mahayanists, is a fully enlightened being who has many more characteristic attributes and qualities than other beings.

> Ten titles: A *Buddha* has ten titles as the *Lotus* states, "At that time there was a *Buddha* named Sun-and-Moon-Glow, a Thus Come One, worthy of offerings, of right and universal knowledge, his clarity and conduct perfect, well gone, understanding the world, an unexcelled Worthy, a Regulator of men of stature, a Teacher of gods and men, a *Buddha*, a World-Honored One."[42]

- □ Thus Come One (*Tathāgata*): He who comes and goes in the same way [as the *Buddha* who preceeded him], *Gautama Buddha*.[43]
- □ worthy of offerings (*Arhat*): A *Buddha* who is still a candidate for *Nirvāṇa*; the highest rank in the Buddhist hierarchy.[44]
- □ of right and universal knowledge (*Samyak-saṃbuddha*): One who has attained to complete enlightenment.[45]
- □ his clarity and conduct perfect (*Vidyācaraṇa-saṃpanna*): perfect in knowledge and of good moral conduct.[46]
- □ well gone (*Sugata*): going well; one who has fared well.[47]
- □ understanding the world (*Lokavid*): Knowing or understanding the worlds.[48]
- □ an unexcelled Worthy (*Anuttara*): best, excellent.[49]
- □ a Regulator of men of stature (*Puruṣa-damya-sārathi*): a driver or guide of men.[50]

- ☐ a Teacher of gods and men (*Śāstā devamanuṣyāṇām*).
- ☐ a *Buddha*.
- ☐ a World-Honored One (*Buddha-lokanātha*, or *Bhagavān*).

> The Ten Powers: The *Lotus* further describes ten powers of the Buddha, "The *Buddha* declared to the *bhikṣus*: 'The king at that time was myself. The seer was he who is at present *Devadatta*. It is thanks to my good friend *Devadatta* that I have been enabled to perfect the six *pāramitās*; tenderness, compassion, sympathetic joy, and indifference to self; the thirty-two marks and the eighty beautiful features; the color of polished red-gold; the ten strenghts; the four kinds of fearlessness; the four inclusive *dharmas*; the eighteen kinds of uniqueness; the power of the Way of the supernatural penetrations."[51] The *Tathāgata's* ten powers of understanding or wisdom[52] are as follows:

- ☐ Perfect understanding of past, present, and future;
- ☐ Perfect understanding of *Buddha* Law;
- ☐ Unimpeded understanding of the whole *Buddha-realm*;
- ☐ Unlimited, or infinite understanding of the whole *Buddha*-realm;
- ☐ Of ubiquity;
- ☐ Of universal enlightenment;
- ☐ Of omnipotence, or universal control;
- ☐ Of omniscience with regard to all living beings;
- ☐ Of omniscience with regard to the laws of universal salvation;
- ☐ Of omniscience with regard to all *Buddha* wisdom.

> The Four Kinds of Fearlessness (*Vaiśāradyas*): *Vaiśāradyas* means "perfect self-confidence, self-satisfaction".

There are four grounds of self-confidence on account of which a *Buddha* boldly preaches the *Dharma* and 'utters a lion's roar.' He knows that he has attained perfect enlightenment and understands all principles and phenomena (*dharmāh*). He knows that the obstacles to the higher life, which he has described, really constitute serious hindrances. He knows that the Way, which he teaches for the cessation of pain and evil (*duḥkha*), really leads to that goal. Thus no one in the entire universe, man or *deva*, or any other being, can accuse him of insincerity or falsehood in this respect. No one can say to him: "(1) You claim to be perfectly enlightened; but here are things that you do not understand. (2) You assert that you have destroyed the *āsravas*; but these are the *asravas* that still remain in your personality. (3) You declared that you have indicated the obstacles to the spiritual life; but some of these practices and ideas are no obstacles at all. (4) You say that you teach the Way that leads to the destruction of pain : but that Way does not help one to attain that end." A *Buddha* knows that no one can justly reproach him in this manner. For this reason, he is always serene, fearless and self-confident, and cultivates a noble and magnanimous spirit.[53]

The Eighteen kinds of uniqueness (*Āveṇika-dharmas*): *Āveṇika* means "special, peculiar, extraordinary, exceptional"[54] or "not connected with anything else, independent."[55]

Āveṇikadharma or *buddhadharma*, the eighteen different characteristics of a *Buddha* as compared with *bodhisattvas*, i.e. his perfection of body (or person), mouth (or speech), memory, impartiality to all, serenity, self-sacrifice, unceasing desire to save, unflagging zeal therein, unfailing thought thereto, wisdom in it, powers of deliverance, the principles of it, revealing perfect wisdom in deed, in word, in thought, perfect knowledge of past, future, and present.[56]

> Compassion (*Karunā*): A *Buddha* is distinguished from other beings by his deep and great pity, love, mercy and compassion for all beings. "For the sake of these beings, I evince thoughts of great compassion."[57] "The room of the Thus Come One is the thought of great compassion toward all living beings."[58] And this *karuṇā* is exalted and personified into *Bodhisattva Āvalokiteśvara*, a well-known figure of *Mahāyāna* Buddhism, who is presented in chapter 25 of the *Lotus*. This word, *karuṇā*, frequents in the *Mahāyāna* literature. It is accompanied by prefix *Mahā* (great) in order to emphasise the importance of this attribute. Psychologically, it is love that awakens in us an intense desire to find the way of emancipating the beings from perpetual sufferings and eternal transmigration. Then, the intellect will endeavor to realise its highest possibilities; the Bodhi will exhibit its fullest strength. When it is found out that this life is an expression of the *Dharmakāya* which is one and eternal, that individual existences have no selfhood (*ātman* or *svabhāva*) as they are due to the particularisation of subjective ignorance, and, therefore, that we are true and real only when we are conceived as one in the absolute *Dharmakāya*, the *bodhisattva's* love which caused him to search after the highest truth will now unfold its fullest significance. And only the *Buddha's* or *bodhisattva's* boundless love for all beings like a mother's or father's feelings towards her or his children does make him complete his duty.

"*Śāriputra*, the Thus Come One is also like this. That is, he is the Father of all the worlds. To fear, terror, debilitation, anguish, care, worry, ignorance, and obscurity he puts an absolute end. Also, completely achieving the might of incalculabe knowledge and insight, as well as fearlessness; having great spiritual power and the power of wisdom; perfecting the *pāramitās* of practical expedients and of wisdom, as well as of great good will and great compassion; constantly unflagging; and constantly seeking the good, he benefits all. Thus he creates the old and rotten burning house of the three worlds and, in order to save the beings from the fires of birth, old age, sickness, death, worry, grief, woe, agony, folly, delusion, blindness, obscurity, and the three poisons, he teaches and converts them, enabling them to attain *Anuttarasaṃyaksambodhi*."[59]

And the following passages quoted at random from Devala's *Mahāpuruṣa* will suggest the value of love (*karuṇā*) as conceived by the Mahayanists. "Of all good virtues, lovingkindness stands foremost.... It is the source of all merit.... It is the mother of all *Buddhas*.... It induces others to take refuge in the incomparable *bodhi*. The loving heart of a *bodhisattva* is annoyed by one thing, that all beings are constantly tortured and threatened by all sorts of pains."

> Many *Buddhas*: According to the Pali tradition, there were six *Buddhas* who lived before *Gautama Śākyamuni*. And this number increases to twenty-four in the Pali *Buddhavaṃsa*. But in the *Mahāyāna* texts there are innumerable *Buddhas*, "the emanations of my body, incalculable *Buddhas*, equal in number to Ganges' sands."[60]

> *Buddha*- realms (*-kṣetras*): A *Buddha* has his realm, which is well adorned and where the *Buddha* converts innumerable other beings.

"The territories of his realm shall be well adorned, having no filth or evil, no tiles or pebbles, no thorns or thistles, no excrement or other impurities. Its soil shall be flat and even, having no high or low, no hills or crevices. It shall have *vaiḍūrya* for earth and jeweled trees in rows. With cords made of gold shall its highways be bordered. It shall be everywhere clean and pure, with jeweled flowers scattered about. The *Bodhisattvas* of that realm shall exist in incalculable thousands of

> millions, and the multitude of voice-hearers shall also be innumerable. *Māra* shall have no business there. Though *Māra* and the subjects of *Māra* shall be there, they shall all protect the *Buddhadharma*."[61]

From the perspective of Buddhist cosmology space, like time, is infinite. Infinite space is full of infinite universes, world systems, stretching to the ten directions (the four cardinal points, four intermediate directions, up and down). Within these infinite reaches some universes are known as *Buddha* fields or *Buddha* lands. Generally, this term denotes an area, a cosmos, where a *Buddha* exerts his spiritual influence.

The concept of a *Buddha* field, while of considerable importance in *Mahāyāna* thought, is not unique to the *Mahāyāna*. The *Mahāvastu*, which is a *Lokottaravāda* text, points out that there are many, many universes or world systems which are devoid of a *Buddha*, for *Buddhas* are relatively very rare. Moreover, the *Mahāvastu* notes, there cannot be two *Buddhas* in the same *Buddha* Field, for this would imply that one *Buddha* is not adequate to his task. And even though *Buddhas* are relatively rare, still, throughout the infinite universes there are innumerable *Buddhas*, and innumerable tenth-stage *boddhisattvas* who are about to become *Buddhas*. Each leads infinite beings to liberation, and yet there is no chance that eventually all will be liberated and no one will be left. For with infinite sentient beings, even if infinite *Buddhas* each liberates another infinite beings, still there are infinite suffering sentient beings left.[62]

The main function of a *Buddha* is to teach sentient beings in his *Buddha* field. But the *Buddha* field is not simply a place where the *Buddha* happens to have appeared. Rather, during his career as a *bodhisattva* the *Buddha*-to-be is said to 'purify' his *Buddha* field, and the *Buddha* field is the result of his great compassion. In other words, the very existence of a *Buddha* field depends upon the *Buddha's* wonderful career as a *bodhisattva*. The *Buddha's* infinite deeds of wisdom and compassion have created his *Buddha* field as an area where he can 'ripen' sentient beings. Beings themselves also contribute, for it is a place where they have been reborn through their deeds. A *bodhisattva* or even a *śrāvaka*, according to the *Lotus*, can himself be reborn in the *Buddha* field of a *Buddha*, in the *Buddha's* direct presence, or travel there in meditation. The *Buddha* field is precisely a place where conditions are obviously advantages to his spiritual progress.

Mahāyāna texts mention three types of *Buddha* field: pure, impure, and mixed. Human beings live in a world sphere called *Sahā* of *Śākyamuni Buddha*, which is not a very pure place and is pretty grim for the pious follower of *Mahāyāna* ! A pure *Buddha* field, on the other hand, such as *Amitāyus' Sukhāvatī*, is something like this:

> "well adorned, having no filth or evil, no tiles or pebbles, no thorns or thistles, no excrement or other impurities. Its soil shall be flat and even, having no high or low, no hills or crevices. It shall have *vaiḍūrya* for earth and jeweled trees in rows. With cords made of gold shall its highways be bordered. It shall be everywhere clean and pure, with jeweled flowers scattered about."[63]

But the greatest *bodhisattvas*, the real *bodhisattvas*, vow to appear as *Buddhas* in impure realms, tainted *Buddha* fields, out of their great compassion. The very fact that *Śākyamuni* appeared in this *Sahā* realm, a ghastly place, indicates his compassion.

Besides, there is another explanation for the purity and impurity of a *Buddha* field as given in the *Vimalakīrtinirdeśa-sūtra*. The impure *Buddha* field is indeed the Pure Land. It only appears impure because of the minds of sentient beings dwelling in it. If there are mountains in this world, and all is flat in the Pure Land, that is because there are mountains in the mind ! *Śākyamuni* is not a deficient *Buddha*. To him all is pure. Thus the real way to attain a Pure Land is to purify one's own mind. This is very much like the *Buddhatā*, *Tathāgatagarbha* assertion that we are already fully enlightened *Buddhas* if we but recognize the fact, and it is only a short step from the *Ch'an* (Zen) notion that the Pure Land is the tranquil, clear, radiant, pure Mind. The Pure Land is truly, therefore, not a 'heavenly abode' but enlightenment itself.

The Unlimited Span of Life of a *Buddha*: The demise of *Śākyamunibuddha* or of the six or twenty-four *Buddhas* of the past as mentioned in Pali canon were not supposed to be living after their *parinirvāṇa*. But according to the *Mahāyāna* texts a *Buddha* can live for many aeons (*kalpas*)[64]. "That *Buddha* shall live twelve minor *kalpas*."[65] "That *Buddha's* life-span being twenty-four *kalpas*."[66] We also find the hint of immortality for the *Buddhas*, "An inconceivable number of thousands of *koṭis*[67] aeons, never to be measured, is it since I reach superior (or first) enlightenment and never ceased to teach the law."[68] Moreover, a *Buddha*, who had already entered into *parinirvāṇa* long ago, suddenly reappears as a living *Buddha* in order to praise the *Lotus*, "At that time, the four assemblies, seeing a *Buddha* passed into extinction for incalculable thousands of myriads of millions of *kalpas* speaking such words as these, sighed in admiration at something that had never been before."[69] Thus, according to the Mahayanists, *parinirvāṇa* does not imply extinction.

Superhuman (*lokottara*): The *Buddhas* are not only numerous and immortal, but they are also superhuman.

They can perform miracles by their skilful means to save all beings from suffering.

"At that time the *Buddha* emitted a glow from the tuff of white hair between his brows that illuminated eighteen thousand worlds to the east, omitting none of them, reaching downward as far as the *Avīci* [the lowest] hell and upward as far as the [highest] gods."[70]

"It should be understood that the present *Buddha's* display of light is also of this sort. It is because he wishes all the living beings to be able to hear and know the *Dharma*, difficult of belief for all the worlds, that he displays this portent."[71]

> Threefold Body of a *Buddha* (*Trikāya*): The doctrine of *Trikāya* is a *Mahāyāna* concept, and yet partly results from the *Hīnayāna* idealization of the earthly *Buddha* with his thirty-two signs, eighty physical marks, clairvoyance, clairaudience, holiness, purity, wisdom, etc. In *Mahāyāna* every *Buddha* possesses threefold body : that of spiritual or essential nature (*Dharmakāya*); that of joy or enjoyment of the fruits of his past saving labours (*Sambhogakāya*); that of power to transform himself at will to any shape for omnipresent salvation of those who need him (*Nirmāṇakāya*).

□ *Dharmakāya* in its earliest conception was that of the body of the *dharma*, or truth, as preached by *Śākyamuni*; later it became his mind or soul in contrast with his material body. In *Mādhyamika*, the *Dharmakāya* was the only reality, i.e. the void, or the immaterial, the ground of all phenomena; in other words, the *Tathāgatagarbha*, the *Bhūtatathatā*. According to the *Hua-yen* (Kegon) School it is the noumenon, while the other two are phenomenal aspects.

□ *Sambhogakāya*, a *Buddha's* reward body, or body of enjoyment of the merits he attained as a *bodhisattva*; in other words, a *Buddha* in glory in his heaven. This is the form of *Buddha* as an object of worship. It is defined in two aspects, (i) for his own bliss, and (ii) for the sake of others, revealing himself in his glory to *bodhisattvas*, enlightening and inspiring them. By wisdom a *Buddha's Dharmakāya* is attained, by *bodhisattva*-merits his *sambhogakāya* is attained.

☐ *Nirmāṇkāya*, a *Buddha's* transformation, or miraculous body, in which he appears at will and in any form outside his heaven, e.g., as *Śākyamunibuddha* on earth.

Not only has every *Buddha* all the three bodies or aspects, but as all men are of the same essence, or nature, as *Buddhas'*, they are therefore potential *Buddhas* and are in and of the *Trikāya*. Moreover, *Trikāya* is not divided, for a *Buddha* in his *Nirmāṇkāya* is still one with his *Dharmakāya* and *Sambhogakāya*, all three bodies being coexistent.

Trikāya is also mentioned in the *Lotus* with the *Prabhūtaratnabuddha* as *Dharmakāya*, *Śākyamunibuddha* as *Nirmāṇakāya* and *Śākyamunibuddha's* emanations as *Sambhogakāya*. In chapter 11, *Apparition of the jeweled stūpa,* there is an unification of three *kāyas* in space, a symbol of *Mahāyāna śūnyatā*[72]:

> "At that time, *Śākyamuni-buddha*, seeing that the *Buddhas* who were emanations of his body had all arrived, and seeing how each, seated on a lion throne, was hearing that the *Buddhas* together wished to open the jeweled *stūpa*, straightway rose from his seat and rested in mid-air. All the four assemblies, rising with palms joined, single-mindedly beheld the *Buddha*. Thereupon with his right finger *Śākyamunibuddha* opened the door of the seven-jeweled *stūpa*, which made a great sound as of a bar being pushed aside to open the gate of a walled city. At that very moment all the

assembled multitude saw the Thus Come One Many Jewels in the seven-jeweled *stūpa*, seated on a lion throne, his body whole and un-decayed, as if [he were] entered into *dhyāna-* concentration. They also heard his words 'Excellent ! Excellent, O *Śākyamunibuddha*! Happily have you preached this Scripture of the *Dharma* Blossom. It is to listen to this scripture that I have come here.'

At that time, the four assemblies, seeing a *Buddha* passed into extinction for incalculable thousands of myriads of millions of *kalpas* speaking such words as these, sighed in admiration at something that had never been before, and scattered clusters of divine jeweled flowers over the *Buddha* Many Jewels and *Śākyamunibuddha*. The *Buddha* Many Jewels, in his jeweled *stūpa*, then gave half his seat to *Śākyamunibuddha*, speaking these words 'O *Śākyamunibuddha*, will you take this seat ?' At that very moment *Śākyamunibuddha*, entering that *stūpa*, sat on half that seat, his legs crossed.

At that time, the great multitude, seeing the two Thus Come Ones in the seven-jeweled *stūpa* on the lion throne, seated with legs crossed, all thought : 'The *Buddhas* sit high up and far off. We wish that the Thus Come One with his power of supernatural penetration, would enable the lot of us together to dwell in open space.' At that very moment *Śākyamunibuddha*, with his power of supernatural penetration, touched the great multitudes, so that they were all in open space,"[73]

c. Savior : The conception of Buddhahood was widened and elaborated as has been indicated above. As a result, a *Buddha* ceased to appeal to the popular imagination as an object of devotion. He had been dehumanised and universalised. He lost personality and became cosmic Law.

So the devotees could not approach the idealised and transcendental *Buddha* of the *Mahāyāna* with prayer and worship. He had become too great, vast, impersonal and incomprehensible for such relations. The Mahayanists turned to the earlier history of *Gautama Buddha*, when he was not the remote metaphysical *Buddha*, but only a charitable, patient and wise *bodhisattva*, a married denizen of this workaday world. As a *bodhisattva*, he had helped many people with gifts of wealth and knowledge as described in *jātakas*. He was a more humane and lovable figure at that stage of his career. The pious worshippers felt easily praying to a *bodhisattva* for health, wealth and mundane blessings, and that was all that they really wanted. Ordinary people are more anxious to secure welfare and happiness in this world than to strive for the distant and doubtful goal of Buddhahood. The *bodhisattvas* were thus chosen for worship and adoration in order to satisfy the needs of the pious Buddhists.

So, the *bodhisattva* doctrine makes a distinction between the *arhat* and *bodhisattva*. Both of them are unworldly idealists, but the *arhat* displays his idealism by devoting himself to meditation and self-developing, while the *bodhisattva* actively renders service to other living beings. Psychologically, an *arhat* is an "introvert" and a *bodhisattva* "extrovert".

5. *Bodhisattva* stages

With the arising of the *bodhicitta*, according to the *Daśabhūmika-sūtra* the *bodhisattva* enters ten stages on the path to Buddhahood as mentioned earlier.[74]

Beyond the tenth stage is the stage of a *Buddha*. The *Buddha* said:

> "And, *Mahāmati*, in ultimate reality there is neither gradation nor continuous succession; [only] the truth of absolute solitude (*vivikta-dharma*) is taught here in

> which the discrimination of all the images is quieted. So it is said : ... The [first] seven stages are [still] of the mind, but here the eighth is imageless; the two stages, [the ninth and the tenth,] have [still] something to rest themselves on; the [highest] stage that is left belongs to me."[75]

II. The Development of the *Bodhisattva* Doctrine

The word *bodhisattva* is very old and occurs firstly in *Pāli Nikāyas*. *Gautama Buddha* speaks of himself as a *bodhisattva*, when he refers to the time before his attainment of Enlightenment. The following clause recurs frequently in the *Majjhima Nikāya*: "*Mayham-pi kho brāhmaṇa pubbbe va sambodhā anabhisambuddhassa bodhisattassa*"[76] (*Brāhmaṇa*, in the days before my Enlightenment, when as yet I was only a *bodhisattva*). That is the times when his figure as a *bodhisattva* was still humane, earthly and the word *bodhisattva* seemed to be the earliest signification of it. However, everything was and is changing. In due course of time, in the third century B.C., the *Kathāvatthu*, a text of *Abhidhamma Piṭaka*, was composed by *Tissa Moggaliputta*. In this text, certain questions are raised with regard to the *bodhisattva's* actions; the marks on his body, his rebirth in a state of pain, and the possibility of his bearing heretical opinions or practising asceticism are discussed.[77] The previous lives of *Gautama Buddha* have now begun to excite interest and speculation; but, there was no new systematic doctrine in this time until the first century B.C. when new ideas about *bodhisattva* occurred in *Mahāyāna* texts. The idea of a *bodhisattva's* renunciation of personal *nirvāṇa* is stated clearly and unequivocally,

> "That is also of a *bodhisattva* the perfection of wisdom, which has gone to a Beyond which is no Beyond, that he does not take hold of form and the other *skandhas*, because no *dharma* has been appropriated. Nor does

> he enter final *Nirvāṇa* prematurely, i.e. before he has fulfilled the Vows, etc. to: the powers of a *Tathāgata*, the four grounds of self-confidence, the four analytical knowledges and the eighteen special *Buddha-dharmas*. And why ? Because all the *dharmas*, including the *Buddha-dharmas*, are no *dharmas*;"[78]

and *Bodhi* is set up as the new ideal in the *Lotus*, "The *Anuttarasamyaksaṃbodhi* of all *Bodhisattvas* in every case belongs to this scripture [the *Lotus*]. This scripture opens the door of expedient devices; it shows the marks of reality."[79] These *Mahāyāna* texts belong mainly to the first century B.C. And the *Mahāyāna* doctrine in its earliest form must be in the second century B.C.

For several centuries (second century B.C. to seventh century A.D) the *bodhisattva* doctrine was modified in its essential features as follows:

1. In the early *Mahāyāna*, the *bodhisattvas* are inferior and subordinate to the *Buddhas*; but they acquire great importance in course of time till they are at last regarded as equal to the *Buddhas* in many respects. They are to be worshipped like the *Buddhas*, or even in preference to them. This gradual exaltation of the *bodhisattvas* in lieu of the *Buddhas* culminates in the apotheosis of *Bodhisattva Avalokiteśvara*, who is declared to be a kind of "*Buddha*-maker". He helps others to acquire Buddhahood, while he himself remains the eternal *bodhisattva*.

> "Good man, if incalculable hundreds of thousands of myriads of millions of living beings, suffering pain and torment, hear of this *Bodhisattva* He Who Observes the Sounds of the World and single-mindedly call upon his name, the *Bodhisattva* He Who Observes the Sounds of the World shall straightway heed their voces, and all shall gain deliverance."[80]

"Good man, if there are beings in the land who can be conveyed to deliverance by the body of a *Buddha*, then to them the *Bodhisattva* He Who Observes the Sounds of the World preaches *Dharma* by displaying the body of a *Buddha*."[81]

2. In the early *Mahāyāna*, Wisdom (*prajñā*) and Compassion (*karuṇā*) are regarded as equally important. In fact, Wisdom is considered to be somewhat more important than Compassion. *Mañjuśrī*, who represents Wisdom, is invoked in the opening part of several treatises, and he is praised in the *Lotus*. The glorification of Wisdom reaches its climax in the writings of the *Mādhyamika* school of philosophy, which was founded by *Nāgārjuna* in the second century A.D. with his *śūnyatā* doctrine. *Prajñā* is extolled while *karuṇā* is not discussed in detail. But the later *Mahāyāna* emphasises *karuṇā* more than *prajñā*. It is emotional rather than argumentative. As this ideal gains ground, *Bodhisattva Avalokiteśvara* increases in importance till he becomes the supreme and unique *bodhisattva*. *Avalokiteśvara* gradually replaces the role of *Mañjuśrī*, occupies the supreme position in the Universe and reigns without a rival.

III. *Bodhisattvas* and their Roles in the *Lotus*

The *Mahāyāna* Buddhists invented their class of saints (*bodhisattvas*) chiefly by personifying the different virtues and attributes of *Gautama Buddha's* personality. They also took up certain epithets that were applied to *Gautama Buddha*, and converted them into the names of some *bodhisattvas*. The *bodhisattvas* thus derive their existence and attributes from the central historical fact of *Gautama Buddha's* life and work. The two chief *bodhisattvas*, *Mañjuśrī* and *Avalokiteśvara*, are personifications of *prajñā* and *karuṇā* respectively. *Bodhisattva Maitreya* typifies *maitrī* (friendliness). Some other *bodhisattvas* owe their names to the adjectives that were first employed to describe the great Teacher. *Buddha* is spoken of as '*samanta-bhadraka*' and '*samanta-bhadra-kāya*' (auspicious or excellent in all ways) in the *Avadāna-śataka* and the *Lalitavistara*; and *Samantabhadra* is the name of a *bodhisattva*.[82] In other cases, the descriptive titles of the Hindu *devas* have been transferred to the *bodhisattvas*. *Vajrapāṇi* and *Kṣitigarbha* suggest the influence of Hindu mythology.

In the *Lotus* appear many *bodhisattvas*, namely, *Maitreya*, *Mañjuśrī*,[83] *Varaprabha* (Fine Luster),[84] *Śrīgarbha* (Womb of Excellence),[85] *Yaśaskāma* (Seeker of Fame),[86] *Mahāpratibhāna* (Great Joy in Preaching),[87] *Prajñākūṭa* (Wisdom Accumulation),[88] four *bodhisattvas*: *Viśiṣṭacāritra* (Superior Conduct), *Anantacāritra* (Limitless Conduct), *Viśuddhacāritra* (Pure Conduct), *Supratiṣṭhitacāritra* (Conduct Standing Firm),[89] *Satatasamitābhiyukta* (Ever Persevering),[90] *Mahāsthāmaprāpta* (Gainer of Great Strength),[91] *Sadāparibhūta* (Never Disparaging),[92] *Nakṣatrarājasaṃkusumitābhijña* (Beflowered by the King of Constellations),[93] *Sarvasattvapriyadarśana* (Seen with Joy by All Living Beings),[94] *Gadgadasvara* (Fine Sound),[95] *Akṣayamati* (Inexhaustible Mind),[96] *Avalokiteśvara* (He Who Observes the Sounds of the World),[97] *Dharaṇiṃdhara* (Earth Holder),[98] *Pradānasūtra* (Brave Donor),[99] *Padmaśrī* (Floral Excellence),[100] *Vairocana-raśmipratimaṇḍitarāja* (Marks of Adornment), *Bhaiṣajya-rāja* (Medicine King), *Bhaiṣajyarāja-samudgata* (Above Medicine),[101] *Samantabhadra* (Universally Worthy).[102]

1. *Bodhisattvas Maitreya*, *Yaśaskāma*, *Mañjuśrī*, *Varaprabha* and *Samantabhadra*:

Just as in the first chapter of most of *Mahāyāna* texts frequently appears *Mañjuśrī* presenting his own questions, and in the last chapter, *Samantabhadra* performing his great vows, just so in the first chapter of the *Lotus Mañjuśrī* explains the doubts *of Maitreya* and of the great assembly on the *Buddha's* supernatural power "For what reason do we have these wondrous and supernatural signs, a great ray emitted which illuminates eighteen thousand lands to the east, making visible all the adornments of those *Buddha*-lands ?"[103], and in the last chapter, *Samantabhadra* vowing to enter the midst of a muddied, evil age in order to guard and protect those who receive and keep the *Lotus*.

* *Maitreya*: Like *Śākyamuni* before his final birth, *Maitreya* now dwells in the *Tuṣita* heaven awaiting an opportune time to descend to the world. Since *Tuṣita* is a heavenly realm and not a Pure Land, it is possible from the point of view of *Mahāyāna* and non-*Mahāyāna* traditions alike to visit there in meditation. *Maitreya* is close to earth. He visits this world in various forms to save and teach. Perhaps the best-known case is that of *Asaṅga*, where in the Tibetan version *Maitreya* takes *Asaṅga* to *Tuṣita* and delivers to him a series of texts containing details of the conduct of a *bodhisattva*, and the doctrine of *Cittamātra* (Mind Only). For this reason devotion to *Maitreya* was a particular concern of those who followed the *Cittamātra*. In China, for example, *Hsüan-tsang* vowed to be reborn in *Tuṣita* with *Maitreya*, and his translation and popularization of *Cittamātra* works (of *Yogācāra* school founded by *Asaṅga*) in China led to the revival of *Maitreya* worship. The *Yogācāra* school criticizes the contemporary philosophical currents, mainly the two extreme views of the existence of everything by the *Vaibhāṣikas* and the voidness of everything by the *Mādhyamikas*, and declares the doctrine of *Vijñaptimātratā*, the doctrine establishes the reality of consciousness-only and rejects the existence of external things outside consciousness, and the school claims that this is the True Middle Path taught by the *Buddha*.

Besides, in *Mahāyāna* Buddhism knowledge is classified as the three natures (*svabhāvas*) or aspects of existence, depending upon the true understanding which we ourselves possess of the things. They are called — (1) nature of imagination-only (*parikalpitasvabhāva*). (2) nature of dependence on others for manifestation (*paratantrasvabhāva*), and (3) nature of Ultimate Reality (*painiṣpannasvabhāva*). The form of knowledge by which the reality of things is assumed, is the imaginative consciousness (*parikalpa*). For things are only imagined to exist and they have no objective reality. The form of knowledge by which we investigate existence is *paratantra* 'depending upon another'. Thus the things are universally mutually conditioned and there is no substantiality of individual objects. The form of knowledge by which we are able to see the nature of reality as it is, is *pariniṣpanna*, perfected. For the followers of the *Wei-shih* (Mind-Only or Mere-Consciousness), however, all those three natures are inseparable from consciousness and its attributes (*caittas*). It means (*CWSL,* p.46c 7-13):

a. The mind and its attributes, together with the manifestations produced by it, the perceiving (*darśana*) and the perceived (*nimitta*), are produced through various conditions. They are thus like the phenomena produced by a magician's tricks which not really existing though they seem to exist, deceive the ignorant. All this is called the *paratantra* (discriminative consciousness).

b. The ignorant then believe in them as *ātman* and as *dharmas*. But they are, in fact, non-existent both in inner nature and external aspect. All this is called the *parikalpita*.

c. These things which are dependent on others and are wrongly regarded as *ātman* and *dharmas*, are, in reality, all void *śūnya*). The genuine nature of consciousness thus revealed by this 'voidness' is called the *painiṣpanna* (absolute consciousness without duality).

According to the *Wei-shih*, *Maitreya*, who is symbolic of the *paratantra* (discriminative consciousness), is unable to understand the marvellous signs, such as a ray of light emitted from the white curls between the *Buddha's* eyebrows illuminating eighteen thousand worlds in the east, which is a symbol of the *Buddhajñāna* or *Painiṣpanna* (Absolute consciousness without duality).

* *Yaśaskāma* (Seeker of Fame): *Yaśaskāma* was in the former life *Maitreya*.[104] *Yaśaskāma* craved advantage and profit, and yet he had planted roots of goodness; consequently, he was assured of Buddhahood by the *Buddha*. But a question may be raised in us, why did the *Buddha* predict Buddhahood to *Yaśaskāma* but not to *Varaprabha* (Fine Luster), the former life of *Mañjuśrī* ? The answer, as conceived by the *Wei-shih* school, may be like this : the way of enlightenment is to change the mind from *parikalpita* to *pariniṣpanna*. *Yaśaskāma* is a symbol of *parikalpita*. That is why the Buddha foretold him about his attainment of Buddhahood. Meanwhile, *Varaprabha* is the lineage of *Buddhajñāna* or *Pariniṣpanna* (Luster refers to wisdom). By virtue of this, *Varaprabha* was not done so.

* *Mañjuśrī*: Just as *Avalokiteśvara* is said to incarnate all the *Buddha's* compassion, just so *Mañjuśrī* manifests the other attribute of Him — wisdom. Of course, both are tenth-stage *bodhisattvas* and in reality have equal attainments. But just as *Avalokiteśvara* is met performing heroic deeds of compassion in the *Lotus*, *Mañjuśrī* is particularly associated with the role of interlocutor on questions concerning the Ultimate Truth in *Mahāyāna sūtras*, such as the *Vimalakīrti*. According to the *Pañcaviṃśati-sāhasrikā Prajñāpāramitā*, a *bodhisattva* who has reached the tenth stage is to be known, quite simply, as a *Tathāgata* — which is to say, a *Buddha*. Although he is not a *Buddha*, from our side he (or she) is so amazing that we could not distinguish him from a *Buddha*. In the *Mañjuśrībuddhakṣetraguṇavyūha* we are told how *Mañjuśrī* many, many aeons ago gave rise to the *bodhicitta*

in the presence of a previous *Buddha*. He would always act for the benefit of sentient beings, always observe complete morality and be perfectly pure. *Mañjuśrī* has now attained the tenth stage of a *bodhisattva*. He is asked why he does not proceed straightway to full Buddhahood. The reply is that in fully understanding emptiness and acting accordingly there is nothing more to do. He has let go off the notion of full Buddhahood. He no longer seeks enlightenment; indeed, in the light of emptiness he cannot attain enlightenment. In so saying, indeed, *Mañjuśrī* indicates that he is already fully enlightened. He had been close to the *Buddhas* in the past. In the *Lotus*, to reply *Maitreya* and the great assembly *Mañjuśrī* said that in the presence of past *Buddhas* he saw the portent : when the *Buddhas* had emitted this light, straightway they preached the great *Dharma*. Thus it should be understood that the present *Buddha's* display of light is also of this sort.[105]

The iconography of *Mañjuśrī* is a relatively late development. In Indo-Tibetan Buddhism he is usually represented as a young prince, seated on a lotus, with a sword in his right hand, held above his head, and a book in the left. The sword is said to be the sword of gnosis which cuts aside the bonds of ignorance. The book is the *Prajñāpāramitā*, usually held to be the *Aṣṭasāhasrikā* version. In Sino-Japanese art in particular, and Central Asian art which is influenced by China, *Mañjuśrī* rides on a lion, and often parallels *Samanta-bhadra*, the *bodhisattva* of the *Avataṃsaka Sūtra*, who rides a six-tusked elephant. Because of the importance of the *Avataṃsaka* in East Asian Buddhism, and also because of his role as guardian of the *Lotus*, *Samantabhadra* has a significant place as a cult figure in Sino-Japanese Buddhism.

* *Varaprabha* (Fine Luster): *Varaprabha* was in the former life of *Mañjuśrī*. In the Indian tradition, light or luster indicates wisdom. It is in this sense, *Mañjuśrī* had his suchlike name. *Mañjuśrī* said : "*Maitreya*, be it known : at that time

can the *Bodhisattva* Fine Luster have been anyone else ? I myself was he. You yourself were the *Bodhisattva* Seeker of Fame. We see these portents, now just as before. For this reason I surmise that the *Buddha* will this day preach a scripture of the Great Vehicle named the *Lotus* Blossom of the Fine *Dharma*, a *Dharma* to be taught to *bodhisattvas*, one which the *Buddha* keeps in mind."[106]

* *Samantabhadra* (Universally Worthy): In the *Mahāyāna* tradition, there are three great *bodhisattvas* — *Avalokiteśvara*, *Mañjuśrī*, and *Samantabhadra* — who represent the great compassion, wisdom, and vows of all *Buddhas* respectively. It is *Samantabhadra's* great vows and his single concern in life to relieve the pains and burdens of all sentient beings which embody the deep religious spirit. On the Chapter "The *Bodhisattva Samantabhadra's* vows" of the *Hua Yen sūtra* reads:

> "Again, O noble-minded men, what is meant by making great offerings to the *Buddhas* ? It means that in making such great offerings one should think:
>
> In the smallest dust-motes of all the worlds, in the three periods of time and the ten directions, throughout the entire realm-of-dharma and the realm-of-space, there dwell *Buddhas* equal in number to the smallest dust-motes to be found in all the universes. Each and every *Buddha* is surrounded by an ocean-wide assembly of *bodhisattvas*. Through the power of *Samantabhadra's* vows, and with deep faith and understanding, I see them as though we were face to face. To them all, I offer superb and wondrous oblations, such as clouds of flowers, heavenly music, celestial tapestries, angelic garments, and so many varieties of perfumes....I present them with lighted lamps of various kinds...the wick of each lamp will be as huge as Mount *Sumeru* and the oil as vast as the expanse of the great oceans. To all the

> *Buddhas*, I humbly offer these oblations. O noble-minded men, the crown of all these offerings is the Offering of the *Dharma*, but what does this include ? It includes the offering of following all the *Buddha's* instructions, the offering of benefiting all sentient beings, the offering of embracing and sustaining all sentient beings, the offering of taking upon oneself the sufferings of others, the offering of vigorously fostering the root of merit, the offering of swerving not from the *Bodhisattva's* duty, and the offering of never departing from the Thought-of-Enlightenment.
>
> I will never abandon, but continue to practice, this vast, great, and supreme offering without cessation. My effort will be ended if the realm-of-beings and the realm-of-space are ended, or if the karmas, sorrows, and passion-desires of beings are ended. But since they are endless, so also will be my offerings, thought succeeding thought without interruption, in bodily, vocal, and mental deeds without weariness...."[107]

In the *Lotus*, *Samantabhadra* vowed to enter the realm of birth-and-death so that he could guard and protect those who receive and keep this *sūtra*:

> "O World-Honored One ! In the last five hundred years, in the midst of a muddied, evil age, if there is anyone who receives and keeps this scriptural Canon, I will guard and protect him, keep him from decline and care, enable him to gain tranquillity, and prevent those who seek to get the better of him from doing so, Be it *Māra*, or a son of *Māra*, or a daughter of *Māra*, or a subject of *Māra*, or one possessed by *Māra*, or *yakṣa*, or *rākṣasa*, or *kumbhāṇḍa*, or *piśāca*, or *kṛtya*, or *pūtana*, or *vetāna*, or any other tormentor of men, none shall get the better of him. If that person, whether walking or standing, reads and recites this scripture, at that

> time I, mounted on a white elephant-king with six-tusks, together with a great multitude of *bodhisattvas* will go to that place and, personally revealing my body, make offerings to him, guard and protect him, and comfort his thoughts. Also, if, as an offering to the Scripture of the Dharma Blossom, that person, seated, thinks on this scripture, at that time also I will appear before that person, mounted on a white elephant-king."[108]

Particularly in the *Lotus*, Chapter "The encouragements of the *Bodhisattva* Universally Worthy" is intentionally arranged at the rear part of the *sūtra*. The *Lotus* is a *sūtra* of religious philosophy, in which practice must accompany the theory, a sort of practical philosophy. In the previous chapters the *sūtra* mentions its philosophy, i.e., the One-Vehicle, then in the latter chapters its religion, i.e.. the activities of deliverance by *bodhisattvas*. Among them *Samantabhadra* is the *bodhisattva* whose single concern in his life is to save all sentient beings. And this embodies the deep religious spirit of the *Lotus*.

2. * *Mahāpratibhāna* (Great Joy in Preaching): From chapter 10 backward to chapter 1 of the *Lotus*, all those who raise questions are well-known in history of the religion. But in chapter 11 the questioner, *Mahāpratibhāna*, is a symbolic figure, who addressed to the *Buddha*,

> "O World-Honored One ! From what causes and conditions comes this jeweled *stūpa*, welling up out of the earth and producing from its midst the sound of this voice?"[109]

Chapter 11 is to show *Buddhajñāna*, *Dharmakāya*, which are symbolized by the jeweled *stūpa* in which seated by *Prabhūtaratnabuddha*. The reason why *Prabhūtaratnabuddha* had been *parinirvāña* very long ago, and yet he would come to attend wherever and whenever the *Lotus* is preached. This is an implication. As aforesaid, the purpose of the *Lotus* is to demonstrate the *Buddhajñāna* to living beings, that is, the *Lotus* is identical with *Buddhajñāna*. *Buddhajñāna* as well as *Dharmakāya*, beyond the control of time and space, are likened unto jewels. Jewels give one happiness or pleasure. In this sense there appears the name *Mahāpratibhāna*.

3. * *Śrīgarbha* (Womb of Excellence or Embryo of Good Fortune): This *bodhisattva* is also symbolic. Those who having done benefit to living creatures and having stored much merit would be assured of Buddhahood.

4. * *Prajñākūṭa* (Wisdom Accumulation): This is a *bodhiṣattva* in the retinue of *Buddha Prabhūtaratna*. He is a symbol of the accumulation of knowledge belonging to duality, discrimination. As far as the speculative standpoint of the *Vijñaptimātratā* is concerned, consciousness actualises in dependence on others (*paratantra*). It is of two kinds — (a) false (*parikalpita*), the defiled aspect of *paratantra*, that refers to discrimination (*vikalpa*) divided into the perceiving (*darśanabhāga*) and the perceive (*nimittabhāga*); and (b) the absolute (*painiṣpanna*), i.e., the pure or real aspect of *paratantra* that refers to *Tathatā*, *Advayatā* (Oneness), *Buddhajñāna*. This is the nature of the *Vijñaptimātratā*. And as soon as one enters and abides in it, he realizes the emptiness of the nature of *dharmas* (*dharmaśūnyatā*) and attains enlightenment. Due to his discriminatory consciousness *Prajñākūṭa* is not able to understand the *Saddharma* (Fine Dharma) and *Buddhajñāna*. Therefore, he wants to go back to his original land.

> "At that time, in the nether region there was a *bodhisattva* in the train of Many Jewels the World-Honored One whose name was Wisdom Accumulation (*Prajñākūṭa*). He reported to the *Buddha* Many Jewels that he was about to return to his original land. *Śākyamunibuddha* addressed Wisdom Accumulation,

saying, 'Good man, wait a bit ! There is here a *bodhisattva* named *Mañjuśrī* whom you would do well to meet, for he will preach the Fine *Dharma* to you, and then you may return to your original land.' "[110]

5. * There are four other *bodhisattvas*: *Viśiṣṭacāritra* (Superior Conduct), *Anantacāritra* (Limitless Conduct), *Viśuddhacāritra* (Pure Conduct), and *Supratiṣṭhitacāritra* (Steadfast Conduct). These are four leaders within the multitude of *bodhisattvas* having the same name '*cāritra*' (conduct), appearing in chapter 15 of the *Lotus* which begins the latter half part of this *sūtra*. In the first half part from chapter 1 to chapter 14 the teaching of reason, truth, and wisdom was portrayed. But if the teaching was not applied in practice, in conduct, it would become limping, nonsense. That is why these four kinds of conduct — superior, limitless, pure, and steadfast — appear here as manifestations of the *Buddhajñāna* or the *Lotus*.

6. * *Satatasamitābhiyukta* (Ever Persevering): This *bodhisattva* is another symbol of *Buddha's* attributes. Those who ever-perseveringly accept and keep the *Lotus*, i. e., lead a life with the *Buddhajñāna* within their *pañcaskandha* bodies will make their six senses pure.

> "If any good man or good woman shall accept and keep this Scripture of the Dharma Blossom....,by means of which virutes he shall adorn his six faculties, causing them all to be pure."[111]

7. *Sadāparibhūta* (Never Disparaging) and *Mahāsthāmaprāpta* (Gainer of Great Strength): These two *Bodhisattvas* appear in chapter 20 of the *Lotus* and they are also symbolic figures.

* *Sadāparibhūta*: The conduct of this *bodhisattva* is to inspire the religious faith among the fellow creatures. To whomever he meets in the way, he says: "I dare not hold you

all in contempt. You shall all become *Buddhas* !"[112] The reason why this *bodhisattva* is so doing because everyone has his own *Buddhatā* or *Buddhajñāna*, as said by the *Śākyamunibuddha* that He for one great cause appears in the world because He wishes to cause the beings to hear of the *Buddhajñāna*, to demonstrate the *Buddhajñāna* to the beings, to cause the beings to understand the *Buddhajñāna*, to cause the beings to enter into the path of *Buddhajñāna*.[113] This *Buddhajñāna*, however, is covered by ignorance. So *Sadāparibhūta* helps all the fellow creatures to awake it.

* *Mahāsthāmaprāpta*: Faith causes strength. When one knows that *Buddhajñāna* or Buddhahood is immanent in him, he becomes self-confident. And this inspires strength in himself. That is why the *bodhisattva*, being said to by the *Buddha*, is named 'Gainer of Great Strength.'

8. *Bodhisattvas* to get rid of *skandhas*

As conceived in Buddhism, when the five *skandhas* are combined according to their previous *karma* and present a temporal existence in the form of a living creature, chimerical minds imagine that they have here an individual entity sustained by an immortal self-substratum. As a matter of fact, the material body (*rūpakāya*) alone is not what makes the ego-soul, nor the sensation (*vedanā*), nor the conception (*samjñā*), nor the actions (*sanskāra*), nor the consciousness (*vijñāna*); but only when they are all combined in a certain condition they make a living being. This combination however is not the work of a certain independent entity, which, according to its own will, combines the five *skandhas* in one form and hides itself in it. Buddhism declares that this combination of the constituent elements is achieved by themselves after their *karma*. Individual existences cannot be real by their inherent nature, but they are illusory, and will never remain permanent as such; for they are constantly becoming, and have no selfhood though they may so appear to our particularising senses on account of our subjective ignorance. They are in reality *śūnya* and *anātman*, they are empty and void of *ātman*. The word '*ātman*' is used by the Buddhists not only psychologically in the sense of soul, self, or ego, but also ontologically in the sense of substance or thing-in-itself or thingness (*svabhāva*). *Vasubandhu* in his treatise on the *Yogācāra's* idealistic philosophy declares that the existence of *ātman* and *dharma* is only hypothetical, provisional, apparent, and not in any sense real and ultimate. Indeed, mutual transformation is everywhere observable; there is a constant shifting of forces, an eternal transmigration of the elements, - all of which tend to demonstrate the transitoriness and non-*ātman*-ness of individual existences. The universe is moving like a whirlwind, nothing in it proving to be stationary, nothing in it rigidly adhering to its own form of existence. Mahayanists condemn the wrong view that denies the consubstantiality and reciprocal transformation of all beings, not only because it is scientifically untenable, but mainly because, ethically and religiously considered, it brings about extremely dangerous consequences. It is this view, born of egoism, which, as the Buddhists understand it, incapacitates us to follow the natural flow of sympathy, love towards our suffering fellow-beings diving in the cycle of birth-and-death under the direction of ignorance. It is in this sense, *bodhisattvas* appear.

In the *Lotus*, in the sense of eradicating the *pañcaskandhas*, five chapters are used for this purpose respectively. They are: (a) chapter 23 "The former affairs of the *Bodhisattva* Medicine King," (b) chapter 24 "The *Bodhisattva* Fine Sound," (c) chapter 25 "The gateway to everywhere of the *Bodhisattva* He Who Observes the Sounds of the World," (d) chapter 26 "*Dhāraṇī*," and (e) chapter 27 "The former affairs of the King Fine Adornment." Out of these five chapters, except chapter 26, *Dhāraṇī*, the remaining four chapters speak of *bodhisattvas*.

a) *Bodhisattva* to eliminate *rūpa-skandha* : In chapter 23 mentions three *bodhisattvas*, i.e., *Nakṣatrarājasaṃkusumitābhijña* (Beflowered by the King of Constellations), *Bhaiṣajyarāja* (Medicine King)[114], and *Sarvasattvapriyadarśana* (Seen with Joy by All Living Beings).

* *Nakṣatrarājasaṃkusumitābhijña*: Chapter 23 starts with the questioner named *Nakṣatrarājasaṃkusumitābhijña*. This *bodhisattva* is also a symbolic figure. His name is 'very beautiful'. Why ? Because according to the law of cause-retribution, those who practise the conduct of *bodhisattva* will get a good reward-body, e.g., as illustrated in the case of *Bodhisattva Sarvasattvapriyadarśana* below.

* *Sarvasattvapriyadarśana* : It is this *bodhisattva* who wipes out *rūpaskandha*. At that time, after a strict self-discipline and hearing the *Lotus* from *Buddha Candra-vimala-sūrya-prabhāsa-śrī Bodhisattva Sarva-sattvapriyadarśana* acquired the *Samādhi* of *Sarvarupasandarśana* (display of all forms or all manner of physical bodies), that is, he realizes the nature of *rūpa-skandha,* i. e., the reciprocal transformation of all *dharmas*, or the principle of *pratītyasamutpāda*, which, *Nāgārjuna* calls *sūnya* or emptiness. Then, to express his gratitude and to correspond to the ground-principle of the philosophy of *Mahāyāna* Buddhism 'All is without self (*sarvam anātmam*),' the *Lotus* creates a 'wonderful event' — *Sarvasattvapriyadarśana* offers to the *Buddha Candra-vimala-sūrya-prabhāsa-śrī* by means of burning his own body. A question may arises in us, 'after burning, this *bodhisattva* would disappear ?' — No. He was reborn in the happy realm of that *Buddha*. Isn't it this means that to attain the goal of *nirvana* one must get rid of egoism ? But if a man eliminates egoism and yet clings to the notion of elimination he would not achieve the Buddhahood. That is why the *Lotus*, again,

creates 'another wonderful event' — *Sarvasattvapriyadarsāna* burns his forearms. The story continues: Before entering *nirvāṇa* the *Buddha Candravimalasūryaprabhāsaśrī* entrusted the *Buddha-Dharma* to this *bodhisattva* on the purpose of spreading it. After the *nirvāṇa* of that *Buddha*, this *bodhisattva* made an offering to his relics by burning his forearms. But by doing so, his body becomes the *Buddha's* gold-colored body ! This is an implication of the *Lotus*.

> "At that time, the *Bodhisattva* Seen with Joy by All Living Beings in the midst of the great multitude took this oath, saying, 'I have thrown away both arms. May I now without fail gain the *Buddha's* gold-colored body! If this oath is reality and not vanity, then may both arms be restored as before !' When he had taken this oath, they were restored of themselves, and achievement due to the purity of this *bodhisattva's* merit and wisdom."[115]

Thus, to achieve the goal of *nirvāṇa* one must reject not only egoism but also the notion of the rejection, as said by *Nāgārjuna* 'emptiness of emptiness.' *Sūnyatā* is not an end in itself. It is a means to lead the mind up to *prajñā*, and should not be thought of as an end in itself. *Nāgārjuna* says:

"Śūnyatā sarvadrṣṭīnām proktā nihsaraṇam jinaih

Yeśām tu śūnyatā drṣṭistan asādhyān babhāṣireh"

(M.K. 13, 8)

> (*Śūnyatā* was declared by the Buddha for dispensing with all views or 'isms'. Those who convert *Śūnyatā* itself into another 'ism' are verily beyond hope or help).

It is the non-*ātman*, altruistic spirit that gives one joy, happiness. This is the sense of *Sarvasattvapriyadarśana*.

b) * *Gadgadasvara* (Fine Sound): This *bodhisattva* in chapter 24 is used to eliminate *vedanā-skandha*. According to the principle of twelve *nidānas*, six sense organs when keeping in touch with their objects, i.e., sight, sound, smell, taste, touch, and idea, produce sensations or feelings. And among these six objects both 'beautiful sight' and 'fine sound' seduce the living beings most and bring about the pain to them. That is why this chapter makes use of the images of 'jeweled bowl' and 'divine music' for illustration. As reported in chapter 24 of the *Lotus*, after being touched by the light emitted from the *Śākyamunibuddha's* knot of flesh and white tuft between his brows, *Gadgadasvara* in the realm of 'Adorned with All Pure Light' was about to come the *Sahā* world for worshipping, making offerings to *Śākyamunibuddha*, *Prabhūtaratnabuddha* and hearing the *Lotus*. But the coming place is ugly, inferior. Thus *Gadgadasvara* possessing of beautiful face and gold-colored body is advised not to arrive there with the discriminative mind, i.e., praise and blame.[116] If doing so, the feelings of pleasure and displeasure will arise. But the thing is how to make the feelings calm, indiscriminative eternally, without the duality of pleasure and displeasure. One must realize that feelings are not real because their existence is dependent on touch. In other words the genuine nature of feelings are void under the *painiṣpanna* knowledge (Absolute consciousness without duality) or *Buddhajñāna*. That is why *Gadgadasvara* meets *Śākyamunibuddha*, *Prabhūtaratnabuddha* and dwells in the *samādhi* of 'manifestation of the body of all forms,' where the genuine nature of things is revealed. Feelings are not real, so pleasure and displeasure are not real either. Feeling aggregate thus can be wiped out. Furthermore, out of six sense organs, ear is the most quick-witted and permanent, for whenever walking, standing, lying, sitting, awake or asleep one's ear can hear sound. Consequently, *Gadgadasvara* (Fine Sound) is also present in the *Lotus*.

C. *Bodhisattva* to eliminate *samjñā-skandha*: In chapter 25 of the *Lotus* appear three *bodhisattvas*, namely, *Akṣayamati* (Inexhaustible Mind), *Avalokiteśvara* (He Who Observes the Sounds of the World), and *Dharaṇiṃdhara* (Earth Holder). Out of these three, *Avalokiteśvara* is used to eliminate *samjñā-skandha*.

* *Akṣayamati*: The questioner in chapter 25 of the *Lotus* is *Akṣayamati*. *Akṣayamati* means endless, uninterrupted ideas or inexhaustible mind. Why does this *bodhisattva* have so much ideas ? This is also an implication. As aforesaid, this chapter is to eliminate *samjñā-skandha*. Man's mind is constantly thinking, worrrying about something, never rest and is likened to ape's mind or horse's ideas. But if he calls upon the name of *Avalokiteśvara*, all the ideas or fear will be stopped and all sufferings end. Why ? because fear or suffering is produced from thinking, imagination. The more he imagines the more he fears, the more he fears the more he suffers. And the fact that *Avalokiteśvara* comes to deliver living beings from pain means that he makes them fearless.

> "Good man, if incalculable hundreds of thousands of myriads of millions of living beings, suffering pain and torment, hear of this *Bodhisattva* He Who Observes the Sounds of the World and single-mindedly call upon his name, the *Bodhisattva* He Who Observes the Sounds of the World shall straightway heed their voices, and all shall gain deliverance."[117]

> "Good men, do not let terror take possession of you ! You all must single-mindedly call upon the name of the *Bodhisattva* He Who Observes the Sounds of the World. For that *bodhisattva* can confer fealessness upon living beings. If you all call upon his name, then from these malicious bandits you shall contrive to be delivered."[118]

* *Avalokiteśvara*: In his (or her) various forms *Avalokiteśvara* is perhaps the most popular of all *Mahāyāna bodhisattvas* and is glorified in chapter 25 of the *Lotus*. Particularly, this chapter frequently circulated as a separated *sūtra* in its own right. It describes how *Avalokiteśvara* will straightway heed those who call upon him, and save them from various kinds of sufferings — fire, rivers, storms on the ocean, murderers, demons and ghosts, prison (whether one be guilty or innocent), and also robbers. He will moreover remove lust, anger, and stupidity. He will grant sons or daughters to those who request him. *Avalokiteśvara* also appears in manifold different forms, whichever are most suitable for aiding, converting, and saving living beings. If a *Buddha* form is suitable, then he appears as a *Buddha*; if a *śrāvaka* form, as a *śrāvaka*; if a god, then as a god, etc. *Avalokiteśvara*, the 'Lord who looks down,' i.e., who looks down with infinite pity on all beings, appears as the typical *bodhisattva*, who refuses to assume Buddhahood until all beings are redeemed. *Avalokiteśvara's* one and only one task is to bring the doctrine of deliverance to all living beings, to help all sufferers, to save them from every distress, and to exercise infinite pity that does not even shrink from sin, and does not stop at the gates of hell. He is the most wonderful compassionate saviour of the universe, constantly and tirelessly acting with all the powers of a tenth-level *bodhisattva* for the benefit of all living beings whithout discrimination. As such, *Avalokiteśvara* is said to be the veritable incarnation of the compassion, essence, and very reason of all the *Buddhas* towards beings.

However, it is mistaken if we base only upon the word-for-word meaning of the passages mentioned above or the like. For example,

> "If there is one who keeps the name of this *Bodhisattva* He Who Observes the Sounds of the World, even if he

> should fall into a great fire, the fire would be unable to burn him, thanks to the imposing supernatural power of this *bodhisattva.*"[119]

Is it true ? Or in the next paragraph,

> "If he should be carried off by a great river and call upon this *bodhisattva's* name, then straightway he would find a shallow place."

Literally, such opportunities are hard to happen. However, one can understand the implications in another way. In the *Śūraṅgama-sūtra*, the *Buddha* said that *Bodhisattva Avalokiteśvara* practised the method of 'turning back to hear his inner auditory nature'. Auditory nature is real, which has no forms or marks and is identical with *Dharmakāya*. A Chinese poem puts the true nature of *Avalokiteśvara* as follows:

> "The *Dharma*-body of *Kuan-yin*[120]
>
> Is neither male nor female[121]
>
> Even the body is not a body,
>
> What attributes can there be ?...
>
> Let it be known to all Buddhists:
>
> Do not cling to form.
>
> The *Bodhisattva* is you:
>
> Not the picture or the image"[122]

So, how can the fire or water burn or submerge the things which have no forms or attributes ? In this sense, the deliverance from calling upon *Avalokiteśvara* has been established.

Again, the next paragraph puts it:

> "If a hundred thousand myriads of millions of living beings enter the great sea in quest of gold, silver...., even if a black wind blows their ship away, carrying it

> off and plunging it into the realm of the *rākṣasa*—ghosts, if there is among them but one man who calls upon the name of the *Bodhisattva* He Who Observes the Sounds of the World, these men shall be delivered from the troubles [caused by] the *rākṣasas*. It is for this reason that he is called Observer of the Sounds of the World."

Why so ? Because, here, the black wind and realm of the *rākṣasa*—ghosts are symbols of man' anger which create bad *karmas* and hence suffering. Yet *Avalokiteśvara* is symbolic of compassion. And when compassion arises, anger disappears.

Again, as aforesaid, suffering is caused by fear, and fear by imagination, wrong ideas. *Avalokiteśvara* delivers living beings from pain by making them fearless. For this reason he is named *Abhayandada* (i.e. Giver of Fearlessness). This *bodhisattva* is not only the incarnation of *Buddha's* compassion but alśo of *Buddhajñāna*. And, calling upon the name of *Avalokiteśvara* is to return back to *Buddhajñāna* or the so-called *Painiṣpanna* (perfect knowledge), by which, according to the *Vijñaptimātratā* school, we are able to realise the nature of reality as it is, i.e., the emptiness of all things (*dharma-śūnyatā*). This perfect knowledge is identical with Suchness or Ultimate Reality (*chen-ru*) which is beyond conceptions and wrong ideas that are the causes of fear and insecurity. In this sense, the calling upon *Avalokiteśvara* brings about security.

Chapter 25 of the *Lotus* teaches us how to rule out *samjñāskandha*. When entering into the path of *Buddhajñāna*, one eradicates *samjñāskandha*, ends sufferings, and is possessed of the supernatural powers of self-mastery in this suffering world. Consequently, *Akṣayamati* (Inexhaustible Mind) advised the living beings to be mindful and to bow down their heads before *Avalokiteśvara* for the deliverance.

"Therefore one must ever be mindful of them.
From moment to moment conceive no doubts,
For the pure saint Who Observes the Sounds of the World
In the discomforts of pain, agony, and death
Can be a point of reliance.
Fully endowed with all the merits,
His benevolent eye beholding the beings,
He is happiness accumulated, a sea incalculable.
For this reason one must bow one's head to him."[123]

* *Dharaṇiṃdhara* (Earth Holder): He is a *bodhisattva* in charge of the earth, i.e., the *Sahā* world. We have not heard the name of this *bodhisattva* before. Now he suddenly appears, saying,

> "O World-Honored One ! If there is a living being who shall hear this Chapter of the *Bodhisattva* He Who Observes the Sounds of the World, the deeds of self-mastery, the manifestation of the gateway to everywhere, the powers of supernatural penetration, be it known that that person's merit shall not be slight."[124]

He means that those who practise the method of 'turning back to hear one's inner auditory nature,' i.e., 'without discriminating and clinging to the outside sounds' will get the pure mind, brilliant wisdom, which is fraught with merit; hence wonders arise. This is the universal method of cultivation in this *Saha* world. So it is called the Gateway to Everywhere,' which is another title of chapter 25, 'When the *Buddha* preached this Chapter of the Gateway to Everywhere.'[125]

9.* *Bodhisattva Pradānasūtra* (Brave Donor): As above-mentioned, chapter 26 of the *Lotus*, ***Dharani***, is used to eradicate *sanskāra-skandha*. *Sanskāra-skandha* is an activity of mind, which is very fine and not as easily visible as *samjñā-*

skandha. So it must use *dhāraṇī* to rule it out. *Dhāraṇīs* are mystical words, which, when hearing or reading we are not able to understand their meanings, but only experience them. Whilst reciting *dhāraṇī*, one's mind becomes awake, thanks to the *Buddhas'* help,

> "This *dhāraṇī*, this supernatural charm, has been pronounced by *Buddhas* equal in number to the sands of sixty-two millions of Ganges rivers."[126]

Hence *dhāraṇī* can destroy the fine quietness of *sanskāra-skandha*. As usual, when eradicating *samjñā-skandha*, without remaining illusions, the vulgar aspirants (*śrāvakas*) thought that their minds were pure and that was *nirvana* as the *Laṅkāvatāra-sūtra* puts it:

> "*Mahāmati*, at the eighth stage the *Bodhisattva-Mahāsattva*, *Śrāvakas*, and *Pratyekabuddhas* cease cherishing discriminative ideas that arise from the *Citta*, *Manas*, and *Manovijñāna*. From the first stage up to the sixth, they perceive that the triple world is no more than the *Citta*, *Manas*, and *Manovijñāna*, that as it is born of a discriminating mind there is no ego-soul and what belongs to it, and that there is no falling into the multitudinousness of external objects except through [the discrimination of] the Mind itself. The ignorant turning their self-knowledge (*svajñāna*) towards the dualism of grasped and grasping fail to understand, for there is the working of habit-energy which has been accumulating since beginningless time owing to false reasoning and discrimination.
>
> *Mahāmati*, at the eight stage there is *Nirvāṇa* for the *Śrāvakas* and *Pratyekabuddhas* and *Bodhisattvas*; but the *Bodhisattvas* are kept away by the power of all the *Buddhas* from [being intoxicated by] the bliss of the *Samādhi*, and thereby they will not enter into *Nirvāṇa*."[127]

The Chinese *Ch'an* school also compares this state of mind with the eighth out of ten paintings of 'grazing cow,'[128] in which there are no more herdsman and cow. The school calls it "the end of a stick one-hundred-'*truong*'[129] high," over which those who can jump are called heros. The aspirants are usually stuck in this eighth state of mind and they do not know how to proceed. Therefore it must need the supernatural powers of the *Buddhas* to cross over.

So, to cross over the *sanskāra-skandha* or the eighth out of ten *bhūmis* of *bodhisattvas* or the eighth step out of ten paintings of 'grazing-cow' of *Ch'an* school it must take recourse to the external power, *dhāraṇī* of the *Buddhas*. Therefore in the *Lotus* not any *bodhisattva* is assigned to eradicate *sanskāra-skandha*. Instead, there must be a brave spirit to cross over it. That is why *Bodhisattva Pradānasūtra* (Brave Donor) appears in this chapter 26.

10. *Bodhisattvas Padmaśrī* (floral Excellence), *Vairocanaraśmipratimaṇḍi-tarāja* (Marks of Adornment), *Bhaiṣajyarāja* (Medicine King), and *Bhaiṣajyarāja-samudgata* (Above Medicine): These four *bodhisattvas* appear in chapter 27 of the *Lotus*, of which the important point is to destroy or rather to transform the *vijñāna-skandha*. The doctrine of this chapter coincides with that of the *Vijñaptimātratā* school.

In this chapter 27 appear four figures who are representatives of eight consciousnesses of the doctrine of *Vijñaptimātratā* school.[130] They are: a king named *Śubhavyūha* (Fine Adornment), the king's lady named *Vimaladattā* (Pure Virtue), and the two princes named *Vimalagarbha* (Pure Womb) and *Vimalanetra* (Pure Eye). They are representatives of *ālayavijñāna* (the eighth consciousness)[131], *manas* (the seventh consciousness),[132] *manovijñāna* (the sixth consciousness), and *cakṣurvijñāna* (visual consciouness, typical for the first five consciousnesses in relation to the five sense-organs, i.e., eye, ear, nose, tongue, and body) respectively.[133]

The doctrine of *Vijñaptimātratā* (*Wei-shih*) as presented in the *WSSSLS* and the *CWSL*, may thus be summarised. There is definitetly no real *ātman* or *dharma* apart from the three categories of consciousness that is capable of evolution and manifestation, i.e., the *ālayavijñāna*, *manas*, and the six consciousnesses. Each of these eight consciousnesses is the basis for a twofold manifestarion, the perceived division (*nimittabhāga*) and the perceiving division (*darśanabhāga*). *Ātman* and *dharmas* are merely conventional designations of this double manifestation of consciousness, the *nimittabhāga* and the *darśanabhāga*, and there are no real external world or entities apart from these two divisions. As a result, 'all is Mere-consciousness' or 'nothing exists but consciousness', The *WSSSLS* and the *CWSL* illustrate the various developments of consciousnesses, their special characteristics and mutual relations to enable people to realize the emptiness of all things (*dharmaśūnyatā*) and the Ultimate Truth in the path of spiritual practices. In this way, the Masters (*Dharmapāla,* etc.) avoid the two extremes of either adding something to consciousness or reducing consciousness to nothing. The doctrine of the *Vijñaptimātratā* is therefore established to conform the Middle Way. According to the *Vijñaptimātratā*, the reason why all sentient beings suffer is due to the two false beliefs: belief in the real existence of self (*ātman*) and things (*dharmas*). And the understanding of *Vijñaptimātratā* will destroy these beliefs by demonstrating that both 'self' and 'things' are unreal.

As conceived by the *Vijñaptimātratā*, the *ālayavijñāna* is not a universal, but an individual mind or soul, in which the 'seeds' of all things exist in their ideality. And this human or individual mind should be regarded as an individuation of the *Tathāgatagarbha*, the universal or cosmic *Garbha*, in which the essence of Tathāgatahood is intact, and from which issues forth the multitudinousness of things, mental as well as physical.

As above said, this chapter 27 is purported to destroy or transform the *vijñānaskandha*, the last out of the *pañcaskandha*. According to the *Vijñaptimātratā*, this *Vijñānaskandha* is not just six kinds of consciousnesses produced by the objects and six sense-organs. *Kliṣṭa-manovijñāna* the seventh consciousness, but *ālayavijñāna* also, which is the cause and contains the seeds of all the *dharmas*,

> "The first is the strorehouse-consciousness (*ālayavijñāna*) which is also called retributive consciousness (*vipākavijñāna*) and consciousness carrying all seeds (*srvabījaka*)."[134]

This *ālayavijñāna* from the beginningless time flows like a stream and 'ends at the stage of *Arhat*ship' as says *Vasubandhu*. The *āryas* or the saints of three vehicles are called the *Arhats* from the moment of *Vajropamasamādhi*, when they have completely cut off the obstacle (*āvaraṇa*) of the *kleśas*. Because at that moment the gross and heavy *kleśas* are completely dissociated, it is said that the *ālayavijñāna* is arrested.[135] And at the moment of *Vajropamasamādhi*, in the absence of all consciousness bearing *bījas*, the *Arhats* enter *nirvāṇa*—without-residue (*nirupadhiśesanirvāṇadhātu*).[136] It is a pure *dhātu* unimaginable, good and eternal. It is a state of bliss, an 'emancipated body', called the famous law of the great sage (*Śākyamuni*).[137] It is blissful because it is the cessation of all ideas.This is the fifth or final stage which is that of the attainment of the final realization (*bodhi*). This means abiding in the *Anuttarasamyaksaṃbodhi* (supreme enlightenment). Getting out of the veils, the aspirant attains complete enlightenment and is capable of striving for transformation of all sentient beings until the end.

As far as the self-discipline is concerned, the aspirant makes use of his *manovijñāna* (mind consciousness) to understand the *Buddha's* teachings, then transforms his first five consciousnesses from distinction[138] into purity, i.e., the cessation of all ideas of egoness. By virtue of the purity of the six consciousnesses, the *kliṣṭa-mano-vijñāna* becomes pure and *ālayavijñāna* is converted to *Tathāgatagarbha*. For this reason, in this chapter 27 of the *Lotus*, the two princes, *Vimalagarbha* (Pure Womb) and *Vimalanetra* (Pure Eye), after a long practice in the Path trodden by *bodhisattvas*, attained their pure *samādhi* and advised king *Śubhavyūha* (Fine Adornment) and lady *Vimaladattā* (Pure Virtue) to leave the household and follow the *Buddha* Path. These two princes who guide the king and the lady to follow the Path ought to be predicted Buddhahood first, but, on the contrary, the *Buddha* predicted this for the king but not for the two princes. So, this clarifies that *ālayavijñāna*, which changes from illusion to enlightenment and defilement to purity, is the main cause, not the remaining seven consciousnesses, to become *Buddha*. This also clarifies that *ālayavijñāna* is directed by the enlightenment of the six conciousnesses through the praise of the *Buddha* and of the king towards the two princes respectively,

> "O great king ! Do you see these two boys, or do you not ? These two boys have already made offerings to *Buddhas* equal in number to the sands of sixty-five hundred thousand myriads of millions of *nayutas* of Ganges rivers, approaching them with familiarity, doing them humble reverence, before the *Buddhas* receiving and keeping the Scripture of the *Dharma* Blossom, taking compassionate thought for the beings with their crooked views and enabling them to dwell in right view,"[139]

> "These two sons are my good friends. It is because they wished to raise up my wholesome roots of former ages, to confer benefit upon me, that they came to be born in my house."[140]

In chapter 27 the *Buddha* relates a story of the past times to know the present situation. He says that the king of the past times is now *Bodhisattva Padmaśrī* (floral Excellence), the lady now *Bodhisattva Vairocanaraśmipratimaṇḍjtarāja* (Marks of Adornment), the two princes now *Bodhisattvas Bhaiṣajyarāja* (Medicine King) and *Bhaiṣajyarājasamudgata* (Above Medicine). And among these the two *Bodhisattvas Bhaiṣajyarāja* and *Bhaiṣajyarājasamudgata* are worth of notice. Why ? Because the illusions of sentient beings originated from the six consciousnesses are eradicated by these two *bodhisattvas*. Hence their merits are very great as the *Buddha* says,

> "When these *bodhisattvas*, Medicine King and Above Medicine, shall have achieved such great merits as these,.......If any man know the names of these two *bodhisattvas*, then the gods and men of all the worlds must do obeisance to him also."[141]

So, the four *bodhisattvas*, namely, *Padmaśrī*, *Vairocanarśmi-prati-maṇḍitarāja*, *Bhaiṣajyarāja* and *Bhaiṣajya-rājasamudgata* in chapter 27 of the *Lotus* are personified from the eight consciousnesses of the *Vijñaptimātratā* school in order to destroy or transform the *vijñānaskandha*.

In this Chapter V— *Bodhisattva*, *Buddhahood* and *Dhāraṇī* — one can summarize the mutual relation of these three concepts and doctrines as follows:

Bodhisattva is considered as the best candidate to attain the Ultimate Reality, which is identical with Buddhahood or *Nirvāṇa*, and he must have recourse to the *dhāraṇīs* of the *Buddhas*. However, the *bodhisattva* delays this goal and eradicates the ego or *pañcaskandha* in order to accomplish his vows of delivering all living beings from suffering.

Besides, through the analysis of these three concepts and doctrines one can recognise that the *Lotus* makes use of many symbols and personifications of the *Buddha's* attributes or the doctrines of other Buddhist philosophical schools.

References

1. *Majjhima,* i, (*Cūlasaccakasuttaṃ*)
2. *Yo pi so bhikkhave bhikkhu arahay.*
3. *Tathāgato pi bhikkhave arahaṃ.*
4. *Majjhima,* i, (*Cūlahatthipadopamasutta*).
5. *Vinaya,* i, trans. T.W.Rhys Davids and H. Oldenberg, Delhi. 1996. p. 94.
6. *Yo pi so bhikkhave bhikkhu arahay khīṇāsavo.*
7. *Majjhima,* I, (*Vatthūpamasuttaṃ*).
8. Viṇaya, I. 21 *"Caratha bhikkhave cārikaṃ bahu-jana-hitāya bahu-jana-sukhāya lokānukampāya atthāya hitāya sukhāya deva manussānaṃ"*
9. *Caraṃ ce nādhigacchyeyya*

   Seyyaṃ sadisam attano

   Ekacariyaṃ daḷham kayirā

   natthi bāle sahāyatā. (*Dhammapada*, *Balavagga*)
10. *Dūraṅgamaṃ ekacaraṃ*

    asarīraṃ guhāsayaṃ. (*Dhammapada*, *Cittavagga*)
11. *naparay itthattāyati abbhaññāsi.*
12. cf. *Puggala-paññatti,* p. 14.
13. See *The Lankavatara Sutra*, trans. D.T. Suzuki, Boulder, 1978, pp. 86-87.
14. *Scripture of the Lotus Blossom of the Fine Dharma*, tr. Leon Hurvitz, NY, 1976, p. 89.
15. *Śrāvaka-bodhiṃ pratyeka-bodhiṃ....mahā-bodhiṃ.*
16. *Pr. Pā Śata.* (p. 1373, lines 1-6)

17. *Pr. Pā Śata.* (p. 964, lines 19-20)
18. "*Trīṇi yānani śrāvaka-yānaṃ pratyeka-buddha-yānaṃ mahā-yānaṃ Ca*" (Dh.S. II). "*Yāna Kramaḥ... mahāyānaṃ pratyeka-buddha-yānaṃ śrāvaka-yānaṃ hīna-yānaṃ*" (M. Vy. LIX. p. 95).
19. *The Saddharma-pundarika,* tr. H. Kern, Delhi, 1994, p. 18.
20. *Scripture of the Lotus Blossom of the Fine Dharma,* Op.cit., p. 167.
21. *The Lankavatara Sutra*, tr. D.T.Suzuki, Colorado, 1978, pp. 182-3.
22. *The Large Sutra on Perfect Wisdom*, tr. E.Conze, Delhi, 1990, p. 124.
23. *The Lankavatara Sutra*, Op.cit., pp. 52-3.
24. *The Large Sutra on Perfect Wisdom*, Op.cit., pp. 456-7.
25. *Scripture of the Lotus Blossom of the Fine Dharma*, Op.cit., pp. 12-3.
26. Ibid., p. 280.
27. Ibid., p. 63.
28. Skt. Dicy., Monier Williams, p. 685b.
29. Ibid., p. 688.
30. *Mādhyamika Śāstra*, Buddhist Text Society edition, pp. 180-181.
31. *Scripture of the Lotus Blossom of the Fine Dharma*, Op.cit., p.13.
32. Ibid., p. 30.
33. Shoko Watanabe, *Saddharmapuṇḍarīka Manuscripts Found in Gilgit*, Tokyo, 1975, 21.
34. *Scripture of the Lotus Blossom of the Fine Dharma*, Op.cit., p. 25.
35. Ibid., p. 22.
36. Ibid., p. 10.

37. Ibid., p. 130.
38. Ibid., p. 134.
39. Ibid., p. 167.
40. *Prajñāpāramitā*, (trans.) Walleser, M., Die Vollkommenheit der Erkenntnis. Guttingen, 1914, p. 99.
41. Suzuki, D. T., *Studies in the Lankavatara Sutra*, London, 1930. Repr. 1957.
42. *Scripture of the Lotus Blossom of the Fine Dharma*, Op.cit., p. 12.
43. *A Sanskrit-English Dictionary*, M. Monier-Williams, Delhi, 1990, p. 433.
44. Ibid., p. 93.
45. Ibid., p. 1181.
46. Ibid., p. 964.
47. Ibid., p. 1222.
48. Ibid., p. 907.
49. Ibid., p. 33.
50. Ibid., p. 637.
51. *Scripture of the Lotus Blossom of the Fine Dharma*, Op.cit., pp. 196-197.
52. *A Dictionary of Chines Buddhist Terms*, W.E. Soothill & L. Hodous, Delhi, 1987, p. 51.
53. *Pr. Pā. Śata.*, pp. 1448-9.
54. *Pali-English Dictionary*, T.W.Rhys Davids & W.Stede, Delhi. 1993, p. 113.
55. *A Sanskrit-English Dictionary*, Op.cit., p. 156.
56. *A Dictionary of Chinese Buddhist Terms*, Op.cit., p. 45.
57. *Scripture of the Lotus Blossom of the Fine Dharma*, Op.cit., p. 42.
58. Ibid., p. 180.
59. Ibid., p. 61.

60. Ibid., p. 189.

61. Ibid., p. 120.

62. *Mahāvastu*, tr. Jones, 1949-56: I, 96ff.

63. *Scripture of the Lotus Blossom of the Fine Dharma*, Op.cit., p. 120.

64. A kalpa during which a human lifetime increases from ten years to 80,000 years and then decreases back to ten. At the end of the first century the increse is to 11 years; at the end of the second century to 12 years, and so on till a lifetime lasts 80,000 years; then decrease follows in the same ratio till 10 is reached. The whole period of accretion and declension covers a small kalpa, i.e. 16,800,000 years. (*A Dictionary of Chinese Buddhist Terms,* Op.cit., p. 5)

65. *Scripture of the Lotus Blossom of the Fine Dharma*, Op.cit., p. 125.

66. Ibid., p. 128.

67. A *koṭi* is million.

68. *The Saddharma-pundarika*, Op.cit., p. 307.

69. *Scripture of the Lotus Blossom of the Fine Dharma*, Op.cit., p. 188.

70. Ibid., p. 4.

71. Ibid., p. 12.

72. "Those who had formerly been voice-hearers were in mid-air preaching the conduct of the voice-hearer. But now all were putting into practice the Great Vehicle's doctrine of emptiness" (*Scripture of the Lotus Blossom of the Fine Dharma,* tr. Leon Hurvitz, , NY, 1976. p. 198).

73. *Scripture of the Lotus Blossom of the Fine Dharma*, Op.cit., pp. 187-188.

74. In Chapter I, I, A, 4.

75. *The Lankavatara Sutra*, trans. D.T. Suzuki. Boulder, 1978. p. 186.

76. *Majjhima*, i, 17.
77. *Kathā-vatthu*, xxiii, 3, p. 623; iv, 7, 8, pp. 283-90.
78. *The Large Sutra on Perfect Wisdom*, tr. Edward Conze, Delhi, 1990, p. 102.
79. *Scripture of the Lotus Blossom of the Fine Dharma*, Op.cit., p. 179.
80. Ibid., p. 311.
81. Ibid., p. 314.
82. *Ava.Śa*, i, 3.7. *Lal, V.*, 438.6.
83. *Scripture of the Lotus Blossom of the Fine Dharma*, Op. cit., p.4.
84. Ibid., p. 14.
85. Ibid., p. 15.
86. Ibid., p. 15.
87. Ibid., p. 184.
88. Ibid., p. 198.
89. Ibid., pp. 226-227.
90. Ibid., p. 264.
91. Ibid., p. 279.
92. Ibid., p. 280.
93. Ibid., p. 293.
94. Ibid., p. 294.
95. Ibid., p. 303.
96. Ibid., p. 311.
97. Ibid., p. 311.
98. Ibid., p. 319.
99. Ibid., p. 321.
100. Ibid., p. 330.
101. Ibid., p. 330.

102. Ibid., p. 332.
103. Ibid., pp. 4-5.
104. Ibid., p. 15.
105. *Scripture of the Lotus Blossom of the Fine Dharma*, Op.cit., p. 12.
106. Ibid., pp. 15-16.
107. *The Buddhist Teaching of Totality, The Philosohy of Hwa Yen Buddhism*, Garma C.C.Chang, Delhi, 1992, pp. 187-8.
108. *Scripture of the Lotus Blossom of the Fine Dharma*, Op.cit., p. 333.
109. Ibid., p. 184.
110. Ibid., p. 198.
110. Ibid., p. 264.
112. Ibid., p. 281.
113. See. Ibid., p. 30.
114. This bodhisattva will be analysed after.
115. *Scripture of the Lotus Blossom of the Fine Dharma*, Op.cit., pp. 297-298.
116. See, Ibid., p. 304.
117. Ibid., p. 311.
118. Ibid., p. 312.
119. Ibid., p. 311.
120. The Chinese name of *Avalokiteśvara*.
121. In East Asia, *Avalokiteśvara* has changed sex! It is not clear why or how early this happened.
122. Tay, C. N. (1976) 'Kuan-yin: the cult of half Asia'. *History of Religions* 16 (2): 173.
123. *Scripture of the Lotus Blossom of the Fine Dharma*, Op.cit., p. 319.
124. Ibid.

125. Ibid.

126. Ibid., p. 321.

127. *The Lankavatara Sutra*, Op.cit., p. 183.

128. Ten paintings of 'grazing cow' are mentioned in the endnote 38 of chapter 2 of this thesis.

129. A unit of measure equals with ten-feet.

130. According to this doctrine, there is only consciousness. But because the ideas of the self (*ātman*, *Wo*) and the elements (*dharma*, *Fa*) are false, the phenomenal appearances of all kinds arise. These appearances are dependent upon the development (*pariṇāma*, *pien*) of the consciousness. This development is of three kinds: The maturing consciousness (*vipāka*), the consciousness that deliberates (*manana*), and the consciousness that discriminates (*vijñapti*) the spheres of objects. (*WSSSLS* 60a 25).

131. This consciousness corresponds to *vipāka*. It is in perpetual evolution like a violent current, and is renounced in the state of an arhat. (*WSSSLS* 60b7-8).

132. This consciousness corresponds to *manana*. It functions with storehouse-consciousness as its support and object. It has essentially the characteristics of 'cognition'. (*WSSSLS* 60b9-11). It is named *manas* because it is capable of cogitating and reflecting on its object. When it has not yet been revolutionalized, it cogitates upon the supposed *ātman*. After revolution, it meditates upon *nairātmya*. (*CWSL* 22á9-23). It ceases to exist at the stage of *arhat*, in the meditation of annihinlation and on the supramundane path. (*WSSSLS* 60b14-15).

133. *Manovijñāna* and the first five consciousnesses are the six consciousnesses which correspond to the third development of consciousness, *vijñapti*, which has six different categories. Perception of the object is the nature and characteristics of these six consciousnesses. The six categories of consciousnesses are classified in relation to the six sense-organ (*indriyas*) and their respective spheres of objects

(*viṣaya*). They are named as the visual consciousness (*cakṣurvijñāna*) and so on down to the sense-centre consciousness (*manovijñāna*). The six consciousnesses manifest themselves depending on the *manas*, but only the sixth consciousness receives the name of *manovijñāna*, because it is named in accordance with its special point of support, i.e. the seventh consciousness or *manas*, which is not of the same character as the first five consciousnesses. Like this, the first five consciousnesses, in spite of depending on *manas* for support, are named after their special points of support, i.e. the eye etc.

134. *WSSSLS* 60b1-4.

135. See *CWSL* 13a 19-22.

136. Ibid., 13c3-7.

137. *WSSSLS* 61b20-24.

138. They are called six consciousnesses, i.e., *manovijñāna* and the first five consciousnesses, because they distinguish (*paricchid*) the six spheres of the object (*CWSL* 26b3-6). Depending on the root consciousness (*ālayavijñāna*) the five consciousnesses originate in accordance with various conditions, sometimes together, sometimes separately, just as waves originate on water (*WSSSLS* 60c3-6). But the thought consciousness (*manovijñāna*) manifests at all times, except for those who are born in the 'heaven without thought', for those in the two mindless meditations, and for those who are born in the states of unconsciousness (*WSSSLS* 60c7-8).

139. *Scripture of the Lotus Blossom of the Fine Dharma*, Op.cit., p. 330.

140. Ibid., p. 329.

141. Ibid., pp. 330-331.

of waking. They are sometimes ... dreamless ... and ... the ... consciousness ... only ... dependent on the ... body ... with consciousness ... because it is named in accordance with its special point of support ... the ... the same name as the first two ... Like the ... first two consciousness ... dependent on ... for support ... point of support, i.e. the ...

134. MSS ... 3.103.

135. See ... 13 ... 72.

136. Ibid., 13.

137. MSS ... 1.65.

138. The ... called ... the ... first ... consciousness ... Depending on the ... consciousness ... called ... conditions, sometimes ... as takes on ... consciousness ... for those who ... states in the two middle ... them ... scales of ...

139. ... of the Lotus ... p. ... 140.

140. Ibid., p. 329.

141. Ibid., pp. 340–341.

Notes

Chapter VI

Conclusion

It has been the writer's intention in the preceding chapters to throw some light on the following question: What and how is the kind of philosophy that the *Lotus* hides behind its highly symbolic expressions and fully dramatic style, and from which it calls itself the king of all *sūtras*'?

The writer has tried his best to demonstrate that the *Lotus* hides a practical philosophy of Mahāyānism, which advocates knowledge (*prajñā*) and the practice (*sīla* and *karuṇā*) of the Ultimate Reality that the two great Indian Buddhist philosophical schools, *Mādhyamika* and *Yogācāra* call *Paramārtha-satya* and *Pariniṣpanna* respectively. Also, it advocates *Nirvāṇa* and the way to realise it. The *Mahāyāna* philosophy can be mainly analysed into such concepts and doctrines as *Ekayāna*, *Upāya-kauśalya*, *Bodhisattvas*, *Buddhahood* and *Dhāraṇī*.

Chapters I and II of this book, *Introduction* and *The Lotus in Brief,* are given to provide a necessary background for the comprehension of such a philosophical system.

Gotra, the underlying principle as well as the foundation of Mahāyānism, is termed by the *Lotus* as *Ekayāna*, which is identical with *Paramārtha-satya*, *Madhyamā Pratipad*, *Nirvāṇa* and *Buddhajñāna*, etc. Noticeably, it is because of one great cause alone, according to this *sūtra*, the *Buddha* appears on earth, that is, he wishes to help living beings awaken their own immanent *Buddhajñāna*.

To reach *Paramārtha-satya* or the goal of *Nirvāṇa*, however, according to *Nāgārjuna*, *Samvṛti-satya* or pragmatic reality, provisional truth is very necessary. It is the means (*upāya*) for reaching Reality which is the goal (*upeya*). He expressly mentions the importance of *vyavahāra* or empirical reality in attaining *Paramārtha* or Absolute Reality "Without a recourse to pragmatic reality, the absolute cannot be taught. Without knowing the absolute truth, *nirvāṇa* cannot be attained." Likewise, the *Lotus* emphasises the important role of *Upāya-kauśalya* (Skilful means). In this *sūtra*, chapter 2, *Upāya-kauśalya*, and chapter 16, *The Life-span of the Tathāgata* (implying the *Paramārtha-satya*), are the most important ones. *Samvṛti-satya*, according to the *Lotus*, covers the doctrines of the Four Noble Truth (*Catvāri ārya-satyāni*) of *śrāvakas* and Dependent Origination (*Pratītyasamutpāda*) of *pratyekabuddhas*. In *Paramārtha-satya*, however, those doctrines give up their roles to the *Lotus*, which is illustrated by the immaculacy and the complete symbiosis between the petals and seed-pots of the lotus flower.

The *Lotus* is not a text of mere philosophy. It also emphasises the aspect of religion, that is, *Nirvāṇa*. As mentioned earlier, the *Mahāyāna* doctrine is developed, religiously and philosophically, with the *bodhisattva* ideal as its center. A *bodhisattva*, however, is defined as one who strives to gain *Bodhi*, *Buddhahood* and delays such *Nirvāṇa*, as he wishes to save all living beings on earth from suffering. His inward life is in accord at once with the laws of transitory phenomena and with those of transcendental Suchness. He lives in the world like unto the lotus flower, the emblem of immaculacy, which grows out of the mire and yet does not share its defilement. To accomplish his vow the *bodhisattva* must eradicate the *ātman* or *pañcaskandhas*, which obstruct the fluent stream of loving-kindness (*karuṇā*). Thus the *bodhisattvas* in this *sūtra* are even used to eliminate these *pañcaskandhas* except *saṃskāra-skandha*, which requires the help of *Buddha's* supernatural power by means of *dhāraṇī*.

The *Lotus* is not a mere doctrine but a complete symbiosis of theory and practice. This *sūtra* encourages and extols all those who propagate the Ultimate Truth through receiving and keeping, reading and reciting, explaining, copying or writing even a single verse of it or hearing it for a moment. This *sūtra* is not a dead text but a source of life force, and One Vehicle is not only static, invisible but also dynamic, visible. Chapter 14 of this *sūtra* tells us clearly and more sufficiently about the character of the Preacher or Propagator; it asks for the four *dharmas* or conditions in which the roles of *Prajñā*, *Śīla* and *Karuṇā* are highlighted. They are necessary for those who set forth the *Saddharma-puṇḍarīka-sūtra* for the sake of living beings. It means this *sūtra* must be applied in life.

So, the analysis of the *Saddharmapuṇḍarīka-sūtra* or the *Lotus* through the concepts and doctrines of *Ekayāna*, *Upāya-kauśalya*, *Bodhisattva*, *Buddhahood* and *Dhāraṇī* demonstrates that this *sūtra* hides behind its highly symbolic expressions and fully dramatic, lively but formulaic, repetitious style a practical philosophy of the Ultimate Reality, *Ekayāna* or in a sense, the Oneness (*advayatā*) or the Unity in the diversity, the Immaculacy in the defilement. That is why it calls itself the 'king of all *sūtra*' or the like.

List of Chinese Characters

An lo hsing 安樂行
Ch'ang Pu ch'ing p'u-sa 常不輕菩薩
Ch'uan ch'ih 勸持
Cha'n 禪
Chen-ru 真如
Chih 止
Chu lei 囑累
Fa shih kung te 法師功德
Fa shih 法師
Fa 法
Fa-hsiang 法相
Fang pien 方便
Fen pieh kung te 分別功德
Hsien pao t'a 現寶塔
Hsin chieh 信解
Hsu 敍
Hsüan-tsang 玄莊
Hua ch'eng yu 化城喻
Hua-yen 華嚴
Hui-neng 慧能
Hul-wen 慧文
Ju lai shen li 如來神力
Ju lai shou liang 如來壽量
Kuan shih yin p'u-sa p'u men 觀世音菩薩普門
Kuan 觀
Kuan-yin 觀音
Miao chuang yen wang pen shih 妙莊嚴本事
Miao yin p'u-sa 妙音菩薩
P'i yu 譬喻
P'u hsien p'u-sa chu'an fa 普賢菩薩勸發
Pien 變
San-lun 三論
She-lun 攝論

Shou chi ______ 授記

Shou hsueh wu hsueh jen chi ______ 授學無學人記

Sui his kung te ______ 隨喜功德

T'ien-t'ai ______ 天台

T'i-p'o-ta-to ______ 提婆達多

T'o-lo-ni ______ 陀羅尼

Ts'ung ti yung ch'u ______ 從地湧出

Wei-shih ______ 唯識

Wo ______ 我

Wu pai ti tzu shou chi ______ 五百弟子受記

pYao ts'ao yu ______ 藥草喻

Yao wang p'u-sa pen shih ______ 藥王菩薩

Select Bibiliography

A Dictionary of Chinese Buddhist Terms, W.E. Soothill & L. Hodous, Delhi, 1987.

A Sanskrit-English Dictionary, M. Monier-Williams, Delhi, 1990.

A.K. Warder, *Indian Buddhism*, Delhi, 1980.

Alfonso Verdu, *Early Buddhist Philosophy*, Delhi, 1995.

Andrej Gawronski: *The Beginnings of Indian Drama and the Problem of Greek Influence*. Varanasi: Banaras Hindu University, 1965.

Arthur E. Wright, *Buddhism in Chinese History*, London, 1979.

Avadāna-śataka, edited by J. S. Speyer (St. Petersburg 1906, 1909). 2 vols. Bibliotheca Buddhica.

D.T. Suzuki, *Outline of Mahayana Buddhism*, New York, 1963.

__________, *Studies in the Lankavatara Sutra*. London, 1930. Repr. 1957.

__________, *The Essence of Buddhism*, Kyoto, 1968.

Dharma-sangraha, edited by F. Max Müller, H. Wenzel, and K. Kassawara, Oxford, 1885.

Edward Conze, *Buddhism — Its Essence and Development*, New Delhi, 1994.

Encyclopedia of Religion and Ethics, Vol. 8.

Franklin Edgerton, *Buddhist Hybrid Sanskrit Language and Literature*, Banaras Hindu University, Banaras, 1954.

Fumimaro Watanabe, *Philosophy and Its Development in the Nikāyas and Abhidhamma*, Delhi, 1996.

G.Sutton, *Existence and Enlightenment in the Lankavatara Sutra*, New York, 1991.

Garma C.C.Chang, *The Buddhist Teaching of Totality — The Philosohy of Hwa Yen Buddhism*, Delhi. 1992.

Giáo-hôi Phât-giáo Viêt-nam, *Tù-diên Phât-hoc Hán -viêt,* Ha-Noi, 1992.

H.B. Watanabe, *Philosophy and its Development in the Nikāyas and Abhidhamma,* Delhi, 1996.

Hajime Nakamura, *Indian Buddhism — A Survey with Bibliographical Notes,* Delhi, 1989.

Har Dayal, *The Bodhisattva Doctrine in Buddhist Sanskrit Literature,* Delhi, 1975.

Junjiro Takakusu, *The Essentials of Buddhist Philosophy,* Delhi, *1975.*

K. K. Mittal, *Vijñānavāda (Yogācāra) and its tradition,* Delhi, 1993.

__________, *Śūnyavāda,* Delhi, 1993.

K. V. Ramanan, *Nagarjuna's philosophy,* Delhi, 1978.

Kamaleswar Bhattacharya, *The Dialectical Method of Nāgārjuna, Vigrahavyāvartanī,* Delhi, 1990.

Kathāvatthu, edited by A. C. Taylor, London, 1894.

Kazuyoshi Kino (in Engl.) in *IBK.*, Vol. 10, No. 2, Jan. 1962, pp. 380 f.

Kenneth Ch'en, *Buddhism in China*, Princeton, 1964.

Kogen Nizuno, *Basic Buddhist Concepts*, Tokyo, 1994.

L.A. de Silva, *The Four Essential Doctrines of Buddhism*, Colombo, 1948.

La Vallee Poussin, L. de, *Bodhisattva*, Encyclopedia of Religion and Ethics 2: 739-753, 1916.

Laṅkāvatāra, ed. Bunyiu Nanjio, Kyoto, 1923 (Bibliotheca Otaniensis, Vol. 1).

Leon Hurvitz , *Scripture of the Lotus Blossom of the Fine ·Dharma*, translated from the Chinese of Kumārajīva, Newyork: Columbia University Press, 1976.

Lu K'uan Yü, *Ch'an and Zen Teaching*, London, 1960.

M. Mc. Govern, *An Introduction to Mahāyāna Buddhism*, London, 1922.

Madhyamakaśāstra of *Nāgārjuna* with the commentary; *Prasannapadā* by *Candrakīrti*, edited P. L. Vaidya, Darbhanga: The Mithila Institute, 1960.

Mahā-vyutpatti, edited by Sakaki, Kyoto, 1928.

Majjhima-Nikāya, edited by V. Trenckner and R. Chalmers, 3 vols, London, 1888-99.

Mādhyamikavṛtti (*Madhymakakārikas*), ed. L. de la Vallée Poussin, Bibliotheca Buddhica 4, St. Petersburg: The Imperial Academy of Sicences, 1903-1913.

Maurice Winternitz, *History of Indian Literature*, Vol. II, Delhi, 1988.

Michael Pye, *Skilful Means — A Concept in Mahāyāna Buddhism*, London & Texas, 1978.

Minoru Kiyota, *Mahāyāna Buddhist Meditation — Theory and Practice*, Delhi, 1991.

N. Chopra, *Contribution of Buddhism to World Civilization and Culture*, Delhi, 1983.

N.Dutt, *Buddhist Sects in India*, Delhi, 1978.

__________,*Mahāyāna Buddhism*, Delhi, 1978.

N.V. Joshi, *Indian Philosophy — From the Ontological Point of View*, New Delhi, 1977.

Nikkyo Niwano, *A Guide to the Threefold Lotus Sutra*, Tokyo, 1990.

Pali-English Dictionary, T.W.Rhys Davids & W.Stede, Delhi, 1993.

Paul Williams, *Mahāyāna Buddhism — The doctrinal foundations*, London & Newyork, 1998.

Puggala-paññatti, edited by R. Morris, London, 1883.

R.P. Singh and G. F. McLean, *The Buddhist World-View*, Faridabad: Om Publications, 2001.

Radhakrishnan, *Indian Philosophy*, 2 Vols., Delhi, 1993.

S. Dasgupta, *A History of Indian Philosophy*, Delhi: Motilal Banarsidass, 1975.

S. R. Bhatt and Anu Mehrotra, *Buddhist Epistemology*, London: Greenwood Press, 2000.

S. R. Bhatt, *Buddhist Thought and Culture in India and Korea*, Indian Council of Philosophical Research, New Delhi, 2003.

S. R. Goyal, *A History of Indian Buddhism*, Meerut: Kusumanjali Prakashan, 1993.

Saddharmapuṇḍarīka-sūtra, ed. by Kern and Nanjio, Tokyo, 1977.

Sallie B. King, *Buddha Nature*, Delhi, 1992.

Shoko Watanabe, *Saddharmapuṇḍarīka Manuscripts Found in Gilgit*, Tokyo, 1975.

Strug, F., *Emptiness: a study in religious meaning*, Nashville, 1967.